LLEWELL

2022

Witches'
Spell-A-Day
Almanac

Holidays & Lore
Spells, Rituals & Meditations

© 2021 Llewellyn Worldwide Ltd.
Cover design by the Llewellyn Art Department
Interior art © 2018 Laura Tempest Zakroff: pages 9, 29,
47, 67, 85, 105, 127, 149, 171, 193, 215, 233
Spell icons throughout © 2011 Sherrie Thai

You can order Llewellyn books and annuals from *New Worlds*,
Llewellyn's catalog. To request a free copy of the catalog, call toll-free
1-877-NEW WRLD or visit our website at www.llewellyn.com.

ISBN: 978-0-7387-6056-8

Llewellyn is a registered trademark of Llewellyn Worldwide Ltd.
2143 Wooddale Drive
Woodbury, MN 55125

Printed in the United States of America

Contents

A Note on Magic and Spells

The spells in the *Witches' Spell-A-Day Almanac* evoke everyday magic designed to improve our lives and homes. You needn't be an expert on magic to follow these simple rites and spells; as you will see if you use these spells throughout the year, magic, once mastered, is easy to perform. The only advanced technique required of you is the art of visualization.

Visualization is an act of controlled imagination. If you can call up in your mind a picture of your best friend's face or a flag flapping in the breeze, you can visualize. In magic, visualizations are used to direct and control magical energies. Basically the spellcaster creates a visual image of the spell's desired goal, whether it be perfect health, a safe house, or a protected pet.

Visualization is the basis of all good spells, and as such it is a tool that should be properly used. Visualization must be real in the mind of the spellcaster so it allows him or her to raise, concentrate, and send forth energy to accomplish the spell.

Perhaps when visualizing you'll find that you're doing everything right, but you don't feel anything. This is common, for we haven't been trained to acknowledge—let alone utilize—our magical abilities. Keep practicing, however, for your spells can "take" even if you're not the most experienced natural magician.

You will notice also that many spells in this collection have a somewhat light tone. They are seemingly fun and frivolous, filled with rhyme and colloquial speech. This is not to diminish the seriousness of the purpose, but rather to create a relaxed atmosphere for the practitioner. Lightness of spirit helps focus energy; rhyme and common language help the spellcaster remember the words and train the mind where it is needed. The intent of this magic is indeed very serious at times, and magic is never to be trifled with.

Even when your spells are effective, magic won't usually sparkle before your very eyes. The test of magic's success is time, not immediate eye-popping results. But you can feel magic's energy for yourself by rubbing your palms together briskly for ten seconds, then holding them a few inches apart. Sense the energy passing through them, the warm tingle in your palms. This is the power raised and used in magic. It comes from within and is perfectly natural.

Among the features of the *Witches' Spell-A-Day Almanac* are an easy-to-use "book of days" format; new spells specifically tailored for each day

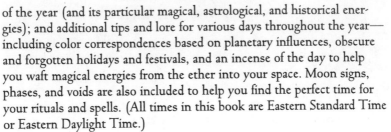

of the year (and its particular magical, astrological, and historical energies); and additional tips and lore for various days throughout the year—including color correspondences based on planetary influences, obscure and forgotten holidays and festivals, and an incense of the day to help you waft magical energies from the ether into your space. Moon signs, phases, and voids are also included to help you find the perfect time for your rituals and spells. (All times in this book are Eastern Standard Time or Eastern Daylight Time.)

Enjoy your days and have a magical year!

Spell-A-Day Icons

New Moon

Full Moon

Abundance

Altar

Balance

Clearing, Cleaning

Garden

Grab Bag

Health, Healing

Home

Heart, Love

Meditation, Divination

Money, Prosperity

Protection

Relationship

Success

Travel, Communication

Air Element

Earth Element

Fire Element

Spirit Element

Water Element

Spells at a Glance by Date and Category*

	Health, Healing	Protection	Success	Heart, Love	Clearing, Cleaning	Home	Meditation, Divination
Jan.	8, 9, 23, 27		1, 11, 25, 26	12, 19	5, 7, 20, 29	3	
Feb.	7, 28	4, 11		5, 8, 14, 15, 24	3, 17	10	12, 18, 21, 26
March	9, 26	7, 17		13	19, 28	11, 17	3, 16, 24, 27, 30
April	7, 9	6, 13, 27		24	2, 14, 17		12, 15, 21, 25
May	8	7, 19		12	6	17, 28	2, 14
June		23, 25, 27	10, 13	12		2, 5, 18, 24	3, 21, 22
July	11, 27	6	14	15, 17	2, 12, 16	20	
Aug.	23	13, 26, 31	28		6, 14, 16, 20		7, 15
Sept.	9	24	1, 4, 29	19, 23	2, 12	3	15, 27
Oct.		3, 12, 29			4, 11, 21	7, 30	15, 26
Nov.	14, 15, 25	7, 16, 21, 27	19	18	1	5, 6	26
Dec.	1, 15	1, 5	3, 29	24, 25, 31	22, 30	16, 21	4, 8, 10, 12

*List is not comprehensive.

2022

Year of Spells

January

Happy New Year! The calendar year has begun and even though we may be in the depths of winter (in the Northern Hemisphere) or the height of summer (in the Southern Hemisphere), we stand at the threshold of fifty-two weeks filled with promise. Legend has it that this month is named to honor the Roman god Janus, a god of new beginnings and doorways, but it is also associated with Juno, the primary goddess of the Roman pantheon. Juno was said to be the protectress of the Roman Empire, and Janus (whose twin faces look to both the past and the future simultaneously) encourages new endeavors, transitions, and change in all forms. Since this month marks the beginning of the whole year, we can plant the seeds for long-term goals at this time, carefully plotting the course of our future success.

In the United States, there are three important holidays occurring in January: New Year's Day, Martin Luther King Jr. Day, and Inauguration Day. Each of these days exemplifies powerful change and transition. The dawn of a new year heralds a fresh start, and whether snow-covered or bathed in summer heat, January offers renewed possibilities for all.

Michael Furie

① January 1
Saturday

4th ♐

☽ v/c 3:16 am

☽ → ♑ 6:02 pm

Color of the day: Brown
Incense of the day: Magnolia

New Year's Day – Kwanzaa ends

The Climb Begins

Now nature begins its climb toward spring and summer, to growth, maturity, and eventually the harvest. We also begin our own climb. We have a clean slate before us. To what heights will you climb this year?

On a sheet of clean white paper, write two or three goals you've set for yourself this year. Or write them in your Book of Shadows. They could be health or diet goals, or perhaps a career or education goal—anything you desire. After you've written them, say:

> Now nature begins its climb
> to growth and the harvest.
>
> I, too, begin to climb and
> to fulfill my wish.

Keep the paper or Book of Shadows on your altar or other special place. Read your goals, meditate on them, and repeat the Words of Power about once a month. As you achieve a goal, you may strive for another. Just repeat the same steps. At the end of the year, even if you haven't met all your goals, throw the paper away and start with a clean sheet next year.

James Kambos

NOTES:

January 2
Sunday

4th ♑

New Moon 1:33 pm

Color of the day: Orange
Incense of the day: Juniper

Gifts of the Shadow

A new moon at the start of a fresh year is the perfect time to reveal any latent gifts seeking expression in the months to come. The darkness of this moon phase provides a safe space for any hidden qualities that might feel a bit vulnerable to emerge.

All you'll need is a mirror and a black candle. In a darkened room, gaze at your shadowy form in the mirror, inviting contact with any unconscious gifts that are ready to be honored. Allow yourself to go into a light meditative state as you look at yourself with a soft focus.

Before lighting the candle on a heatproof surface, hold it in both hands and charge it with new moon energy. Then light the candle where it casts light onto the mirror. Gaze at yourself once more and allow any insights to arise. What within you wants to be seen, heard, and lived? How can you express these gifts in the days and weeks to come? When done, snuff out the candle with thanks.

Melissa Tipton

January 3
Monday

1st ♑

☽ v/c 11:21 am

☽ → ♒ 5:44 pm

Color of the day: Silver
Incense of the day: Clary sage

Magical Snowflake Window Art

Window art is a great way to create a screen of privacy and protection between your home and the outside world. For this spell you'll need paper, scissors, and tape.

Start with a square of paper. Trace the four corners with your finger and speak your intention aloud. Fold the paper to create a triangle. With every fold, imagine the power of your intention doubling. Fold the paper again to make a smaller triangle. Fold it again to make a triangular crease at one-third of the triangle. Repeat from the other side to create a tiny triangle with two "tails." Cut the tails off so the edges are smooth. As you cut shapes in the folded paper, say:

With every cut, I call to me

Protection and privacy.

It's a fortress, you can see.

So move along, good day to thee.

Once you feel the paper will convey your meaning, open it up and envision it working. Tape your magical snowflake up in a window.

Astrea Taylor

January 4
Tuesday

1st ♒

☽ v/c 7:45 pm

Color of the day: Gray
Incense of the day: Cedar

Grow Your Wealth

Magically clarify and bless your financial goals today so your savings account will grow throughout the year. Put a little potting soil in the bottom of a pot. Crumple up a dollar bill into a loose ball and hold it in both hands. Close your eyes and bring to mind the amount of money you'd like to have in your savings account by the end of the year. In your mind's eye, imagine checking your account and seeing this number. Feel the joy of having already accomplished your financial goal. Place the dollar in the pot and put a little more soil on top. Then pot a jade plant on top of the dollar. Once the jade is potted, water it. Choose to be open to creative ideas for earning and receiving money. Also vow to take continuous action toward earning the money you desire. As you care for your jade plant throughout the year, know that money is constantly coming to you, from both expected and unexpected sources.

Tess Whitehurst

January 5
Wednesday

1st ♒

☽ → ♓ 7:17 pm

Color of the day: White
Incense of the day: Lavender

Chakra Clearing Spell

The beginning of the year is a good time to do all sorts of cleansing, clearing, and balancing spells. One that is particularly useful is a chakra clearing spell. Chakras are the energy centers of the body, and are vital to the flow of physical energy. Because they are connected to emotions as well, when the chakras are blocked, you can feel sluggish, unhappy, and out of balance.

The seven chakras are located at the root (base of the spine), sacrum (lower abdomen), solar plexus (belly), heart, throat, third eye (middle of forehead), and crown (top of the head). Each chakra is associated with a color in this order: red, orange, yellow, green, light blue, dark blue/purple, and violet or white.

To do this spell, sit quietly and visualize each chakra, starting at the bottom. See it glow with color and strength, and say this spell for each of the seven in turn until you feel them clear and the energy moving freely:

Chakra strong and chakra clear,

Bring me energy for this year.

Deborah Blake

January 6
Thursday

1st ♓

Color of the day: Purple
Incense of the day: Carnation

A Spell for hibernation

Avoid the winter blues by embracing hibernation. For this spell, don comfy clothes and fuzzy slippers. Have dark chocolate or a cup of hot chocolate ready. Set a blue candle in a dish of crushed ice—blue for the winter blues and the subtle blue of ice and snow. Sit before the candle on a comfortable couch or chair, wrap yourself in a blanket (again, fuzzy is good!), and repeat:

As the depths of winter near,

May I sleep deep like the bear.

Curling up in dark embrace,

Nurturing soul with calm and grace.

Meditate for a moment on the quiet benefits of winter's cold depths. Imagine yourself slowing down and feeling the patient rhythm of the season. Munch the chocolate or sip the cocoa, feeling it sustain you. Blow out the candle and place it on your altar. Each morning, light the candle for a moment and pause, considering how you will embrace winter's rhythms that day. Blow out the candle and carry on.

Susan Pesznecker

January 7
Friday

1st ♓

☽ v/c 5:23 pm

Color of the day: Rose
Incense of the day: Cypress

Looking Forward, Not Back

Janus is the two-headed Roman god of beginnings and endings. Because January is named after him, this is a great month to work magick with him. For this spell you will need a piece of flash paper, a pencil, a fireproof bowl, and a candle.

Set up your items in a safe space and then reflect upon the past calendar year. What is the one mistake, relationship, or embarrassing moment that you'd like to leave in the past and discard going forward? When you've decided what that is, write it down on your piece of flash paper.

Using your candle, light the flash paper and place it in the bowl while saying:

Janus, god of beginnings and endings,

Within your fire I seek cleansing.

I now leave this bad memory behind,

Entering the new year with piece of mind!

When done, blow out your candle. No longer dwell upon what you wish to be forgotten. It is past.

Ari & Jason Mankey

January 8
Saturday

1st ♓

☽ → ♈ 12:26 am

Color of the day: Blue
Incense of the day: Rue

Midwives Day (Bulgaria)

B rigid is the goddess of many dominions, including fertility and childbirth, which is the focus of today, as it's Midwives Day in Bulgaria. We will focus on Brigid as maker and one of her animals, the pure white bull.

Our work honors Brigid for looking after babies, and those either wanting to have a child or who are pregnant and ready to soon give birth. This is an offering from your heart to her spirit and familiars. If this is not right for you at the moment, gift it to a family member or friend. Goddess Brigid leads and commands ale production, and she should be feted for that too. She and her white bull love cakes, and with that in mind, let's construct an offering.

On your doorstep, place a freshly baked cake next to a mug of ale, with a full head of foam. Around the ale, place a few coins to pay Brigid for her generosity and assistance.

Stephanie Rose Bird

January 9
Sunday

1st ♈

2nd Quarter 1:11 pm

Color of the day: Yellow
Incense of the day: Almond

Shedding Some Light

S undays are associated with Apollo, Ra, and other deities of the sun. We can use the influence of solar energy to shed light on and bring clarity to issues that remain obscured to us. This spell is best done during the day when the sun is at its zenith.

Sit outside in the full sun. If you can use some lemon incense or lemon essential oil to work with the sun energy, do so. As you inhale the lemon scent, picture the issue that you are having trouble understanding or seeing clearly. See it being surrounded by a dense fog. Lift your face to the sun and feel its warmth radiating around you and see it burning off that fog. As the fog lifts from around the issue you are dealing with, look at it with fresh eyes. Use any information you can garner in order to change your perspective on the situation.

Charlynn Walls

January 10
Monday

2nd ♈

☽ v/c 2:23 am

☽ → ♉ 9:47 am

Color of the day: White
Incense of the day: Narcissus

Brain Freeze, Be Gone!

If you've been experiencing any sort of mental blockage or "brain freeze," take a walk outside to meet the brisk January air at sunset. Stand in one place and focus on your breath while facing west. Close your eyes and bring to mind those mental blockages from which you wish to break free this year.

With each issue that comes to mind, take a deep belly breath through your nose and forcefully exhale through your mouth. Continue this with each thought that comes up, and feel free to do so multiple times for each issue. Multiple thoughts may come quickly.

To add an extra boost, consider taking a handful of sea salt and/or any of the herbs vervain, nettle, or clove. With each forceful exhalation, throw a little bit of the salt or herbs to the thought you are offering to the setting sun.

Raven Digitalis

January 11
Tuesday

2nd ♉

Color of the day: Maroon
Incense of the day: Basil

Good Numbers for the New Year

Let's use numerology as we move into this new year. Today's date is 1-11-2022. Here's how to add it up:

$$1 + 1 + 1 = 3 \text{ (day + month)}$$
$$2 + 2 + 2 = 6 \text{ (year)}$$
$$3 + 6 = 9$$

The number 9 signifies, among other things, the end of a cycle. (After 9, we begin again with 10 = 1.) Nine also means "awakening." Before we awaken, of course, we've been asleep. Consider your current life and at least one issue, belief, or habit that you've been "asleep" about. What do you want to end so that you can awaken to something better?

In the tarot, card 9 of the major arcana is the Hermit. This figure is very wise and can help you review your "old stuff."

Cast your circle (if you wish), light black and white candles, and set card 9 in the center between them. Speak to the Hermit and ask for help in finding what you need to end as this new year begins. Ask the Hermit what you need to awaken to.

When you have answers, speak both resolutions aloud:

I am ending _____.

I am awakening to _____.

Let the two candles burn down safely, then open your circle and move into your awakened life.

Barbara Ardinger

NOTES:

January 12
Wednesday

2nd ♉

☽ v/c 2:39 pm

☽ → ♊ 10:08 pm

Color of the day: Topaz
Incense of the day: Bay laurel

handy Love Magic

The second week of January is Letter Writing Week. We hardly write letters anymore, but it's time for a Hand-Written Love Letter Spell. In touch with the paper and pen, handwriting is personal and, like your fingerprints, distinctive.

Gather paper, a pen, an envelope, a glue stick, and decorative items such as stickers, cut-out pictures, ribbons, or dried flowers. Start with "Dear ___," and tell them what makes them so dear to you. It doesn't have to be written to a lover, partner, or spouse. Why not write a love letter to a friend, family member, or yourself? Express love in words, channelling heart energy down through the pen and onto the paper. Sign your name and decorate with hearts, stars, and pictures. Place the letter in the envelope and seal it. Post the "handy" love letter, stamped and addressed, knowing you're sending a personal, unique, and timeless gift—something they can hold onto forever.

Dallas Jennifer Cobb

January 13
Thursday

2nd ♊

Color of the day: Green
Incense of the day: Balsam

Stick on Magic

January 13 is Sticker Day, which celebrates stickers of all kinds—from utilitarian labels to the fun and colorful ones that brighten our books, laptops, and vehicles. The date was chosen because it's the birthday of R. Stanton Avery, who is on record for creating the first commercially viable self-sticking peel-off labels.

Besides helping us label things, mail packages, and decorate things, stickers can also be used for magical means. They can transform and beautify a surface, aiding in glamour magic. A sticker can signify ownership or membership, adding protection or inclusivity. Then there's the fact that you're literally affixing it onto something—which may help a certain idea "stick." You can certainly buy pre-made stickers, but you can also get some adhesive paper and draw your own. The latter method is especially great when drawing sigils that may work best when applied to certain places or objects.

Laura Tempest Zakroff

 January 14
Friday

2nd ♊

☽ v/c 9:22 pm

Color of the day: Coral
Incense of the day: Orchid

Transformative Magick

The Julian calendar is thirteen days behind the Gregorian one. That makes today the Old New Year! So, if you still need to reset and make some magickal resolutions, you still can. Transformative magick is powerful, and you can tap into that energy to make change in your life.

Take a piece of moonstone that speaks to you, and place it in a bowl or other container with some water and a pinch of salt. Set the bowl on a windowsill or near a window through which you can see the moon. The energies of the moon will be absorbed into the stone over the course of the night. Then say:

*Allow me to transform and change
for my highest good. So mote it be.*

Keep the stone with you daily or place it on your altar so you can continue your transformation throughout the year.

Charlynn Walls

January 15
Saturday

2nd ♊

☽ → ♋ 11:11 am

Color of the day: Gray
Incense of the day: Sage

A Pine Purification Spell

For this spell you'll need two small pine branches or two pine cones. Bless them according to your spiritual path. After blessing them, hold them and think of something you wish to purify in your life. Perhaps you want to clear away a habit or a situation. Next, safely light a small fire in a heat-proof container, cauldron, or fireplace. Burn the branches or cones in the fire. Visualize the flames purifying your life. "See" the burning pine cleansing the issue from your life. Let the fire burn safely out. When the ashes are completely cool, scatter them away from your home. It is done.

James Kambos

 January 16
Sunday

2nd ♋

Color of the day: Amber
Incense of the day: Marigold

Spiritual Technology Sweep

In the days of old, we spent a lot of time spiritually cleansing our homes, especially the floors with magickal floor washes. Now we spend so much time at our desks that it's good to charge them too.

Smudge your work area with a sage smudge stick. Light it and tamp out the flame. Smudge everything, including inside the drawers and underneath the desk and chair, and be careful to smudge the corners.

Wipe down your desk with an organic cleanser featuring lemon or pine, as both are purifying and energizing.

To the east, put an amethyst crystal. It is known to aid in communication and business matters. Amethyst will usher in prosperity and abundance. Ultimately this stone will bring peace, calm, and love to your life, and it will manifest through your workstation.

Stephanie Rose Bird

January 17
Monday

2nd ♋

☽ v/c 6:48 pm

Full Moon 6:48 pm

☽ → ♌ 11:03 pm

Color of the day: Ivory
Incense of the day: Hyssop

Martin Luther King Jr. Day

Prayer to Mildgyth

The youngest and least famous of a trio of saintly sisters, St. Mildgyth is linked with the theological virtue of hope—which is sometimes all we have when things go amiss. Look into tonight's full moon (the same that Mildgyth looked on herself) and invoke her:

Maiden

In the cloister

Living by the sea,

Divine intervention

Give unto me.

Yearning for peace when I cannot cope,

There is your presence, there is

Hope.

Chant this prayer to St. Mildgyth when hope is lost. Say her name—she will help you find it.

Natalie Zaman

January 18
Tuesday

3rd ♌

Color of the day: Gray
Incense of the day: Ylang-ylang

Magick of the 18th Path

In the Qabalistic Tree of Life, path 18 is associated with the Chariot card of the tarot. In many depictions, two strong beasts, often one black and one white, are leading the chariot. In our daily lives, we are constantly working to unite opposing desires and initiatives. We want to sleep in, but we also want to pay rent. We want to blow up at our partner in a moment of anger, but we also want to maintain our relationship.

Finding a way to steer the chariot of our lives, without being yanked this way or that, is one of the greatest challenges of adulting, and this magical boost will help heal discord between opposing elements within.

Sit between two lit candles, one black and one white, situated on heatproof surfaces, and chant the following spell:

This or that, either or.

Pass between—the inner door.

My mind is clear,

My heart does know,

And every choice divinely flows.

Snuff out the candles with thanks.

Melissa Tipton

January 19
Wednesday

3rd ♌

☉ → ♒ 9:39 pm

Color of the day: Brown
Incense of the day: Honeysuckle

Mirror Magic for Self-Love

Today the moon is in fabulous, fiery Leo, which helps us extend more love to ourselves. Everyone has lovable features, and this spell brings them out. You'll need a red or pink candle, a lighter, a piece of rose quartz, a small bowl of water, five rose petals, and a mirror set up on your altar.

Light the candle. Place the rose quartz in the bowl of water and sprinkle the rose petals over the water. Gaze into the mirror at the flame as you stir the water clockwise nine times with increasing intensity. Say:

Like the fire burning bright,

My features bring sublime delight.

Anoint yourself with your wet finger and say:

I love _____ (feature).

Name at least nine of your features. Gaze into the mirror and see how truly beautiful they are, like the bright flame. Give thanks. Blow out the candle and pour the water in a potted plant or outdoors. Keep the rose quartz on your altar.

Astrea Taylor

January 20
Thursday

3rd ♌

☽ v/c 3:15 am

☽ → ♍ 9:02 am

Color of the day: Turquoise
Incense of the day: Jasmine

Clarity and Charity

A closet purge today will create greater clarity in your life and remove blocks to abundance and self-love. First, pull everything out of your clothes closet. (Really, everything.) Next, physically clean your closet: dust, vacuum, etc. Then clear the energy in your closet with sage smoke, incense smoke, or a mister of water containing a few drops of essential oils, or use a chime or bell to clear the space with sound. Now consider each item one at a time. Ask yourself, "Do I love this? Do I use this? Do I need this? Does it boost my energy and mood?" If the answer is no to all of these, put the item in one of three piles: give away, recycle, or trash. If the answer is yes to any of them, put it back in your closet. Remember, the Virgo moon today loves details, so if there are numerous knickknacks or keepsakes in your closet, repeat the process with every single one of them.

Tess Whitehurst

January 21
Friday

3rd ♍

Color of the day: Purple
Incense of the day: Mint

A Day for Quiet

One of the benefits of winter is that it is a calmer, quieter time. Spring is full of rebirth, noisy and energetic. Summer is busy, as we try to take advantage of the nicer weather and get outside to work or play or take vacations. Fall is harvest time or going back to school. But in the winter, things slow down a bit.

If you live in a northern clime, the snow might blanket the ground and bring its special hush. Even in warmer places, the beaches may empty of crowds. Take time today to embrace that quiet, slower pace. Whether you choose to meditate or take a walk or chop vegetables for a pot of soup, try to be fully present in whatever you do. Let the silence speak to you. And when it feels right, say this spell:

Winter quiet,

Work your magic.

Calm my spirit

And soothe my soul.

Deborah Blake

January 22
Saturday

3rd ♍
☽ v/c 2:46 pm
☽ → ♎ 5:03 pm

Color of the day: Indigo
Incense of the day: Patchouli

Talking with Your Pet

Did you know that January 22 is Answer Your Cat's Questions Day? We didn't either until working on our spells for this year's almanac. While we doubt it's possible to answer all of your cat's questions, we thought it might be worth a try. (This is not limited to cats either. Dog owners are welcome.)

Start by invoking the goddess Bast into your space (or another deity of your choosing). After invoking Bast, sit next to your pet, or better yet, convince your pet to sit in your lap. Close your eyes and begin petting your animal, feeling their presence next to you. Now open to whatever feelings and energies are coming from your pet. Visualize these in your mind's eye, and when you are done with the exercise (or your pet is), write them down. Use any insights you've gleaned to grow closer to your pet.

Ari & Jason Mankey

 **January 23**
Sunday

3rd ♎

Color of the day: Gold
Incense of the day: Hyacinth

A Cup of Wellness

Winter is cold and flu season, and you can add magical and physiological support with this spell-crafted tea.

In your favorite cup or mug, grate some fresh ginger (or use ¼ teaspoon powdered ginger) and squeeze in one tablespoon lemon juice and a bit of freshly grated lemon peel. Ginger is known magically for warming and healing, while lemon has strong solar connections and is associated with health and longevity; both ginger and lemon are full of antioxidants, and lemon is also packed with vitamin C. Add some honey to sweeten the tea and to imbue it with healing vitality and an antiviral kick.

Fill the mug with near-boiling water and stir sunwise (clockwise) for extra energy. Sip slowly while it is hot, visualizing the tea fighting off viral invaders. Bonus: add a dram of whiskey (or your favorite spirit) for an even deeper soul-warming effect. Repeat as needed.

Susan Pesznecker

January 24
Monday

3rd ♎

☽ v/c 5:10 pm

☽ → ♏ 10:57 pm

Color of the day: Lavender
Incense of the day: Neroli

Gold Rush Day Ritual

Gold is stunning, captivating, and connected with the sun. Let's celebrate gold, along with the element of water, used for panning, for this is Gold Rush Day, embodied by Agni.

The Indian deity Agni, god of fire, melded his powerful eyes with water from his semen to yield gold. Agni represents transformative energy. He cleanses all that is unlucky and foul. Agni represents immortality and the alchemy of fire and water.

For this ritual you will need:

• A red medium pillar candle

• ⅓ cup ghee (clarified butter)

• A golden fireproof plate

• ¼ cup lightning water (rain collected during a lightning storm)

Take your red candle, which represents vitality, transformation, and passion, and dress it with ghee. To dress, focus on Agni's powers and rub ghee from the center of the candle upward and then from the bottom of the candle to the center, all around

the candle. Then light the candle and place it on a firesafe golden plate. Recite:

Agni, this Gold Rush Day, I invite your cleansing energy into my life.

Repeat twice more. After reflection, dip fingers of your dominant hand in the lightning water and snuff out the candle.

Stephanie Rose Bird

NOTES:

January 25
Tuesday

3rd ♏

4th Quarter 8:41 am

Color of the day: Red
Incense of the day: Ginger

Five Stones of Success

This spell creates a focus to enhance success. First you need some beading thread or wire and a gold-tone sun charm. You also need five semiprecious stone beads representing different aspects of success:

Sodalite: Success of the mind

Bloodstone: Success of the body

Amethyst: Success of the spirit

Garnet: Success of the heart

Tiger's-eye: Success of the magic

The sun charm selects success from the various things that each stone can do. Hold each bead and concentrate on its aspect. Then string them together along with the sun charm and fasten the ends of the thread.

You can use this as a pendant, key chain, pocket charm, or whatever you like. Carry it with you as a reminder of your goals. Whenever you encounter an obstacle on your way to success, rub your fingers over the beads for added power. Then look again for a way to move forward.

Elizabeth Barrette

January 26
Wednesday

4th ♏

Color of the day: Yellow
Incense of the day: Lilac

The Parking Space Word

No matter where we live, if we drive a car, we need to park it somewhere. Whether we're at work or at the mall or at home in an urban neighborhood that has more multi-family dwellings than there are parking spaces, we need to park our car.

Speak the Parking Space Word:

ZZZZZAAAAAAZZZZZ.

Speak it loud and with great energy. It seems to work best if you plan ahead and say where you want to park. Speak the Word, therefore, when you turn a corner or enter the parking lot:

ZZZZZAAAAAZZZZZ.
Parking space at_____.

Be aware that the Word doesn't always work immediately. Sometimes you have to drive around the block or around the lot. Repeat the Word every time you turn a corner. It will work.

Barbara Ardinger

January 27
Thursday

4th ♏

☽ v/c 12:28 am

☽ → ♐ 2:34 am

Color of the day: White
Incense of the day: Clove

Shedding the Wintery Veil

For many people in the world at this time of year, it feels like winter may never end. When our body becomes accustomed to a season, it can be difficult to imagine that it will ever shift.

If you're feeling any wintery blues, doldrums, or general ennui, take a black veil, blanket, or cloak and step outside to a private location. Hunker down and bring focus to the warmth of your breath as you hide beneath a cloak of darkness.

As many times as you'd like, repeat these words:

Breaking free from winter's strife,
I give thanks and rise tonight.

When it feels right, quickly throw off your covering and look up at the sky. Raise your arms and breathe in the cosmic energy of seasonal change.

Even if we can't always feel it, the clock is always ticking and the Wheel of the Year is always turning.

Raven Digitalis

January 28
Friday

4th ♐

☽ v/c 2:00 pm

Color of the day: Pink
Incense of the day: Thyme

Keep a Secret Spell

Do you have a secret you need to keep? Maybe it's something someone else told you, but you're super excited about it so you're finding it hard to maintain self-control. Or perhaps it's something you want to keep quiet until the time is right for it to be revealed. Either way, this charm can help you out—as long as you don't have a fear of spiders.

All you need to do is find a spider that is tending to a web and whisper your secret to her, if she's willing. Be sure to keep within a respectable distance so you don't invade her space. Ask, "Can I tell you a secret?" and watch. If yes, speak this charm:

Sister Spider, spinning your web,

Catch my words, curiosity fed.

Sticky silken threads holding tight,

Secrets kept quiet, out of sight.

Share your story and thank her. The secret will catch in the web and stay put.

Laura Tempest Zakroff

 ## January 29
Saturday

4th ♐

☽ → ♑ 4:09 am

Color of the day: Black
Incense of the day: Ivy

Releasing Negativity

Today we can combine the energetic properties of both Saturday and the waning moon to release that which no longer serves us or is beneficial in our lives.

Gather items that represent what you want to release from your life. You can use any object that has meaning to you. For instance, if you have a toxic individual that you need help removing from your life, you can use a photo of them. Hold the first item over a container and say:

There is no room in my life for this energy. I cast you out.

Then drop the item in the container. Continue the process until no items are left. Next, use some incense or sage to clear your space. Dispose of the items after you complete your spell.

Charlynn Walls

△ **January 30**
Sunday

4℞ ♑
☽ v/c 11:44 pm

Color of the day: Amber
Incense of the day: Frankincense

Incense Clock

A geisha's time entertaining is often marked by incense sticks called *ohana*. Her fees are determined by how many ohana have burned while she sings, dances, and tells stories—an incense clock. The average stick of incense burns for sixty to ninety minutes, which is plenty of time to utilize its cleansing smoke to lift and carry away what no longer serves you.

Choose a scent that corresponds with your situation (e.g., rose for love and relationships, dragon's blood for anxiety and negativity, and lavender for healing and cleansing). Roll the stick gently between your fingers and tell it your troubles. Light the incense and let the smoke envelop you. You can go about your business while it burns safely or stay and meditate on what needs to be cleansed. Reset this incense clock as many times as needed to cleanse your spirit.

Natalie Zaman

January 31
Monday

4℞ ♑
☽ → ♒ 4:43 am

Color of the day: Gray
Incense of the day: Lily

Winter Wish-Craft

There was a huge billboard overlooking a major intersection in a city where I once lived, showing a runner, in winter, in the slush. The caption read something like "Winter. We've only had it for 100 million years. Get used to it." That poster inspired me to engage in winter wishcraft. I longed to change winter from a season I dreaded and barely tolerated to something I embraced and enjoyed.

I realized that enjoying winter necessitated having the right gear for the weather. I started wishing and made a list: Stylish, warm, waterproof boots. A full-length, lightweight down coat. Attractive bright-colored mittens and hats. Soft, warm wool socks. Gradually my wishes came true. I acquired the gear needed to enjoy winter weather every day.

These days I snowshoe, hike, and even go winter camping. Do you want to get outdoors and be active? Acquire good gear. Make a wish. Make a list.

Dallas Jennifer Cobb

February

The word *February* is based on the Latin *februa* and refers to the Roman festival of purification of the same name. This festival later became integrated with February's infamous Lupercalia. Since ancient times, February has been observed as a month of cleansing, cleaning, purification, and preparation for the warm months ahead. We see the Celtic Imbolg (Candlemas) celebrated in February to perpetuate the summoning of solar light. In many parts of the world at this time, the promise of sunlight seems bleak, even imaginary. The world around us is slowly awakening from its wintery slumber, and some semblance of excitement begins to grow in the hearts of those attuned to the seasonal tides.

Daylight hours are short in February, so this time of year can sometimes feel depressive. We must actively cultivate our inner light through regular exercise, solid sleep, meditation, yoga, ritual, studying, artwork, and planning ahead for the year. When performing magickal work this month, remember that your energy levels may be lower than usual and you must summon your own inner light to strengthen and illuminate your efforts. Do whatever it takes to stay on top of your game, keep energized, cultivate happiness, and embrace February's cleansing rebirth!

Raven Digitalis

February 1
Tuesday

4th ♒

New Moon 12:46 am

☽ v/c 6:01 am

Color of the day: Scarlet

Incense of the day: Bayberry

Lunar New Year (Tiger)

Tiger Water

Today marks the start of Lunar New Year, which honors the Water Tiger this year. Those who are born in a year of the Tiger are said to be charming, confident, and very brave, but also competitive and at times unpredictable. The element of water brings calmness, insight, innovation, and good judgment. The new moon is a wonderful time to plant the seeds for new habits, so why not let the Water Tiger inspire you?

Fill a cotton satchel with the following herbs: ginger root, orange peel, holy basil, and vervain. Dried, fresh, or a combination is fine. Blend the herbs together first in a mortar and pestle, thinking about Tiger energy. You may even want to recite William Blake's "The Tyger." Place the satchel in a small ceramic bowl full of purified water and let it sit overnight. In the morning, transfer the water to a jar and store in the fridge. Anoint yourself daily until the next full moon.

Laura Tempest Zakroff

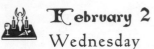

 February 2
Wednesday

1st ♒

☽ → ♓ 6:00 am

Color of the day: White

Incense of the day: Marjoram

Imbolc — Groundhog Day

New Candle Blessing for Imbolc

As a festival of the returning light, Imbolc is the perfect time of year to replace any dying candles on your altar or in your ritual space. Start your ritual/magickal work as usual, including lighting the old candles that you will be replacing. Ritually cleanse your new candles with salted water or by running them through a purifying incense.

Now light one of your new candles with the flame from an old candle. As you do so, say:

I transfer this sacred Witch's flame to its new home. Long may its light shine!

By transferring your old candle's light to your new one, you are also transferring its energy and history in your ritual space. Once your new candle is lit, blow out the old one and say:

Thank you for your service, and now your flame will burn anew!

Transfer your new candle to where the old one stood. Repeat for each new candle.

Ari & Jason Mankey

February 3
Thursday

1st ♓

Color of the day: Crimson
Incense of the day: Apricot

A Simple Banishing Spell

Use this banishing spell to cut ties with someone or something causing you stress or even harm. If possible, perform this spell during the waning moon or dark (new) moon.

You'll need a small black candle, a small burning bowl or cauldron, a black crayon, a piece of paper, something connected to the person or situation (a photograph, an item, etc.), and a grater.

Place the candle in the bowl or cauldron. Use the crayon to write the person's or situation's name/description on the paper, then tear the paper into small bits and add them to the bowl along with the item representing what's being banished. Grate the tip of the crayon over the candle, then break the crayon into pieces and add to the bowl.

Light the candle and speak your banishing intention aloud. Light the paper bits and allow the bowl contents to burn safely until little remains. Bury the remnants in a deep hole, saying "Gone from me" as you cover it.

Susan Pesznecker

February 4
Friday

1st ♓

☽ v/c 4:41 am
☽ → ♈ 9:57 am

Color of the day: Rose
Incense of the day: Vanilla

Saving Winter

Winter used to be something that people wanted protection from. Now climate change means that winter itself needs protection. According to the Celtic calendar, today is King Frost Day. Traditionally, people gathered to ask King Frost and the Queen of the Snowflakes to end winter and bring spring. Today you can flip this around and ask them to stay longer.

For this spell you need a window crystal or other ornament shaped like a snowflake. Take it outside in the cold winter air and say:

King Frost and Snowflake Queen,

Hold back the creeping green.

Let winter linger more

While spring is yet in store.

Find some snow or ice and touch the snowflake crystal to it. Repeat the verse again. Finally, take the snowflake crystal back indoors and hang it in your window as a reminder to protect winter and its guardian spirits.

Elizabeth Barrette

February 5
Saturday

1st ♈

Color of the day: Brown
Incense of the day: Pine

A Self-Love Spell
to Begin the Day

After you have showered, had tea or coffee, performed yoga, or whatever your daily routine happens to be, stand in front of the bathroom mirror and look yourself in the eyes.

While it may feel uncomfortable at first, gazing into your own "windows to the soul" can be a very positive practice. Although it is natural for the mind to enter a judgmental place while practicing such an activity, you must stay focused on the beauty of your physical frame. Repeat these words:

Beauty above, beauty below,
beauty within, beauty without.

Slowly admire your facial features, from the texture of your skin to the shape of your eyebrows. Disallow your thoughts from entering a state of judgment. Bring your focus back to beauty.

Conclude by looking yourself in the eyes, admiring their perfect hue and depth. Repeat the words, smile, and know that you are beautiful on every level.

Raven Digitalis

February 6
Sunday

1st ♈

☽ v/c 12:21 pm
☽ → ♉ 5:52 pm

Color of the day: Gold
Incense of the day: Heliotrope

Finding the Valuable
in Ordinary Life

One of the plot lines in Shakespeare's *Merchant of Venice* concerns how Portia is to be married. Suitors are to pick a casket of gold, silver, or lead. The gold casket bears this inscription: "He who chooses me will get what many men want." The silver casket says, "He who chooses me will get what he deserves." The lead casket bears a blunt warning: "He who chooses me must give and risk all he has." Like Bassanio in the play, choose lead today.

Cast your circle with ordinary "leaden" objects in the four elemental corners. Light a gray candle. Speak aloud the inscription on the lead casket (altering the wording as you wish):

He who chooses me must
give and risk all he has.

Say it several times and contemplate your ordinary symbols of earth, air, fire, and water. For what part of your ordinary life would you risk all you

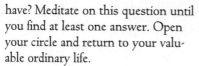

have? Meditate on this question until you find at least one answer. Open your circle and return to your valuable ordinary life.

Barbara Ardinger

NOTES:

February 7
Monday

$1st \, \vartheta$

Color of the day: White
Incense of the day: Hyssop

Celebrating Amethyst

February's birthstone is amethyst, the lovely violet-colored quartz. Violet represents spirituality and is connected to Archangel Michael. He carries very protective energies of your possessions while instilling inner strength. Moreover, violet brings the welcomed peace, calm, and stillness we need after the busyness of the holidays. It even encourages sobriety and helps heal wounds.

Obtain a magickal amethyst crystal. You will find that one will call out to you and feel tingly, special, or heavier than the others.

Now charge the amethyst during the waxing moon. Bury it outdoors in sea salt or earth. After a week, dig it up and feel if it has a higher vibration. If not, bury and repeat during the next waxing moon period.

Now you have a powerful stone to put in your mojo bag and use as an amulet or as an ally for your intentions regarding spirituality, strength, protection, healing, sobriety, love, and much more.

Stephanie Rose Bird

February 8
Tuesday

1st ♉

2nd Quarter 8:50 am

☽ v/c 11:48 pm

Color of the day: Black
Incense of the day: Geranium

Uniting with Love

In India, February 8 is known as Propose Day, a popular time to profess one's love for a significant other. In a twist on this theme, today's spell is an opportunity to propose to the most important person you will ever meet: you.

Throughout life, we all discover aspects of ourselves that don't meet with societal approval or match the identity our ego holds dear. These rejected parts, relegated to the unconscious, can weaken what is known as the unified will: a powerfully cohesive sense of self and conduit of inner wisdom.

This self-love declaration is designed to help unite the parts within, unifying your will and supercharging any of your efforts, magical and mundane.

Gazing at yourself in a mirror, conjure up waves of self-love as you recite:

Inner, outer, light, and dark,

I unite all things within my heart.

My being entire, I am whole,

And the light of truth
shines in my soul.

Melissa Tipton

NOTES:

February 9
Wednesday

2nd ♉

☽ → ♊ 5:27 am

Color of the day: Brown
Incense of the day: Lavender

Show Some Love

What you send out returns to you multiplied. So send out some positive energy today. Make a list of five people you feel grateful to know. You can choose people you see all the time or people you rarely see. Take some deep breaths. Place both hands on your heart and envision bright light at your heart. Now open up your hands like a book so your palms are radiating outward. Envision sending that light to the first person on your list. Then write that person a brief text or email. The important thing is that you let them know you appreciate them. For example:

Hey, _____! I'm thinking about how glad I am to know you. That's all. Bye!

Or:

Hi, _____! Remember when you helped me move when everyone else was busy? That was awesome. Thank you.

Repeat this process with the other four people on your list. Finish up by feeling even more gratitude.

Tess Whitehurst

February 10
Thursday

2nd ♊

Color of the day: Purple
Incense of the day: Mulberry

Peaceful Sleep Spell

Sleep is so important to our everyday lives, but a lot of people don't get enough of it. There are many reasons why this may be, and this spell works to solve them.

With a pen and paper, write down any worries or regrets you may have. Bury the paper in the earth with the knowledge that you can't change your regrets and worrying is a waste of energy.

Next, write a list of everything you want to do. Put the paper on your fridge and draw a star on it.

Lastly, combine one teaspoon of chamomile, lavender, and salt in a bowl with a piece of howlite or amethyst. Stir them together slowly and repeat this ten times:

When it's twilight, I will sleep,

Tucked away in dreamtime deep.

Sprinkle the mixture in the corners of your room and under your bed. Place the stone in a safe place. When it's time for sleep, speak the spell again. Breathe deeply and let go.

Astrea Taylor

 February 11
Friday

2nd ♊

☽ v/c 3:23 am

☽ → ♋ 6:27 pm

Color of the day: Pink
Incense of the day: Alder

Put a Curse on Ice Spell

Ice, one of the greatest forces of nature, can help weaken and remove a curse. If you feel you've been cursed and you know its source, this spell will help weaken the curse with harm to none. Write the name of the curse's source on a small piece of paper. Fold the paper. Place the paper in a small freezer bag, and add enough water to cover the paper. Then place the bag in the freezer. When frozen, remove the bag and say this charm:

With ice, the opposite of fire,

Free me from this curse as I desire.

With ice this curse's power is locked.

As it melts, the curse's power will stop.

Allow the ice to melt. When melted, pour the water and paper on the ground away from your home. The ice will serve to lock or "freeze" the curse's power. As the ice melts, the curse will weaken and eventually be stopped.

James Kambos

February 12
Saturday

2nd ♋

Color of the day: Blue
Incense of the day: Sandalwood

Looking at Love

With Valentine's Day right around the corner, it's not unusual for our thoughts to turn to love. Love can manifest in many ways. Maybe you're looking for clues to finding a new love or need help with an ongoing relationship. For some, love is less about romance and more about family, friends, or even pets.

Either way, this is a good day to take a peek at what the future holds for you where love is concerned. If you have a tarot deck, you can shuffle it and pull a card. If rune stones are more your thing, pull one of those. You can even try scrying in a dark bowl full of water. No matter how you choose to do it, empty your mind and fill your heart with all the love you can muster. Then say this spell and see what the universe has to tell you:

Love today and love to be,

Show me what I need to see.

Deborah Blake

February 13
Sunday

NOTES:

2nd ♋

Color of the day: Yellow
Incense of the day: Eucalyptus

Lucky Thirteen

The number 13 has so often been deemed unlucky. Office towers are built with no thirteenth floor, restaurants lack a number thirteen table, and there is even superstition about Friday the 13th being unlucky. Have you ever wondered why our culture practices *triskaidekaphobia*, the fear of the number thirteen? Thirteen is the number of moon cycles in a year, and was a sacred number long ago when time was told with a lunar calendar.

Let's take thirteen back as a lucky number, a sacred number. Rub your hands together until they are warm and you feel them tingle. Say:

> *Lucky thirteen, bless these*
> *hands with luck.*

Touch your eyes, ears, and mouth. Say:

> *Lucky thirteen, bless all I see,*
> *hear, and say today with luck.*

Touch your thighs. Say:

> *Lucky thirteen, bless all I do today.*
> *May the powers of the moon be mine*
> *and lucky thirteen bless me in every*
> *way. Lucky thirteen, lucky day.*

Dallas Jennifer Cobb

Ḟebruary 14
Monday

2nd ♋

☽ v/c 5:27 am

☽ → ♌ 6:17 am

Color of the day: Silver
Incense of the day: Narcissus

Valentine's Day

A Basket of Love

Craft yourself a Basket of Love—a charm to keep love and gratitude close throughout the year. You will need:

- A number of items corresponding to love and harmony (e.g., rose quartz, rose petals, lavender flowers, allspice or juniper berries, lapis, moonstone, red or pink beads, or other items that speak your love language)

- A round piece of pink, red, lavender, or floral fabric, 6 to 8 inches in diameter

- A 12-inch length of red or pink cord

- A medium-size basket or bowl

Place the correspondence items on the fabric round. Gather up the edges, hobo-style, and tie the fabric closed with the cord. Then place in the basket or bowl.

Now, every day or as the spirit moves out, begin adding items to the bowl that remind you of love, harmony, and gratitude, such as photographs, movie tickets, lines of poetry, written memories, or fabric scraps. Look at the bowl daily, seeing its fullness and memories as visible evidence of the love in your life. On days when you're feeling wistful, dip into the bowl, pull out an item, and remember.

Susan Pesznecker

NOTES:

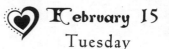

♥ February 15
Tuesday

2nd ♌

Color of the day: Maroon
Incense of the day: Cedar

Love Reset Spell

February 15 not only is the day after Valentine's Day, but has also come to be known as Love Reset Day. This is an ideal time to shift away from society's expectations and preconceived notions about love and journey deeper to explore self-love. Take yourself on a date, buy yourself some flowers, or make a special meal and set the table as you would for company. Start the day off with a cleansing bath or shower—use a fancy soap or similar bath item if you've got one! Then before you get dressed, face the mirror and say this blessing:

To you, myself, I do bring
the gift of self-love.

I recognize the divine below and above.

Your heart is worthy, open,
beautiful, and kind.

In all its forms, the love
within I shall find.

Take a favorite oil or perfume and anoint your navel, then your heart, and finally your forehead. Throughout the day, remember to be kind to yourself and have some fun!

Laura Tempest Zakroff

☾ February 16
Wednesday

2nd ♌

☽ v/c 11:56 am

Full Moon 11:56 am

☽ → ♍ 3:42 pm

Color of the day: Yellow
Incense of the day: Honeysuckle

Charging Your Magickal Tools

Every practitioner has tools that they prefer to use for their Craft. To make the most of your tools and your energy, you should recharge your ritual items at least once a year. If you happen to have snow in your area at this time, you can include that in your spell. If you do not, you can utilize shaved ice for a similar effect.

Place the tools and/or stones that you wish to recharge in a bowl. Then top them with snow and any herbs you wish to use. Chamomile is a good choice, if you have it handy, as it works to purify. The snow works toward purification and a clean slate, and it will work slowly and steadily as it melts throughout the night under the full moon. Place the bowl on your altar and say:

Lady, may your light illuminate
my work in the months to come.

Leave the items to soak overnight, then remove the next day and pat dry.

Charlynn Walls

February 17
Thursday

3rd ♍

Color of the day: Turquoise
Incense of the day: Myrrh

To Encourage Happiness in Yourself

Take a piece of rose quartz and hold it in your dominant hand. Close your eyes and think of the three happiest moments of your life. As you visualize each thought, feel the energy it generates moving through you, and transfer that energy into your piece of rose quartz. As you remember past joys, chant quietly:

Happy thoughts, happy thoughts...

As you charge the rose quartz, it will continue to grow warmer. Your crystal is fully charged when it won't hold any more of your energy.

Place the rose quartz in a magickal space, and going forward, whenever you feel sad or depressed, pick up your rose quartz and feel the happy energies and memories within it. Hold the rose quartz until you feel refreshed, renewed, and a bit happier.

Ari & Jason Mankey

February 18
Friday

3rd ♍

☉ → ♓ 11:43 am
☽ v/c 6:20 pm
☽ → ♎ 10:51 pm

Color of the day: White
Incense of the day: Yarrow

Aleuromancy: Divination with Flour

This evening, when the energies feel calm and your mind is winding down for the night, grab a handful of flour and sit calmly at a table by the light of only one candle. Think about a life issue that you'd like to gain insight into as you slowly dump the flour into a pile on the table. (You may wish to use a black tablecloth or covering.)

Close your eyes and run your hands through the flour while focusing on the issue at hand. Allow your fingers and palms to make imprints, swirls, or anything that feels natural.

When it feels like the time is right, lift your hands and examine the images you created in the flour. Try blurring your eyes and looking at the pattern from different locations around the table. Make note of any images you see, and determine their meaning to the best of your ability. Extinguish the candle.

Raven Digitalis

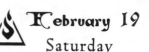

February 19
Saturday

3rd ♎

Color of the day: Black
Incense of the day: Patchouli

Warm Memories

In winter, fire is a vital source of light and heat. However, it's not convenient to carry a fire everywhere you go, and not every place is necessarily heated as much as you'd like. This spell captures the memory of heat from a fire to warm you in its absence. You will need a small square of sturdy cotton cloth in any fire color and some string.

Place a small amount of ash from a campfire, woodstove, etc., on the cloth. Concentrate on your memories of warm, cheerful fires. Then say:

Wood is the food of fire.

Ash is the bone of fire.

Warm me with their memories,

For this is my desire.

Repeat the verse with each fold of the cloth. Begin by folding the top third of the cloth toward you, covering the ash. Fold again toward you to the bottom edge. Fold the left third of the roll over the top to the middle. Fold the right third underneath, forming a flat S shape. Bind with string. Carry with you for warmth.

Elizabeth Barrette

February 20
Sunday

3rd ♎

Color of the day: Amber
Incense of the day: Marigold

Green Money

We all feel impoverished at times. Speaking in a strong voice, tell the Goddess what you need. Show her your piled-up bills or your overcharged credit cards. Explain to her what your obligations are and how, with her help, you expect to be able to meet them. Next, tell her that you deserve to be prosperous and remind her—and yourself—of the ways you're already rich: in family and friends, good grades in school, a good job or career.

When you're sure she's listening, cast a circle around yourself and raise power by clapping, shaking a rattle, or drumming. Visualize cash, checks, dividends, and stocks flying to you. Visualize job offers and gifts pouring in and piling up around you. Invoke prosperity:

The things I need,

The people I've seen,

The wealth I'm deserving—

Make everything green!

Green money, green,

Bright silver and gold—

Come to me swiftly,

Come in from the cold.

Barbara Ardinger

February 21
Monday

3rd ♎

☽ v/c 12:02 am

☽ → ♏ 4:19 am

Color of the day: Lavender
Incense of the day: Neroli

Presidents' Day

Tarot Spread for the Unseen

Today is Card Reading Day. Many people will reread greeting cards, but you can also read tarot cards. With the waning moon in Scorpio today, there's an added dimension of going deep. This tarot spread picks up on your blind spot, or that which you keep hidden from yourself.

Hold a deck of tarot cards and connect with it. Pass it around your waist widdershins (counterclockwise) three times and say:

Deck of cards, tell me true,

Reveal what's hidden,
through and through.

Shuffle the cards and think about your blind spot. Choose four cards from the middle of the deck that intuitively feel right.

Card 1: The blind spot—what is hidden from you

Card 2: How you perceive it

Card 3: How others perceive it

Card 4: How to make friends with it

Write the messages down in your journal and meditate on the meanings. Negative cards may indicate that shadow work is needed.

Astrea Taylor

NOTES:

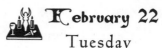

February 22
Tuesday

3rd ♏

Color of the day: White
Incense of the day: Basil

Contemplating Ibeji Altar

Today is a unique day. It's a date filled with twos, as in 2/22/2022. This brings to mind the Yoruba orisha Ibeji, the sacred twins: Taiwo (first born) and Kehinde (second born). Yorubaland, a place in and around Nigeria, has a 5 percent twins birth rate. Twins are revered there and are considered one soul in two bodies. Ibeji brings fun, mischief, childish curiosity, and abundance. On this ideal day to conjure the twins, create an altar to draw them near.

On a small red and blue piece of fabric, set out a nonmetallic plate (earthenware or wood). On this plate, place candies, cakes, and baby bananas (Manzanos). Make the Ibeji's favorite dish: *arroz con pollo* ("rice with chicken"). There are wonderful recipes for this dish online. Put this in a Pyrex or wooden bowl. Do some reflection on the magickal qualities of Ibeji and divination to let you know when to dispose of these items and take apart your altar.

Stephanie Rose Bird

February 23
Wednesday

3rd ♏
☽ v/c 4:24 am
☽ → ♐ 8:29 am
4th Quarter 5:32 pm

Color of the day: Topaz
Incense of the day: Bay laurel

Spark Your Inner Light

By February, our new-year enthusiasm might begin to wane as resolutions fade and a feeling of routine settles in. This is a great time to rekindle your inner spark, and all you need is a candle in the color of your choice.

Come into a meditative state, allowing each inhale and exhale to lead you to a place of calm. At your solar plexus, midway between the belly and the heart, imagine a golden yellow sun. Feel the energy of this sun spreading outward, filling your entire body and energy field.

Holding the unlit candle, allow this golden energy to pour down your arms and into the candle. Then place the candle on a heatproof surface and light it. Give thanks for the power of light, and feel your renewed sense of purpose and passion burning bright. Allow the candle to burn down safely, or simply snuff it out with thanks.

Melissa Tipton

❤ February 24
Thursday

4th ♐

☽ v/c 10:24 pm

Color of the day: Green
Incense of the day: Nutmeg

Draw a New Love

Today is the Romanian holiday of Dragobete. In addition to being considered the first day of spring and a day for honoring love and lovers, Dragobete is also a magical day for gathering plants for love magic as well as collecting snow to be melted and used in potions.

Today, obtain one red rose. Scatter its petals across a small baking sheet lined with parchment and bake for ten minutes at 275°F. Once the petals are cool, place them in a bowl and empower them in sunlight for a minute or two. (If there's no sunlight available, you can just envision them being filled with golden white light.) Bundle the petals, along with a garnet, into a piece of red flannel. Tie it closed with ribbon or twine. Hold the charm to your heart and conjure up the ecstatic feeling of falling in love. Place the charm on your altar or sleep with it under your pillow until your new love has appeared.

Tess Whitehurst

▽ February 25
Friday

4th ♐

☽ → ♑ 11:27 am

Color of the day: Pink
Incense of the day: Rose

Consecrating Water

February is a month when many of us see water in one form or another. Depending on where you live, that could be rain, snow, fog, or some combination of them all. Water is necessary for life. It washes the land clean and nurtures the plants. Plus, of course, it is one of the four elements that many Witches integrate into their magical work.

Today, collect some water to use in your rites, blessing and consecrating it for your own magic. If you can, gather water from a source outside. If Mother Nature isn't cooperating, tap water will do. It all comes from the same source. Put the water in a container you can keep on your altar or with your magical tools, and say:

*I bless and consecrate this
water for magical use.*

*The essence of life, the tears of
the sky, gift of the Goddess.*

So mote it be!

Deborah Blake

February 26
Saturday

4th ♑

Color of the day: Gray
Incense of the day: Rue

The Goddess Awakens Meditation

Snow may still cover the ground in many regions, but the Goddess, the life force of planet Earth, begins to awaken now. Ice begins to melt, buds swell, and early crocus bloom. With this meditation you can honor the Goddess for this miracle. On your altar place the Empress card from your Tarot deck faceup. Beside it set a small dish of soil. Potting soil or garden soil would be fine. Study the card and meditate on it as you crumble the soil with your fingers. Then say:

> Goddess, you control nature and the life force,
>
> You set the seasons upon their course.
>
> With shades of green and flowers you clothe the earth.
>
> Thank you, Divine Mother, for this season of rebirth.

Meditate for as long as you like, thinking about how the Goddess awakens quietly beneath the earth. When done, return the card to your deck and scatter the soil outside as an offering to the Goddess.

James Kambos

February 27
Sunday

4th ♑

☽ v/c 9:49 am
☽ → ♒ 1:36 pm

Color of the day: Orange
Incense of the day: Almond

Ellen Terry, Queen of Swords

Happy birthday to Ellen Terry, the model for the Queen of Swords in the Rider-Waite-Smith tarot deck. The image created by Pamela Colman Smith may have been inspired by a role Terry played on stage: the Viking queen Hjordis, whose name means "sword goddess."

In the Tarot, swords represent air, knowledge, and ideas, and the Queen is the subtle wielder of that element. Invoke the power of the Queen of Swords when you need the knowledge of strength to cut to the heart of the matter. Hold Pamela Colman Smith's image before you and chant:

> Sword in hand, rosaries at your wrist,
>
> You wear velvet gloves, hide mailed fists!
>
> Share your knowledge, share your wealth,
>
> That I may take it into myself.

Natalie Zaman

February 28
Monday

4th ♒

☽ v/c 9:01 pm

Color of the day: Ivory
Incense of the day: Rosemary

Magical Sleep Technique

Sometimes insomnia can make us crazy as we lie awake at night, worrying or thinking. A lack of sleep can negatively impact our physical, mental, and emotional health. What if you had a magic spell that helped you fall asleep when you wanted to? This magical technique can both pro-voke and invoke sleep when you want or need it, whether you wish to get to sleep at night, go back to sleep after waking, or nap in the afternoon.

Lie down and close your eyes. Place your hands on your thighs, palms down. Begin to gently tap your fingers against your thighs for about three minutes, and become aware of your breathing. Breathe deep into your belly, and as you exhale, release all tension. Gradually slow down the tapping, and keep breathing. Notice how your breath slows, your body relaxes, and your mind quiets. Before you know it, you will be asleep. Magically.

Dallas Jennifer Cobb

NOTES:

March

March is upon us! March is a month of unpredictable weather. Will the weather spirits decide to bring us a last hurrah of winter in the form of a blustery snowstorm or instead bring us signs of spring's beginning in the form of budding trees and perhaps rain showers sprinkled with mild, sunny days? There really is no telling! However, for those of us who follow the Wheel of the Year, the spring equinox is a time of new beginnings, regardless of the weather.

Rituals of spring and new beginnings will take place around the globe this month. Druids still gather at Stonehenge to welcome the rising sun on the morning of the equinox. March also is the time to celebrate the festival of Holi, popular in India and Nepal. People engage in paint fights, covering each other in festive splatters of vibrant color, welcoming the arrival of spring and all its vibrancy.

In March, however you choose to celebrate, work the magick of new beginnings!

Blake Octavian Blair

March 1
Tuesday

4th ♒
☽ → ♓ 3:53 pm

Color of the day: Red
Incense of the day: Bayberry

Mardi Gras (Fat Tuesday)

The Triple Flames of Success

Mardi Gras is a day of celebrating life's riches, and this spell aligns with this energetic current to empower your magic. You'll need three candles, which can be purple, green, and gold/yellow, or any color(s) you choose. Set the candles in a row on a heatproof surface.

Choose a desired magical outcome, and spend some time in meditation, really conjuring up the sights, emotions, sounds, and maybe even smells and tastes of enjoying this success.

Start by lighting the candle on the left. This candle is your present moment, and you're setting it alight with the energy of your successful outcome. Use this candle to ignite the second one, which represents the stepping-stone stage, where the energy of your spell is weaving the threads of your magic into fruition. Finally, light the third candle, sparking the flame of your successful outcome. Give thanks, and let the candles burn down safely or snuff them out with gratitude.

Melissa Tipton

March 2
Wednesday

4th ♓
New Moon 12:35 pm

Color of the day: White
Incense of the day: Marjoram

Ash Wednesday

Dark Moon Divination

The dark (new) moon is a prime time for divination, with Earth's energies quiet and pulled inward.

You'll need a tarot or oracle deck and a dark cloth. Find the date and time of the next new moon (2:24 a.m. EDT on April 1). Work in a quiet room and wear dark clothing.

Spread out the cloth. Shuffle and/or cut your deck, pausing to see what comes to mind. You may already have a question to ask the cards, or perhaps something will occur to you. If nothing comes, proceed.

Deal one card in the center of the cloth, then lay cards at 9:00 (on a clock face), 12:00, 3:00, and 6:00.

The center card represents you. The 6:00 card is your current situation; the 9:00 card reveals emotional obstacles; the 12:00 card (full moon position) shows the situation's future possibilities; and the 3:00 card points to obstacles outside of yourself.

Let meanings flow between the cards. Keep them on your altar until the next new moon.

Susan Pesznecker

March 3
Thursday

1st ♓

☽ v/c 4:45 pm

☽ → ♈ 7:52 pm

Color of the day: Purple
Incense of the day: Carnation

Ancestral Magic

March is Women's History Month, a good time to perform ancestral magic. Envision the women of your lineage: your mother, grandmothers, great-grandmothers, and beyond; your cousins, aunts, and great-aunts. Maybe you have photos of them you can place on your altar, or things of theirs, such as jewelry or dishes. As you look at them, invoke the resilience of these strong women who survived, thrived, and had children. Their strength and resilience are written in your DNA. Envision a strand of light connecting you to them. Inhale strength and resilience, then exhale healing back along the ancestral line. Incant:

I call on the brave women of my lineage to bless me with strength, resilience, wisdom, and joy. Let the good lives of these women live in me always. May I know the collected wisdom of my foremothers and be held in their tender care, and may I heal all genetic wounds I carry. So mote it be.

Dallas Jennifer Cobb

 March 4
Friday

1st ♈

Color of the day: Coral
Incense of the day: Cypress

Swan Sewel

On this day in 1877, *Swan Lake* debuted on stage in Moscow. The ballet tells a love story affected by elements of stability (the white swan) and chaos (the black swan). White and black, light and shadow, are part of life and are necessary for balance. Create a sewel (a charm made of string and feathers) to aid in this work. Find or purchase a black feather and a white feather (swan feathers if you can!). Tie a string to each, saying as you do so:

White swan, bring structure.

Blank swan, bring spontaneity.

Tie the strings together and say:

Bless me with the light to see

And the adventure of what will be.

Hang the sewel over your doorway or by your bed to bring the balance of swan magic to your life.

Natalie Zaman

March 5
Saturday

1st ♈

☽ v/c 11:02 pm

Color of the day: Blue
Incense of the day: Ivy

Self-Care

Self-care is important not just in your daily life but in your magickal practice as well. If you take the time to heal yourself, then you will have the energy you need to tap into later.

To restore your energy, take a ritual bath or shower. Add any scent you associate with strength to the water. The herbs and oils in the mint or citrus family are some of my favorites. Allow yourself to soak in the water and feel yourself taking in what you need from the herbs in order to remove stress or anxiety. As the bath is drained or the water from the shower is flowing down the drain, say:

As the water flows down, may
my strength rebound.

Follow up this spell with a solid night's sleep for best effect.

Charlynn Walls

March 6
Sunday

1st ♈

☽ → ♉ 3:00 am

Color of the day: Yellow
Incense of the day: Heliotrope

The Witch's Cottage

Today, take stock of what really recharges you. As much as possible, limit your usage of electricity and devices. Whenever I do this, I imagine I'm in a witch's cottage in the woods, with no electricity or internet. It really connects me with my body and the energy at hand.

When you're ready to begin, put your devices away and say:

Here and now, disconnected,

I find myself better than expected.

Without a phone or any wattage,

I'm peaceful in my witch's cottage.

Ground into your body and feel the energy around you. Do what comes naturally. Instead of watching television, read a book, make art, or take a walk. When it gets dark, light candles instead of turning on lights. Send psychic messages instead of texts. Before going to sleep, blow out the candles and think about what recharged you. Send gratitude to yourself for this fun experiment.

Astrea Taylor

March 7
Monday

1st ♉

Color of the day: Silver
Incense of the day: Lily

A Threshold Protection Spell

Use this spell to protect your threshold and keep negative energy from entering your front door. You'll need three cloves of garlic, some salt, and a broom. First, peel the garlic cloves and rub each one with a bit of salt. Bury the garlic near your front door. Then sprinkle a small amount of salt along your front door's threshold. Now take your broom and sweep the salt away. From your threshold, continue to sweep the salt away from your door, off your porch, and down your front steps. Sweep to the street if that's possible. As you sweep, say:

Protect this home, garlic and salt,

I command all negative energy to halt.

This spell is good to use after a negative person has left your home and you need to restore positive vibrations. Repeat once a year or when you feel the need.

James Kambos

March 8
Tuesday

1st ♉

☽ v/c 9:35 am
☽ → ♊ 1:40 pm

Color of the day: White
Incense of the day: Ylang-ylang

International Women's Day

Today, light a white candle on your altar. Relax, center your mind, and say:

Great Goddess, I call on you. Lend your light and strength to all women, of all races, in all countries now. May the Divine Feminine and Divine Masculine come into complementary balance in human culture, for the highest good of all. Thank you.

Extinguish the candle. Next, look through your library or do a web search to choose a woman from history (recent or ancient) who inspires you, and whom you'd like to emulate in some way. Create, print out, or obtain an image of her that you like. Frame it and place it on your altar near the candle. Light the candle for a few minutes daily until the next full moon (on March 18 at 3:18 a.m. EST) while gazing at her image. Invite her powerful qualities into your being so that you can carry on the legacy of her unique expression of strength, while also making it your own.

Tess Whitehurst

March 9
Wednesday

1st ♊

Color of the day: Brown
Incense of the day: Lilac

heat In, Cold Out

Spring is a season of sniffles and chills. After the long winter, everyone wants to run outside as soon as the weather warms, even if it's nippy and raining. Some people can't wait to start gardening, no matter how dank and soggy the ground is. That often leads to a lot of folks catching cold.

For this healing spell, brew a cup of hot tea. Echinacea boosts the immune system but lacks a pleasing taste. Add lemon (for vitamin C), peppermint (to soothe coughing), or ginger (warming) to improve flavor and effects. Hold the cup in your hands. Feel the heat and breathe in the warm steam. Breathe out, saying:

Herbs and water, brewed about,

Heat come in and cold go out!

Strengthen body, bolster will,

Drive away the springtime chill!

Drink the tea, focusing on the healing properties of the herbs. Repeat the verse one last time as you finish the cup.

Elizabeth Barrette

March 10
Thursday

1st ♊
2nd Quarter 5:45 am
☽ v/c 11:43 am

Color of the day: Green
Incense of the day: Mulberry

Reach Out and Say hello

Many of us have a tendency to hibernate during the winter, and that's not necessarily a bad thing. But as the weather warms and spring approaches, now is a good time to reach out to folks you might not have seen or talked to for a while. Is there a friend or family member who has been showing up in your thoughts or dreams? Perhaps there is someone about whom you have been thinking, "I should really check on so-and-so" or "I really should stop by one of these days." Say this spell to point you toward the people who need to hear from you the most, or to give you that push in the right direction for an impromptu visit.

Time to call and say hello,

A good day to go far and near.

Send me where I need to go,

Tell me who most needs the cheer.

Deborah Blake

March 11
Friday

2nd ♊

☽ → ♋ 2:24 am

Color of the day: Purple
Incense of the day: Alder

Find Your Household Deity

People all around the world have honored gods and goddesses who bless and protect their homes. Where did your ancestors live? Search back as far as you can, not just to the city your grandparents lived in but to the land where your many-times-great-grandparents lived. Read about the history of that land, about the beliefs of the people. Find the household god or goddess in your family history—a food giver, perhaps, or one who protects the hearth or the pantry, or a giver of hospitality.

Set up a new household altar in a place where you'll never have to move it. Cast a circle that encloses your entire home (including the garage and the garden, if applicable). Invoke your ancestral deity:

Beneficent one, _____ (name of deity),

As my foremothers and forefathers honored and called to you,

I also ask for your protection and blessing of my home.

Live with me. Bless my home.

Bring harmony, comfort, and happiness in my home.

Barbara Ardinger

NOTES:

March 12
Saturday

2nd ♋

Color of the day: Indigo
Incense of the day: Magnolia

Flower Magick

For some people, winter is grueling, with long, dark days and very cold weather. For others, it is more foggy, damp, and dreary. The advent of spring opens new windows of magickal possibilities, represented beautifully by the unfurling of new bright green leaves and flowers. Today is just the day to engage with flowers, as it is Plant a Flower Day. Narcissus is a readily available, heady-scented harbinger of spring. Moreover, its aromatic possibilities in the home are endless. Its scent has a very positive effect by uplifting the spirits. Narcissus also brings prosperity and wealth, good luck, clarity, and inspiration. In temperate zones it is still too cold to plant outdoors, but this activity is a great way for anyone to engage in nature.

Fill a three-to-four-inch container without drainage holes with tiny pebbles or small river rocks. Pack some narcissus bulbs into the container. Gently place the bulbs so they are balanced on the stones. Do not bruise or break the bulbs. Add enough water to cover the bottoms of the bulbs. Add a splash of alcohol to the water.

Breathe in the deep, floral high notes of your narcissus once they bloom and feel your spirits soar!

Stephanie Rose Bird

NOTES:

March 13
Sunday

2nd ♋

☽ v/c 11:44 am

☽ → ♌ 3:32 pm

Color of the day: Amber
Incense of the day: Frankincense

Daylight Saving Time
begins at 2:00 a.m.

Daylight Saving Time Meditation

The discovery of the planet Pluto was announced on this day in 1930. Then eighty-five years later, photographs revealed a heart-shaped area on its surface.

Today, as we spring ahead and light returns to the world, chant this mantra as a reminder that light and love can penetrate the deepest darkness across time and space:

The heart of darkness

Sends forth its rays

Of love and light

To the lengthening days.

Repeat as needed whenever you need to be reminded of the presence of light and love.

Natalie Zaman

 March 14
Monday

2nd ♌

Color of the day: Ivory
Incense of the day: Hyssop

Circle of Friends

Write your name in the middle of a blank sheet of paper. Around your name, write the names of friends you are trying to strengthen relationships with. We find this spell is especially helpful when you write down the names of people who live a distance away.

After you've written down the names of your friends, draw a circle connecting them all together, with spokes from that circle pointing back to you. As you draw the circle and the spokes, say:

May the bonds we have
forged remain strong,

So we might share life's
happiness, pain, and song.

May we be connected as long
as our friendships last.

This spell of friendship
has now been cast!

Place your piece of paper in a safe place. Retrieve it and redraw the circle and spokes if you feel a friendship slipping away from you.

Ari & Jason Mankey

March 15
Tuesday

2nd ♌

☽ v/c 6:56 am

Color of the day: Scarlet
Incense of the day: Geranium

Planting the Seed of Abundance

Honensai, or Harvest Festival, is a Japanese celebration of fertility and prosperity. So today, reflect on the abundance that is already richly flowing through your life, and contemplate what you'd like to channel this energy into next. A creative project? A budding friendship? Your physical health?

Once you've chosen a focus, select a crystal that symbolizes your desire, such as aventurine for new friendship, apatite for creative projects, or clear quartz as a multipurpose crystal ally. Come into a meditative state, holding the crystal, and imagine it as a potent seed, containing the spark of your desired outcome at its core. Visualize this seed germinating and flourishing, putting forth an abundance of divine energy in relation to your goal as you recite:

I call upon (crystal name)
as I plant this seed,

Open to abundance, ready to receive.

My heart's desire unfolds most true,

With love and gratitude,
in comes the new!

Keep the crystal in your pocket or display it where you can see it often.

Melissa Tipton

NOTES:

Page 56

March 16
Wednesday

2nd ♌

☽ → ♍ 12:59 am

Color of the day: Topaz
Incense of the day: Honeysuckle

Purim begins at sundown

Revealing Inner Truth

Today the moon is waxing, and it is a good time to do reflective meditation work. To begin this meditation, find a place that is comfortable and quiet. Light a white candle to represent the inner truth you seek. Take a black mirror or other reflective surface and set it behind the candle to reflect the flame. Sit quietly and meditate on the reflection you see. When you feel ready, bring the meditation to a close. Say:

In the dark there is truth. See it reflected and revealed to me.

Repeat this phrase three times, then snuff out the candle. What needs to be revealed to you soon will be.

Charlynn Walls

March 17
Thursday

2nd ♏

Color of the day: Crimson
Incense of the day: Balsam

Saint Patrick's Day

Serpent Wisdom Spell

The snake is an ancient symbol of wisdom, creation, transformation, magic, and healing. Serpentine tattoos and wearing snake jewelry can help call upon the protection of the serpent spirit, but sometimes you need something more subtle on your body.

Infuse some olive oil (or similar oil) with powder made from dragon's blood resin in a small bottle just before the moon is full. Set it on your altar and shake it gently in the morning and evening for at least three days. Then dip your finger in the oil and draw a snake on your arm or leg, from wrist to elbow or ankle to knee. Start with a full fingerprint to make the head, then draw the body slithering, with the tail pointing toward the center of your body. Say:

Serpent dwelling within,
protect me without,

Slithering above, below,
and all about.

Watchful eyes, long fluid spine,
and sparkling scales.

Guide and bring me safely
through dangerous trails.

Refresh as needed.

Laura Tempest Zakroff

NOTES:

March 18
Friday

2nd ♏
☾ull ☾oon 3:18 am
☽ v/c 4:11 am
☽ → ♎ 7:26 am

Color of the day: Rose
Incense of the day: Orchid

Rainbow Positivity Charm

The Virgo full moon arrives early this morning, and it coincides with the popular Indian holiday known as Holi, when festivalgoers celebrate love, laughter, forgiveness, and the arrival of spring by taking to the streets and gleefully coloring other people with colored powder as well as color-filled water balloons. Today, empower seven 6-to-8-inch ribbons in sunlight (or candlelight, if the sun isn't out, but be careful to hold them a safe distance away from the flame), one for each color of the rainbow. As you empower them, feel that they are absorbing the energies of joy and positivity. Braid them together, and see yourself weaving bright light into them as you braid. Bunch or coil the braid and hold it to your heart with both hands. Feel even more bright light at your heart and send it into the charm. Hang it above your front door for all-around positivity, or place it near a photo of anyone you'd like to bless with positive energy.

Tess Whitehurst

March 19
Saturday

3rd ♎

Color of the day: Brown
Incense of the day: Sandalwood

A Magical Spring Cleaning

With the spring equinox approaching, it's a perfect time to cleanse magical items and spaces. If you have a room or sanctum devoted to your Craft, start there. Vacuum or sweep, perhaps with a new broom/besom. Work sunwise (clockwise), finishing in the center of the room. Wash the windows; dust the walls and wash them with lavender- or mint-scented water. Dust everything, and shine any wood with honeycomb wax or linseed oil.

Next comes the altar space. Wipe or dust the altar as needed and place a clean altar cloth there. Cleanse altar tools and items, using soap and water if needed. Dry with a soft cloth and bless or anoint items with a favorite essential or consecrated oil. Place new candles on the altar, retiring the old ones for spellwork.

In addition to cleansing and blessing your tools, it's a good time to charge them under sunlight or moonlight. It's also an excellent time to make or purchase new tools.

When all is done, pause for a ritual of gratitude in your new space.

Susan Pesznecker

March 20
Sunday

3rd ♎

☽ v/c 8:40 am

☉ → ♈ 11:33 am

☽ → ♏ 11:45 am

Color of the day: Orange
Incense of the day: Juniper

Spring Equinox – Ostara

Ostara Collage

We've had half a year of dark. Now we're yearning for the light, for spring to rain on us, for green shoots to rise to our ankles. We're listening to hear the little chirpy birds and see the bees and butterflies. This is mid-spring, the season when the Goddess comes back to earth. Everything she brings to us is new.

Instead of building an altar to celebrate Ostara, begin a creative project: a springtime collage of light and darkness. Buy a piece of poster board in your favorite springtime color and cut it in a circle. Look in magazines and catalogs or search online for images that suggest light and darkness, like shadowy meadows or sunlit gardens. Add images of solar and lunar gods and goddesses.

Paste your images on the poster board and add glittery stickers and other decoration. You may find you've created a collage that looks like the familiar yin-yang symbol, where there is a seed of darkness in the light half and a seed of light in the dark half. Good for you!

Barbara Ardinger

NOTES:

▽ **March 21**
Monday

3rd ♏

Color of the day: Gray
Incense of the day: Clary sage

Showering Off the Day

This evening, after the day has come to a close, light a single candle and hop in the shower while holding a hand of sea salt. Before stepping fully into the water, place the salt on your head and imagine it absorbing energies that have accumulated around your mind and aura.

Step slowly into the running water until you're fully submerged. Speak to the water, thanking it for cleansing your mind, body, and spirit, as well as for nourishing your life and the life of the world.

Dim your vision as the salt washes down, noticing if insights come to your psychic mind. Humbly communicate with the water, asking for its assistance with any particular "releasings" you desire.

Conclude by rinsing off your whole body and meditating somewhere while you dry. Take it easy tonight, knowing you'll wake up refreshed and ready to go when the morning comes! Be sure to extinguish the candle.

Raven Digitalis

▽ **March 22**
Tuesday

3rd ♏

☽ v/c 12:01 pm
☽ → ♐ 2:59 pm

Color of the day: Maroon
Incense of the day: Ginger

Cleansing Bath Magic

As the day begins, the moon is waning in the deep water sign of Scorpio. It's the perfect time to use water magic to cleanse yourself of any negative energy you may have.

This spell uses three handfuls of bath salts, a teaspoon of lavender flowers (or three drops of lavender oil), and a hot bath.

Soak in the bathtub with the salt and the lavender. Imagine that the hot water is drawing out any negative energy from you, like a tea bag releasing tea.

When you're ready to leave, pull the plug and envision the bad energy staying in the water. As the water drains, say:

Negativity, I leave you behind me.

The cleansing waters have set me free.

As the water swirls down the drain,

May we never meet again.

Towel off, knowing you've left it behind you for good. Walk away without looking back.

Astrea Taylor

March 23
Wednesday

3rd ♐

Color of the day: Yellow
Incense of the day: Lavender

A Grass Spell for the Garden

Ordinary grasses are known for their protective qualities. When charged with magical intent, they're excellent for protecting the garden. Early in the spring, cut some tall grasses. Just a handful will do. Tie the bunch of grass in the middle with some jute twine or a few more stems of grass. As you stand in your garden, hold the bundle of grass. Charge it with these words:

Green and noble grasses,

Guard this garden as
each season passes.

Guard the seeds I plant
with my own hand.

Protect the vegetables and
the flowers so grand.

Lay the bundle of grass in a corner of your garden. Leave it undisturbed. Let it return to the earth from where it came. Repeat this spell next spring if you wish.

James Kambos

March 24
Thursday

3rd ♐

☽ v/c 8:59 am
☽ → ♑ 5:54 pm

Color of the day: Purple
Incense of the day: Apricot

Thawing Incantation

When the winter winds arrived, we drew our necks down, bundled up, and became guarded against the cold. As the winter weather begins to show signs of easing up, let's do a thawing spell to release and awaken the frozen parts of ourselves. This spell is best done indoors.

Standing in a safe and private space, gaze down at your feet. Say:

I thaw what holds me stuck in place.

Place your hands on your belly. Say:

I thaw the anger I have held so tight.

Place your hands over your heart. Say:

I thaw my passionate, tender feelings.

Press your hands together in front of you, perhaps rubbing them lightly. Say:

I thaw my creativity and skill.

Holding one hand to your throat and one to your heart, say:

It is safe to thaw out, to speak out,
to feel fully and be real. I thaw myself
and stand here, fully present.

Dallas Jennifer Cobb

March 25
Friday

3rd ♑
4th Quarter 1:37 am

Color of the day: Pink
Incense of the day: Yarrow

Balancing Spring

Spring is a season of balance, poised between winter and summer. It's also a time of opposites and extremes, like a tug-of-war between the two seasons to see who rules for the day. This makes it a good time to work on balance in your life.

Think about the different aspects of balance. There is static balance when things are level and calm. Then there is dynamic balance when things are equally matched but rocking back and forth.

Consider how balance moves through your life. Sometimes it helps you stay calm. Other times it pushes you this way and that.

Make a list of things in your life. Try to match pairs of good and bad influences that counterbalance each other. Where the good things seem weak, think about how to strengthen them. Where there is a gap, imagine how you could fill it. If it's actually going well, consider positive challenges you could add. Balancing exercises can also help. You might explore something like yoga or tai chi.

Elizabeth Barrette

March 26
Saturday

4th ♑
☽ v/c 7:51 pm
☽ → ♒ 8:55 pm

Color of the day: Blue
Incense of the day: Patchouli

A Ritual When Waking in the Night

Anxiety enters the lives of even the happiest people; life is like that. There may be times when anxiety troubles your sleep—an essential element of self-care when dealing with troubling issues. If you find yourself awake in the wee hours, try this breathing meditation and spell to help you slip back into sleep. The number four represents stability, and a firm foundation is the basis of this work.

1. Breathe in for four counts.

2. Hold for four counts.

3. Breathe out for four counts.

4. Hum (or chant a single sound) for four counts.

   4 x 4 x 4 x 4

Repeat as many times as needed.

Natalie Zaman

March 27
Sunday

4th ♒

Color of the day: Gold
Incense of the day: Hyacinth

Doodle Meditation

It's a wonderful day to strengthen your divination abilities and meditate on abundance at the same time. Today is National Scribble Day!

First, utilize the fire element to aid your work in two ways:

1. Light an orange candle for energy and a green candle for abundance.

2. Light some rose incense to invoke creativity and the goddess Lakshmi.

Beautiful Lakshmi, of the Hindu pantheon, will shower your day with fruitful relationships, steadfast love, money, and abundance.

First, obtain a piece of plain brown paper (paper bag or kraft paper) of the desired size.

Tape the paper to a sturdy, smooth surface, like your desk or, if working smaller, a clipboard.

Set an intention having to do with abundance.

With any pen or pencil of your liking, begin scribbling. Take some cleansing breaths, relax your body, and scribble some more. Do this until you feel like you've expended your energy on your full intent.

Gaze deeply at your scribbling. What does it suggest you do to allow abundance to flow into your life? Extinguish the candles and incense when you're done.

Stephanie Rose Bird

NOTES:

March 28
Monday

4th ♒

☽ v/c 10:11 am

Color of the day: White
Incense of the day: Neroli

Magical Spring Cleaning

Spring is here and it is time to do some magical housecleaning. If you want to be really efficient, you can combine this with actual physical cleaning and do both at one time. If it is warm enough where you are, open as many windows as you can. If it is still too cold for that, open one window at the start and one at the end, and close them right away.

Take a sage wand or your favorite cleansing incense and walk through all the rooms of your home, concentrating on clearing away any stagnant or negative energy. Send it out the windows, replacing it with the new clear air. Then take a bowl of salt and water and sprinkle it throughout each room to wash it clear. As you do your cleansing, repeat this spell:

My home is clear and clean,

Filled with fresh energy and light.

Deborah Blake

March 29
Tuesday

4th ♒

☽ → ♓ 12:32 am

Color of the day: Red
Incense of the day: Cedar

Flour in the Wind

By the end of March, we are often imagining the places we want to visit in the summer. To aid in our travels, we like to perform this spell that honors the wind and the spirits of air.

On a windy day, take a small handful of flour and go outside to a place where you won't be disturbed. In your mind's eye, visualize where you wish to travel this year. Visualize yourself arriving there safely as you feel the spring breeze whirl around you.

Open your hand and lightly blow the flour in your palm into the wind. As you blow the flour, visualize your journeys being picked up by the winds and scattered to where you wish to go, and then say:

May the spirits of air take me where I want to go.

Let my journeys be where the kind winds blow!

Ari & Jason Mankey

March 30
Wednesday

4th ♓

Color of the day: Brown
Incense of the day: Bay laurel

Automatic Drawing Exercise

March 30 celebrates a humble tool that is often overlooked in favor of fancy pens and markers—the wondrous pencil. If you're into coloring books, you might have already discovered the joys of colored pencils. The quality ones are very smooth to draw with, which makes them a great choice for the mediumistic practice of automatic writing or drawing. This is a relaxing exercise that can yield some amazing results.

All you need is some paper and a dependable pencil. Set yourself in a quiet, comfortable place with a reliable surface to draw on. If you have a specific question for a guide, spirit, ancestor, or deity, ask it now. Otherwise you can just see what comes. Put the pencil point to paper, close your eyes, take some slow, deep breaths, and relax. Let your hand move as it wants across the page for as long as it needs. Once it becomes still, look at the paper and see what shapes or words have formed there to divine your answer.

Laura Tempest Zakroff

 ## March 31
Thursday

4th ♓

☽ v/c 2:37 am
☽ → ♈ 5:30 am

Color of the day: Turquoise
Incense of the day: Carnation

Back to the Roots

Spring is springing and the roots of Mother Earth's flora are beginning to grow in strength. Let's do a little work on our own roots.

Sit calmly in a comfortable spot outside, wearing minimal or comfortable clothing (or none at all!). Visualize your root chakra growing down into the earth in a dark red color. While doing so, repeat the Sanskrit word *Muladhara*. (This is the ancient Vedic Hindu name for the base chakra.)

Visualize this root going deep into the earth's molten core, feeding your body with comforting warmth. Then imagine the root slowly ascending back into your body, and take a number of deep breaths while you see its nourishing energy filling your whole being.

Cross your arms in front of your chest and speak words affirming that you are a child of Mother Nature. Consider performing yoga or additional visualizations that connect you with the Mighty Mother.

Raven Digitalis

April

This month we move from dark to light, from cold to warm, from brown to green. April is a magical month that starts with April Fools' Day and ends on the eve of May Day, begins with a joke and ends with an outdoor sleep-out. Here in Ontario, Canada, the average temperature at the beginning of April is close to freezing. It's common to have snow on the ground. Throughout April a magical transformation occurs: the temperature climbs as high as 66 degrees Fahrenheit (19 degrees Celsius) and flowers bloom.

Post-equinox, the days grow longer. Between April 1 and 30, the daylight increases from 12 hours and 46 minutes to 14 hours and 8 minutes. As the sun travels northward, it climbs in the sky. Not only do days lengthen, but shadows shorten as well. It is inviting to get outdoors. Like the plants that need sunlight to conduct photosynthesis, we humans need sunlight to help manufacture vitamin D.

This month, make time to enjoy the outdoors. Get out in the daylight, take evening walks in the twilight after dinner, contemplate your garden, and turn your face toward the sun at every chance. With winter coming to an end, now is your time to transform.

Dallas Jennifer Cobb

April 1
Friday

4th ♈

New Moon 2:24 am

Color of the day: Coral

Incense of the day: Mint

April Fools' Day – All Fools' Day

Grand New Start

This spell takes advantage of the new moon today to create paths and connections where there were none before. You'll need the Fool tarot card, a white chime candle, a candleholder, honey, meadowsweet, and a lighter.

At your altar, place the Fool card before you upside down. Dress the top quarter of the candle with honey, and think about how sweet your new beginning will be. Sprinkle the meadowsweet over the top of the candle while imagining you're being showered in blessings. Say:

With candle, honey,

Fire, and meadowsweet,

I conjure a Grand New Start!

A new path appears before me!

Secure the candle in the candleholder—envision you're planting your new beginning in the fertile earth. Light the candle. When you feel a new road opening before you, turn the Fool card upright. Stay with the candle until it has burned down completely. Place the Fool card back in your deck.

Astrea Taylor

NOTES:

April 2
Saturday

1st ♈

☽ v/c 9:51 am

☽ → ♉ 12:50 pm

Color of the day: Gray
Incense of the day: Sage

Ramadan begins at sundown

A Crafty Downsizing

Let's do some spring-cleaning! It's time to bust out that occult incense, mix up that Hoodoo floorwash, get brooms in hand, and sanctify that salt water. But first, let's take an inventory.

Take a couple hours to examine your space as objectively as possible. Close your eyes, take three very deep breaths, and declare:

I am Witch, I am wise. I see the truth now through my eyes.

With pen and paper in hand, and perhaps various bins labeled "donate," "sell," and "trash," slowly make way around your living space. While looking at your belongings, remember that everything around you is temporary and is only on loan to you in this lifetime. Bravely do away with items to which your intuitive mind says "nah," remembering that downsizing is a positive practice. Have fun and get creative as a first step in magickal spring-cleaning!

Raven Digitalis

April 3
Sunday

1st ♉

Color of the day: Amber
Incense of the day: Eucalyptus

Rainbow of hope Spell

April 3 is National Find a Rainbow Day, an excellent reminder to look around for hope—not just in the sky, but all around us and in each other. If you need a bit of a hope pick-me-up, this heartwarming spell can help dispel the clouds. You'll need a sheet of paper and a set of crayons or markers with the seven colors of the rainbow. In any color you wish, draw a five-pointed star, about two inches across, in the center of your paper. Then, in a clockwise motion, draw each circle of color around the star, expanding out, as you say:

Red is for a warm and open heart.

Orange is for a brand-new start.

Yellow is for the sun to shine.

Green is for growth like a vine.

Blue is for clean water and air.

Purple is for kindness to share.

Violet is for a mind so true.

All together, bring hope to view!

Fold the paper three times and carry it with you.

Laura Tempest Zakroff

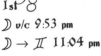

April 4
Monday

1st ♉

☽ v/c 9:53 pm

☽ → ♊ 11:04 pm

Color of the day: Lavender
Incense of the day: Lily

Invite in Wealth

It's a good day to start a new habit, and this particular habit is also a spoken spell. When you do it every day, it will increase your wealth and prosperity over time.

In the morning, perhaps after you have your morning beverage, open your front door as far as it will go. Stand on the threshold so you are both inside and outside your home at once. Say:

> I now attune to the vibration of ever-expanding wealth. I am a master at manifesting money, and I now invite in my endless good.

Now step just outside your door and say the same thing. (If you're worried about what the neighbors will think at any point, you can think the words instead of saying them out loud.) Finally, step just inside the door and repeat the spoken charm a third and final time as you feel that you are indeed inviting in an ever-increasing stream of blessings and wealth.

Tess Whitehurst

April 5
Tuesday

1st ♊

Color of the day: Black
Incense of the day: Cinnamon

Altar Renewal Spell

Spring cleaning is not just for our homes; it's also something we should do periodically for our magickal altars. Start by taking everything off your altar and setting it in a safe space. Now dust off your altar and give it a thorough cleaning. As you wipe down your altar, do so with a counterclockwise motion. As you clean, say:

> I renew this space so that it might serve me magickally.
>
> Dirt, dust, and negative energy must now all flee.
>
> Cleansed and renewed I make this sacred space.
>
> My magick will be forever strong in this place.

As you place your magickal items back on the altar, dust and clean them all as necessary. Before putting each newly cleansed item on the altar, say "renewed" to signify that it's been cleaned and made ready for another year of magick.

Ari & Jason Mankey

April 6
Wednesday

1st ♊

☽ v/c 11:15 pm

Color of the day: Topaz
Incense of the day: Marjoram

Foot Track Protection Magick

Footsteps reveal mood, intention, direction, health, and desires. Let's explore the intent of the footstep as we open ourselves to the magickal possibilities of Hoodoo's foot track magick. For the sake of brevity, foot track magick uses footsteps, paths, shoes, and boots to bring intended results. It's frequently used for heart, home, protection, and health magick.

Today we'll use just four tools: your favorite shoes, two Mercury dimes (or the oldest dimes you have), High John the Conqueror root powder, and some steel dust.

1. Take out your best walking shoes.

2. Sprinkle a pinch of each powder on the inner sole of each shoe's heel.

3. Put a dime under the sole of each shoe's heel.

High John the Conqueror root is a beloved and powerful herb of Hoodoo. When it is coupled with the strong curio of steel dust and the protective energies of dimes, you have some mighty protection magick afoot. Walk as far and as many times as you can today to seal in your shoes' protection powers.

Stephanie Rose Bird

NOTES;

April 7
Thursday

1st ♊

☽ → ♋ 11:30 am

Color of the day: Green
Incense of the day: Nutmeg

Mental and Spiritual healing

Today is World Health Day, a day to bring attention to global health issues. Mental health is often disregarded as a true health issue. Today we can work toward creating more mental stability for those in the world who need it.

On your altar, set up a white and a green candle. The white candle represents the mental and spiritual self, and the green candle is to promote health and wellness.

First, light the green candle, saying:

*This candle represents
the power to heal.*

Next, light the white candle from the green candle, saying:

*For those who need healing of mental
or spiritual wounds, let it now begin.*

Allow the candles to burn out completely if it is safe to do so. This will allow the healing to flow to those who need it the most.

Charlynn Walls

April 8
Friday

1st ♋

Color of the day: White
Incense of the day: Rose

For Those in Need

Today you get a twofer: two nearly identical spells with the same intention. You've seen people who are in need of enough to eat, a safe place to live, and adequate medical care. These twin spells are intended to help those in need.

Whenever you're out, pay attention to what's around you. We know that people are careless. They drop coins and ignore pennies. But pennies add up! Every time you see a penny, pick it up with your receptive (non-dominant) hand and place it in your pocket. As you do this, say aloud:

For those in need.

This might be you, or it might be someone you know or a stranger. Save those pennies on an altar with Dame Fortuna in the center until you get a sum that you can do something useful with. Do that something.

Alternatively, buy a roll of dimes. As you go about, leave a dime or two here and there, each time saying:

For those in need.

People will pick them up.

Barbara Ardinger

April 9
Saturday

1st ♋

2nd Quarter 2:48 am

☽ v/c 9:01 pm

Color of the day: Blue
Incense of the day: Pine

Bandage Sigil Spell

Bandages protect cuts and scrapes on our bodies from the outside world as we heal. They're also blank canvases that we can use to help the healing process move a little faster. For this spell you'll need a clear quartz crystal, a pen, paper, and a bandage.

Hold the crystal in one hand and imagine your wound is all healed up. Feel how good that would be. Write down four words that describe that feeling. Convert them into symbols, and combine the symbols to create a sigil. Meditate on the healing power of this sigil for a few breaths. When your energy feels higher, draw the sigil on your bandage and place the crystal over it. Say:

Healing sigil, helpful sign,

Bring me back to health divine.

After a few breaths, remove the crystal and go about your day. Whenever you see the bandage, send your body positive energy. When you need to replace the bandage, redraw the sigil and charge it up with the spell.

Astrea Taylor

April 10
Sunday

2nd ♌

☽ → ♌ 12:00 am

Color of the day: Gold
Incense of the day: Almond

Palm Sunday

The Magic of the Palm

Today is Palm Sunday, a sacred day for Christians, which celebrates the triumphant entrance of Christ into Jerusalem. The people greeted him by scattering palm branches in his path. In modern-day observances, willow and yew are often substituted where palm is not available.

If you wish to observe the day in a more witchy fashion, the palm tree is associated magically with fertility and is also kept near the front door of a home to prevent evil from entering. Take a palm branch, if they grow nearby, or the branch of any other tree. Hold it up and say this spell:

Let my life be fertile and
full of abundance.

May my home be protected from evil.

May all the gods, old and new,
lend me their blessings.

So mote it be!

Deborah Blake

♔ April 11
Monday

2nd ♌

Color of the day: Silver
Incense of the day: Narcissus

A Prosperity Spell Jar

In the US, it's tax season, and many of us are thinking a lot about money and prosperity. Create a prosperity jar to ease your mind and see to your future prosperity.

You'll need a lidded pint-size jar, an LED tealight candle, a small piece of paper, a green ink pen, and some or all of the following items: a green gem, stone, or crystal (citrine, malachite, jade, moss agate, or fluorite); a number of coins; a four-leaf clover (make one with green paper if you can't find a real one); a bay leaf; some rosemary; a small gold item; and a one-dollar bill, rolled and tied with a gold or green cord.

Place everything but the tealight in the jar. On the paper, write:

PROSPERITY LUCK MONEY GOOD FORTUNE

Roll this into a scroll, add to the jar, and screw on the lid.

To use, turn on the LED candle and place it on or behind the jar, illuminating its contents. Repeat:

Providential energies; may luck and prosperity come to me.

Susan Pesznecker

👁 April 12
Tuesday

2nd ♌

☽ v/c 6:16 am

☽ → ♍ 10:07 am

Color of the day: Gray
Incense of the day: Basil

Dreams to Reality

Summer seems so far off, but it really is just a tick in time away. Gather your calendar and a pen and do a manifesting spell. Cast a circle for protection. Call in the directions:

East, bring the winds of inspiration.
South, fan the fire of dreams.
West, fill me with watery creation.
North, make real what I need.

On your calendar, mark out times to take vacations: a half day spirited away from work, a weekend escape, or a weeklong absence from your work, home, town, and chores.

Say this out loud:

My calendar is marked, and I have planted the seeds.

I consciously tend this garden of dreams.

Growing joy, freedom, and relaxation,

Manifest my desired summer vacations.

Time in nature, with family and friends,

This is what my calendar portends.

So mote it be.

Dallas Jennifer Cobb

April 13
Wednesday

2nd ♏

Color of the day: Yellow
Incense of the day: Lavender

Written on the Door

In the Middle Ages it was not uncommon to write spells of protection around a door jamb—the portal through which the occupants of a house (or barn) came and went. For extra protection to guard against illness as the weather changes and allergy season approaches, write this spell in chalk around the inside of your front door:

To all who come and go from here,

Health and wellbeing shall adhere!

Bring nothing back that carries ill,

So mote it be, this is my will!

Renew the words as needed as the year progresses.

Natalie Zaman

April 14
Thursday

2nd ♏

☽ v/c 2:11 pm

☽ → ♎ 4:46 pm

Color of the day: Turquoise
Incense of the day: Clove

Take It Back Spell

Have you ever wished you could take back a spell and make it powerless? This ritual will help you do that. You'll need two candles, one red and one black. Place the candles on your altar. The red candle should be on the left and the black candle on the right. Safely light each candle, and sit before them. Ground and center. Think of your spell and why you think it went wrong. Then look at the candles and say:

Spirits red, spirits black,

Somehow I went off track.

Spirits red, spirits black,

I cancel the spell and take it back!

Now safely snuff out the red candle. Let the black candle continue to burn. In your mind, see the flame of the black candle absorbing the original spell's power until it's gone. Then snuff out the black candle safely. When both candles are cool, throw them away.

James Kambos

April 15
Friday

2nd ♎

Color of the day: Rose
Incense of the day: Thyme

Passover begins at sundown –
Good Friday

Growing into Spring

Today is Good Friday (Christian), and Passover begins at sundown (Jewish). Good Friday recommends virtues such as silence or selflessness, while Passover favors faith and hope. Also, spring is a good time for any magical work that relates to growth.

Look up a list of virtues. Which ones appeal to you and which don't? Which are things you already practice, and which are ones you would like to acquire?

Mark the virtues you would like to acquire. Look up each one and explore what it would mean to embody that virtue. Whittle down your list until you have one virtue that you most want to learn.

Meditate on your new virtue. Think about ways to express it in your life. What, if anything, will you need to add? What, if anything, will you need to give up?

Take a walk in the greening spring. Draw its energy into yourself. Seek opportunities to try out your new virtue for the rest of the day.

Elizabeth Barrette

April 16
Saturday

2nd ♎

Full Moon 2:55 pm
☽ v/c 5:57 pm
☽ → ♏ 8:23 pm

Color of the day: Indigo
Incense of the day: Rue

Scrying with the Moon

On the night of the full moon, fill a dark-colored bowl with fresh water and place in a spot where it will reflect the light of the moon. This can be outdoors or near a window. Once you see the image of the moon in your water, take the index finger of your dominant hand (or a wand or athame) and gently stir the water in a clockwise direction. As you stir the water, relax your visual focus and say:

Power of the moon, shining bright,

Let me see the future tonight.

In these waters grant me second sight,

Visions powered by the moon's light!

Let your mind wander as your unfocused eyes look upon the swirling water. The power of the moon should charge your water and help you peek into the future. After any vision received, stir the water once again to reset your scrying.

Ari & Jason Mankey

April 17
Sunday

3rd ♏

Color of the day: Orange
Incense of the day: Juniper

Easter

National Haiku Poetry Day

In addition to Easter Sunday, today is National Haiku Poetry Day. Compose a haiku to describe and represent what you will be releasing during the waning moon. As you may know, a haiku is a Japanese form of short poetry composed of three lines only, the first and third lines containing five syllables and the second line containing seven. There are two other traditional elements to include. First, a "cutting word" (*kireji*) should be placed at the end of the second or third line. Think of this as a question, an exclamation, or another incisive word that breaks up the verse or otherwise asks the reader to pause. Second, a seasonal reference (*kigo*) is also included in a haiku, so you may also want to include a word or phrase that is evocative of spring. Take your time until your haiku feels just right, then place it on your altar as a reminder of what you are releasing. Leave it there until the dark moon on the 29th.

Tess Whitehurst

April 18
Monday

3rd ♏
☽ v/c 7:55 pm
☽ → ♐ 10:16 pm

Color of the day: White
Incense of the day: Rosemary

Spirited Communication

On this day in 1857, *The Spirits Book* by Allan Kardec was published, and today's working is inspired by the teachings of spiritism. You'll need something that can serve as a pendulum, which can simply be a length of string with an object tied to one end.

Begin by casting a circle of protection by tracing an energetic circular path with your finger, making three passes around the space. Recite:

This circle protects me from harm on all levels, allowing in only the energies most harmonious for this working and blocking out all other energies.

Enter a light meditative state and ask to communicate with a spirit that comes in perfect love and perfect trust. Holding the pendulum, ask what a "yes" looks like. Allow the pendulum to move as it will, then ask what a "no" looks like. Then ask any questions you have, and close with thanks to the spirit.

Melissa Tipton

▽ April 19
Tuesday

3rd ♐

☉ → ♉ 10:24 pm

Color of the day: Red
Incense of the day: Ylang-ylang

Magickal Prayer Stones

Let's get down to earth. As the Wheel of the Year is cycling into a time of manifestation, it's important to consider what we wish to bring into not only our own lives but also the lives of those around us and those across the globe.

Take some time to gather some small stones of any size. Keep these in a box, bag, or tote. When you've collected about thirty to fifty stones, take a walk in a quiet area where you can focus on the bountiful earth.

Using your right hand, grab one stone at a time and make a wish. Grasp a stone and say:

With this stone, I manifest _____.

You may fill in the blank with anything from "global sustainability" to "personal balance," or whatever feels intuitively right. Drop each stone on the ground as you make the wish.

Once finished, kiss the earth and thank the Great Mother for hearing your magick.

Raven Digitalis

☀ April 20
Wednesday

3rd ♐

☽ v/c 4:56 pm

☽ → ♑ 11:52 pm

Color of the day: Brown
Incense of the day: Bay laurel

herbal Communion

All kinds of herbs have their place in witchcraft. Herbs are often used because their spirits are potent and they like to help with magical applications. This spell creates a spiritual connection with an herb. It's best performed on an empty stomach.

All you need for this spell is an herb. Fresh herbs are better, but dried herbs will do as well. Any herb can be used as long as it's not poisonous. If you don't know where to start, try basil, dill, or thyme.

Hold the herb gently in your left palm and say:

Helpful spirit, herbal one,

Share with me your true wisdom.

Start to converse with the herb's energy. Take a whiff of it, and connect with the aromatics. Take a bite and revel in the taste.

How does the herb make you feel? What messages does the herb's spirit have for you? Explore these questions in your Book of Shadows, and use the answers in your magic.

Astrea Taylor

April 21
Thursday

3rd ♑

Color of the day: Crimson
Incense of the day: Myrrh

The Art of Bibliomancy

It's National Library Week, the perfect time for a little bibliomancy! Bibliomancy is the art of divining the future or receiving spirit-directed guidance from a book. This method is pretty simple, but it's surprisingly effective—often serving up just the right information for the moment.

Some folks use a Bible, but I prefer to run my fingers down a bookshelf with my eyes closed and pull at whatever book catches or gives a little vibe. You could also use a favorite book of poems, lore, or other text that means something to you.

From there, I will either let the book fall open, if it's a hardcover, or fan the pages with my fingers, if it's a softcover, opening where it stops. Wherever my eyes fall first is the passage to read, but other people like to draw their finger down the page and stop where they feel is right. What you find and read will be a message of inspiration for you.

Laura Tempest Zakroff

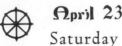

 April 22
Friday

3rd ♑
☽ v/c 11:53 pm
Color of the day: Purple
Incense of the day: Violet

Earth Day

Earth Day

Today is Earth Day, the holiday we have set aside to honor our planet and Gaia, the Greek goddess who embodies abundance, nurturing ability, strength, and even destruction. So that you can always have a personalized Gaia around for your home, hearth, or altar, let's make a figurine of her. You will need:

- 4 cups flour
- 1 cup iodized salt
- 1¾ cup warm water
- Optional: acrylic paints, water, and brushes

Thinking of the importance of this day and the goddess Gaia, pour the flour into a bowl, followed by the salt, and mix with a wooden spoon. Add water and blend with the spoon. Turn out on a floured table and knead for fifteen to twenty minutes.

Focus as you form Gaia's image. Create with intent and love. When your figurine is completely dry, begin using it, or paint it if you wish.

Stephanie Rose Bird

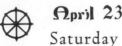 **April 23**
Saturday

3rd ♑
☽ → ♒ 2:17 am
4th Quarter 7:56 am
Color of the day: Brown
Incense of the day: Sandalwood

Passover ends

Cleansing with Bitter Herbs

Today is the last day of Passover, an important holiday in the Jewish religion. Passover celebrates the freeing of the Jews from slavery and is observed in a number of different ways. The best known of these is a meal called the Seder, which features many specific foods with symbolic meanings. This includes the eating of bitter herbs, including horseradish, endive, or romaine lettuce.

There are many different kinds of slavery, including addictions, bad relationships, and destructive habits. To symbolize your intention to free yourself from anything that enslaves you, chew on some bitter herbs and say:

*I give up the bitter and
embrace the sweet,*

*Freeing myself from all
forms of enslavement*

*And allowing my spirit
to expand and grow.*

Then follow this up by eating something sweet.

Deborah Blake

April 24
Sunday

4th ≈

☽ v/c 8:33 pm

Color of the day: Yellow
Incense of the day: Hyacinth

A Spell for St. Mark's Eve

Who shall be your partner in life?
Maybe a husband, maybe a wife?
Tonight is the eve of good St. Mark,
So wait until it's good and dark.
Then light and burn a candle bright,
And hold a cloth up to the light.
In its threads thy shall behold
Thy true love's face in flames foretold.
A warning though that thou must heed:
Bring the cloth not too near the flame,
Lest the thing should catch afire
And burn away love and desire!
Is this legend or is this spell?
Try! It's the only way to tell.

Natalie Zaman

 April 25
Monday

4th ≈

☽ → ♓ 6:15 am

Color of the day: Gray
Incense of the day: Clary sage

To Life!

In *Fiddler on the Roof*, Tevye sings, "L'chaim!" which means, "To life!" The circumstances of his life aren't good—he's a Jew living in anti-Semitic Russia around the turn of the last century—but he manages to find little things to celebrate. Let us emulate Tevye. What little things in your life can you celebrate?

Alone or with your coven or circle, set up an altar filled with growing plants and symbols of happiness, such as musical instruments, a glass of milk, favorite jewelry, or emails from friends. Add whatever brings more life into your life.

Surround your "lifey" things with a whole rainbow of birthday candles. As you light each candle, tell yourself and your friends what's good in your life. What kind of life does this April bring? Ask your friends to speak about their lives. Sit together with your altar and think about renewed and ever-renewing life until the candles burn down safely. Then you and your friends can get up and dance.

Barbara Ardinger

April 26
Tuesday

4ᵗʰ ♓

Color of the day: Scarlet
Incense of the day: Ginger

Seed and Garden Blessing

Springtime heralds the arrival of gardening in most locations, and carrying out a seed and garden blessing will start the season off right.

You'll need some packets of seeds, a trowel or small shovel, some organic fertilizer, and a cup of water.

Carry the items to your garden location. Hold the seeds skyward and say:

I honor these seeds, each carrying the essence of new life and the gifts of food, warmth, and shelter. May I learn the lessons of these seeds and respect their perseverance.

With the trowel, dig a small hole in the garden soil, saying:

I honor the Earth, from whom the great mystery of life springs.

Pour the fertilizer and water into the hole, saying:

May these gifts of food and water be repaid in favored bounty. May the fruits of my labor show love and respect for this process.

Cover the hole. Place the seed packets on your altar until planting time.

Susan Pesznecker

April 27
Wednesday

4ᵗʰ ♓

☽ v/c 9:36 am
☽ → ♈ 12:10 pm

Color of the day: White
Incense of the day: Honeysuckle

Bless Your Babes

Whether you have children, animal companions, plants, or creative babies (like books, paintings, or music that you're working on and growing), today is a great day to bless your babes.

Sit quietly. Draw the image of each of your "babes" to you. Bless them one at a time, giving each your full attention. Picture them in your mind's eye. Inhale deeply, then exhale and surround them with white light. Incant:

Mother Earth, keep my babes safe.

Inhale deeply, then exhale and surround them with blue light. Say:

Goddess, let my babes be peaceful.

Inhale deeply, then exhale and surround them with pink light. Say:

Divine One, may my babes be happy.

Inhale deeply, then exhale and surround them with red light. Say:

Goddess, let my babes feel loved.

Inhale deeply, then exhale and surround them with green light. Say:

May my babes be healthy.

Inhale deeply, then exhale again, envisioning your babes in a blessed state: safe, peaceful, happy, loved, and healthy. Say:

Divine Mother, bless my babes.
For this I am thankful.

                              Dallas Jennifer Cobb

NOTES:

April 28
Thursday

4th ♈

Color of the day: Purple
Incense of the day: Jasmine

A Flowering Garden

Today is Floralia, the Roman festival in honor of Flora, the goddess of flowers and other growing things. Druidic lore has Blodeuwedd, whose name means "flower face." Think of how some flowers such as pansies have a "face" on their petals.

Spend the day worshipping your garden. If you have used an off-season cover crop, you can till it under for green manure. Otherwise, dead leaves or cut grass can be worked into the soil to add more organic matter. Composted animal manure also works, though it goes a bit farther from Druidic tradition. Turn over the top layer of soil onto the unbroken surface beside it, work in the organic matter underneath, then put the clean soil back on top. As you work, say:

Garden Goddess, Flower Face,

Lay your blessing on this place:

Everywhere the ground gives room,

Let the earth now burst in bloom.

Plant hardy spring flowers, such as pansies, primroses, or pinks. They will grow well with fresh food underneath and a blessing to bolster them.

                              Elizabeth Barrette

April 29
Friday

4th ♈

☽ v/c 5:38 pm

☽ → ♉ 8:19 pm

Color of the day: Coral
Incense of the day: Vanilla

Raise the Roof

In honor of International Dance Day, this spell utilizes the energy of movement. This can be as simple, yet powerful, as clapping your hands, or more complex movements of your choice.

Begin by casting a magic circle to contain your ritual space, then imagine an energetic umbrella or jellyfish shape hovering above you, collecting energy as it rises from the earth. As you focus on your magical intention, begin to move your body, perhaps stomping your feet, clapping your hands, swaying your hips, or any movement that feels natural and accessible.

Imagine these movements drawing up earth energy as your body funnels it up and into the umbrella. Continue until the umbrella feels ready to pop with fullness, and loudly exclaim your intention as you visualize and sense the energy bursting free, coursing through the universe to carry out your magical aim.

Melissa Tipton

April 30
Saturday

4th ♉

New Moon 4:28 pm

Color of the day: Blue
Incense of the day: Ivy

Solar Eclipse

A Solar Eclipse Meditation

Today we have a new moon and a solar eclipse occurring. Many occultists believe, however, that the day of a solar eclipse isn't a good day to work magic. When the earth is in the "shadow" of an eclipse, magic could go awry. But this is an excellent day to meditate about new directions or projects you wish to take on.

You'll need one orange candle and the Hermit card from a Tarot deck. The candle will represent the sun, while the lantern or torch that the Hermit is carrying will represent the wisdom you're seeking. Place the candle on your altar, but don't light it yet. In front of it lay the Hermit card faceup. Gaze at the card and ask for its help in guiding you along the correct path to achieve your goal. Then safely light the candle. Visualize the sun shining after the eclipse, lighting your way. Meditate on the Hermit guiding you. When done, safely snuff out the candle. Return the card to its deck. Record any thoughts in a journal.

James Kambos

May

Welcome to the famously merry month of May! Though it was originally named after the Greek fertility goddess Maia, the Catholic Church has since designated this month as sacred to the Virgin Mary, even referring to her as "the Queen of May" during this time. Day one of this flower-filled month is the beloved holiday of Beltane, during which the veil that usually conceals the world of the fairies fades, and our power to make contact with them reaches its yearly peak. Indeed, May's birth flower is a fairy favorite: the lily of the valley. As for our skies, this month they host the Eta Aquariids meteor shower, which reaches its peak around May 6 and is most visible before the sunrise.

May is also the month when the light half of the year begins to assert itself in earnest, and we sense the days lengthening, the sun growing warmer, and the leaves filling out the trees. This allows us to gaze bravely into our own brilliance and to courageously release anything that has been holding us back from being our most radiant, expansive, beautiful selves. Indeed, May's bright presence reminds us to claim the vital prosperity that is our birthright and our natural state.

Tess Whitehurst

May 1
Sunday

1st ♉

Color of the day: Amber
Incense of the day: Heliotrope

Beltane – Ramadan ends

May Day

May Day is a highly significant day on many pagan paths, including Hoodoo. One of Hoodoo's original informants reported on a washing ritual that has come to be known as Edward Marshall's May Day Wash. His rite was designed for the Mississippi River, but a river (or other natural body of water) near you will do, if you have strong intentions.

In Hoodoo, it is believed that running water, as in a river, can cleanse, protect, and banish ill health and the problems that cause them. Wear all white for sacred intent. Head to a nearby river (or other natural body of water) with your towel. Submerge your body and visualize your troubles floating like your clothing. Chant:

> On this auspicious day of May,
>
> Let the healing powers of water shield, cleanse, and protect me,
>
> Shield, cleanse, and protect me,
>
> Shield, cleanse, and protect me.
>
> Blessed be!

Stephanie Rose Bird

May 2
Monday

1st ♉

☽ v/c 6:13 am
☽ → ♊ 6:47 am

Color of the day: Lavender
Incense of the day: Rosemary

Enhance Psychic Awareness

Cleanse three moonstones by placing them in bright sunlight or cool running water for a few minutes or by bathing them in sage smoke. Hold your hands in prayer pose, with the stones between them. Then move your hands to touch your heart. Close your eyes, take some deep breaths, and say:

> Great Goddess, help me to be a clear channel of divine energy and wisdom. Cleanse my perception and open up my awareness so that I may clearly see, hear, know, and understand. Thank you.

Move your hands, still in prayer pose, up to touch your forehead. Then recline comfortably. Place one moonstone on your heart center (the center of your chest), one on your throat, and one on your third eye (the center of your forehead just above your eyebrows). Relax as you feel your psychic sensitivity growing. After a few minutes or when this feels complete, place the moonstones on your altar. If you'd like, you can repeat this process before any psychic or intuitive work.

Tess Whitehurst

NOTES:

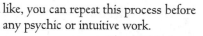 **May 3**
Tuesday

1st ♊

Color of the day: White
Incense of the day: Cinnamon

honor the Sun

On May 3, 1978, Sun Day was established by President Jimmy Carter. It is now recognized as World or International Sun Day. It is a day devoted to solar energy and the power it has to propel life.

Now is the time to honor our sun and its life-giving energies. Decorate your home and your altar with items relating to the sun. Use the colors orange and yellow in the form of sun-flowers or daisies if available. You can also include oranges, sunstones, or agates in your decor.

At sunrise or sunset, honor the sun by lifting your arms to the sky to absorb the radiant energy. As you do so, close your eyes, take a deep breath, and slowly exhale. Repeat this action several times, feeling the ener-gy of the sun increase the element of fire within you.

Charlynn Walls

May 4
Wednesday

1st ♊

☽ v/c 4:37 pm

☽ → ♋ 7:05 pm

Color of the day: Yellow
Incense of the day: Marjoram

Bird on the Wing

Today is Bird Day. In its various incarnations, it draws attention to migratory birds in particular and encourages conservation of birds in general. Like all flying creatures, birds represent the element of air. For this reason, they often figure into travel spells. This can mean air travel but also applies to travel over land or water.

For this spell you will need a charm shaped like a feather or a bird (preferably in flight) and something to string it on, such as a necklace, bracelet, or key chain. Toss the charm gently in the air, catching it in your hand, and say:

Bird on the wing, bird in the air,

Carry me safely from here to there.

Light as a feather on the tail,

Watch over me upon my trail.

String the charm on its carrier. You can wear it to protect yourself, or attach it to a vehicle to protect that. If you put it on your key chain, you'll always have it when you need it.

Elizabeth Barrette

May 5
Thursday

1st ♋

Color of the day: Turquoise
Incense of the day: Nutmeg

Cinco de Mayo

Sweeten Up and Chill Out

If you find yourself in an argument, dispute, or otherwise disagreeable situation with another person, simply write their name on one side of a piece of paper and your name on the reverse.

Put this paper in a small self-sealing bag and add water, filling it enough to cover the paper. While doing this, say:

By the power of water, we invoke empathy between us.

Add a handful of sugar to the water. While doing this, say:

By the power of sugar, we invoke sweetness between us.

Seal the bag and put it in the back of your freezer. While doing this, say:

By the power of ice, we invoke chill vibes between us.

Once you feel resolution has occurred with this person, toss the frozen bag in a public trash receptacle so it can be buried in the landfill, thereby offering the spell to the earth with gratitude.

Raven Digitalis

May 6
Friday

1st ♋

Color of the day: Pink
Incense of the day: Alder

Clean Sweep

This spell is designed to clear out energy that no longer serves, neutralizing and recycling it back into the cosmic flow where it can be put to better use. You'll need to gather some sort of natural debris that you can sweep away without littering, such as sticks, leaves, pebbles, or sand.

In a ritual mindset, arrange the debris intuitively while bringing to mind the situation or pattern you wish to clear. Allow the debris to become a symbol of this situation. Spend a few minutes in meditation, contemplating how this energy has affected your life, expressing gratitude for its lessons, difficult as they may be.

When you're ready, say farewell and sweep the arrangement away, completely dispersing the energy and returning it to the greater cycle of life, where it can be composted and reused. Take a few minutes to enjoy a new sense of liberation and clarity.

Melissa Tipton

May 7
Saturday

1st ♋

☽ v/c 6:26 am
☽ → ♌ 7:50 am

Color of the day: Black
Incense of the day: Sage

A Pet Protection Spell

Traditionally early May was when farmers would hang pine in their barns to protect their livestock from bad luck. Then they would walk their livestock around bonfires in a rite of purification. This spell is similar and helps you bless your pets. You'll need a small pine twig and a small amount of your pet's fur. Safely ignite the pine in a heatproof container. Add the fur and say:

*My furry friend, you'll
remain at my side,*

By my rules you will abide.

I promise to feed you and to protect,

I'll care for you without neglect.

*I'll give you a cozy place
to lay your head,*

Be it by my door or by my bed.

When the ashes are completely cool, sprinkle them near your front door. End by giving your furry friend some extra attention so they know how much you care.

James Kambos

May 8
Sunday

1st ♌

2nd Quarter 8:21 pm

Color of the day: Gold
Incense of the day: Almond

Mother's Day

Mothering Sunday Meditation

A good mother loves her children and teaches them to love themselves. Today is Mother's Day, and while there are many good mothers we should celebrate, there are also many people who don't come from a good mother. Let's expand and extend this day, making it inclusive to all (and not exclusive to those lucky enough to have a good mother).

Sit quietly and meditate. Focus on the qualities of a good mother: someone who is loving, caring, nurturing, and kind; someone who feeds, protects, cuddles, and teaches. Drop your attention down through your root chakra into Mother Earth, reaching awareness there. Know that timeless, abiding strength and wisdom are there for you to meet your deepest needs. Draw mothering energy up from the earth, through your body, and around your heart. Mother yourself: cultivate self-love, self-protection, self-care, and kindness. Claim good mothering as yours as a child of the great mother, Earth.

Dallas Jennifer Cobb

May 9
Monday

2nd ♌

☽ v/c 8:39 am

☽ → ♍ 6:53 pm

Color of the day: White
Incense of the day: Neroli

Make a Port-a-Pagan

D oing ritual in our own spaces is always simple, but what if we're caught in a new location, burning with the desire to carry out ritual or spellwork but without the tools to do so? Of course, you may say ritual doesn't absolutely require any tools—and that's true. But sometimes we want the tools. The answer? The Port-a-Pagan, a miniature set of spellcrafting materials.

Start with a small lidded tin, one that closes snugly. Add items to it, considering which tools you typically use for ritual and spellwork. These might include:

- A small altar cloth, such as a bandana or handkerchief
- Birthday cake candles
- Bits of dried herbs
- Small stones or crystals
- Divination tools: miniature tarot cards, small rune stones or sticks, coins, small dice, a scrying mirror, etc.

- Vials of salt, oil, and charged water
- Large beads in basic colors
- A collapsible cup/chalice
- Chalk
- Strike-anywhere matches
- Other items as desired

Carry this with you for use anytime.

Susan Pesznecker

NOTES:

May 10
Tuesday

2nd ♏

Color of the day: Gray
Incense of the day: Bayberry

Nurture Nest Spell

It can be difficult to manifest a goal that doesn't have something easily tangible for you to work with (such as love, truth, health, etc.). This spell will help make your goal more physical for you.

Locate a small roundish pebble (about one to two inches long) that feels good to you. After cleaning it, draw a symbol on it that represents what you're looking for, or write the word itself. This is now the "egg" containing the idea you will nurture. Create a little nest for it. This can be as simple as a little box that you decorate, a swath of fabric, or a nest largely formed of dried herbs that align with your goal.

Set your egg in the nest upon your altar (or a safe place) and visit it daily, even for just a couple of minutes. Add little items that inspire and feed your idea until it has manifested! Afterward, you may return the pebble to the earth and recycle your nest as necessary.

Laura Tempest Zakroff

 ## May 11
Wednesday

2nd ♍

Color of the day: Topaz
Incense of the day: Bay laurel

Shower Song

Some people get their best ideas in the shower. It's a great place to get physically clean, but all that water can also wash away fogginess and stress.

Turn your morning (or evening) routine into a refreshing ritual. Chose a soap scent with meaning (and that uses real herbs or essential oils). Mint is refreshing, citrus is happy, and vanilla and cinnamon are warming. While in the shower, as the water pours over you and you're enveloped in soap, sing this simple song and visualize what you want out of the shower (brightening, wakening, clarity, etc.):

Bubble, bubble

Shower and scrubbable,

I feel _____!

Fill in the blank with your desired outcome (Awake! Refreshed! Calm! At peace!).

Natalie Zaman

May 12
Thursday

2nd ♍

☽ v/c 12:00 am

☽ → ♎ 2:34 am

Color of the day: Green
Incense of the day: Carnation

Springtime Love

Who doesn't feel the love in the air after Beltane? That celebration of love and fertility can last all month. Are you in the mood for love with someone who's near you? Someone far away? Are you feeling May's currents of passion?

Set up your altar with all the love trinkets you can find—candy hearts, chocolate kisses, bright jewelry, photos of the one you love, cut flowers in a vase, or anything else you're inspired to add. As you light a pink candle (of course), recite these lines from the poem "The Bait" by John Donne and fling them out toward your desired beloved:

Come live with me, and be my love,

And we will some new pleasures prove

Of golden sands, and crystal brooks,

With silken lines and silver hooks.

Collect some of that golden sand (in a heart-shaped dish) and visualize those silken lines and silver hooks on your altar. Invite your desired beloved to create some special springtime love.

Prove some new pleasures. And go to a good concert. (Be sure to extinguish the candle.)

Barbara Ardinger

NOTES:

 May 13
Friday

2nd ♎

Color of the day: Rose
Incense of the day: Yarrow

harmony in a Bottle

Friday the 13th is typically a day filled with superstition. Today, try to bring harmony into your world. Create a magickal water to boost your spirits and keep you in balance.

You will need distilled or spring water to mix with your essential oils, herbs, and crystals in a container. Some possibilities of herbs or oils to incorporate include heather, lilac, and thyme. Crystals or gemstones to use could include quartz and moonstone. Use what works for you. When adding your ingredients to the container, say:

> When my days are in disarray,
> allow me to find harmony today.

Store this in a container with a tight seal on it. If you have a small spray bottle, transfer some to it for easy use. Once you have the spray mixed up, use it throughout the day as needed. If there is any left over, you can use it whenever you feel like you are in a state of imbalance.

Charlynn Walls

May 14
Saturday

2nd ♎

☽ v/c 4:07 am

☽ → ♏ 6:34 am

Color of the day: Indigo
Incense of the day: Magnolia

Divination with Spring Flowers

"He loves me. He loves me not," she says as she plucks the petals from a recently picked flower. It sounds cliché, but flowers are a lovely way to do a little springtime divination. Flowers don't leave a lot of room for interpretation, so this works best with questions that can be answered with a "yes" or a "no." For best results, pick your own flower, preferably in the early morning hours, when the possibilities of a new day are at their strongest.

Before plucking your flower, say:

*Spring flower picked in
the morning dew,*

Show me my future, may it be true!

Hold whatever question you have in your mind as you pluck off the petals, beginning with the affirmative answer ("Yes, it will happen!") before moving to the negative ("No, it will not."). The last petal will give you your answer. If the answer you receive is positive, save the petals and keep them for good luck.

Ari & Jason Mankey

May 15
Sunday

2nd ♏

Color of the day: Yellow
Incense of the day: Eucalyptus

May Flowers

There is a saying "April showers bring May flowers." The saying, however, doesn't specify which flowers or what you should do to make the most of that abundant May energy. I suggest turning your attention to flowering herbs, which can be made into healing teas, tinctures, and ointments and, of course, used for magic. Which herbs are in flower will vary depending on where you live, but you can either plant them in your yard or garden on purpose or take a walk and see what has sprung up without human intervention. (Just make sure that any herbal flowers you pick are safe and readily identifiable.) When you have found some lovely May flowers you wish to use, put them in a vase or bowl on your altar and say this spell:

April showers bring May flowers.

*May those flowers bring me
healing and magic and joy.*

So mote it be!

Deborah Blake

May 16
Monday

2nd ♏

🌕 **Full Moon** 12:14 am

☽ v/c 5:28 am

☽ → ♐ 7:50 am

Color of the day: Ivory
Incense of the day: Narcissus

Lunar Eclipse

Dream Processing and Remembrance

It's a well-known fact that our subconscious mind communicates messages to us in the dreamscape. Additionally, our time of rest allows our brain, our mind, and our consciousness to assimilate previous experiences. Sleep also allows the body to repair itself on a cellular level.

The full moon is a time of illumination and insight. Before going to sleep tonight, meditate with a large piece of amethyst in the dark. Speak nine times to the stone (nine being the esoteric Qabalistic number of the moon) the following words:

*I remember and feel my dreams tonight;
they will provide me healing insight.*

Put the stone in a glass of water on your bedside table. It's even better if the water can receive some moonlight!

Upon waking, meditate while slowly sipping the water. Make note of any dream insights or memories, and consider repeating the spell on other full moons.

Raven Digitalis

NOTES:

May 17
Tuesday

3rd ♐

☽ v/c 11:59 pm

Color of the day: Black
Incense of the day: Geranium

Safe, Magical Neighborhood

Magic can raise the energy, safety, and positivity of your area. This spell requires a printed map of your neighborhood, a pencil, six small bags, and a marker.

On the map, circle your home. Next, draw a pentagram over your neighborhood, with your house in the middle. Number the points 1–5.

Take a walk to the first point. Get as close as possible to it without trespassing. Secretly collect a small sample of dirt, grass, rocks, or leaves, and place it in a bag. Number that bag "1" with the marker. Repeat this for all five points. Collect a sample from your home area as well. At your altar, arrange the materials on the map according to their number. Trace the pentacle with your finger and say:

Rock, grass, leaf, and debris,

A safe, magical community.

A pentacle creates unity.

Trace a circle around the points to form a pentacle. Leave the map out for a day. Store the materials in a jar to seal in the magic.

Astrea Taylor

 May 18
Wednesday

3rd ♐

☽ → ♑ 8:02 am

Color of the day: White
Incense of the day: Lilac

Beginning of La Fête de la Nature

La fête de la nature (the Party of Nature) occurs every year around International Day of Biodiversity. To celebrate, we'll create Nana Buluku. This fierce wisewoman and powerful witch created the universe. Nana Buluku is called Lady of the Swamp and Lady of the Clay. Prominent in West Africa's Fon, Ketu, and Yoruba pantheons, she rose up from the primordial swamp and loves everything connected to it. We'll conjure her energies outdoors; she's too powerful for magick indoors.

Gather these materials:

+ 8 cups (or more) soil

+ Jug of spring water

+ Cowrie shells (or other seashells)

+ Rose petals and buds

+ Freshly collected leaves

To invoke Nana Buluku's energy, make an earth mound, symbolic of her fertility. Think loving thoughts of gratitude as you conjure creativity from this divine herbalist.

Moisten the soil with the water, just enough to be able to work it.

Shape an earth mound with your hands. (Do not use a knife or any metal, as this will anger her.) Decorate with the shells, rose petals and buds, and leaves.

Stephanie Rose Bird

NOTES:

May 19
Thursday

3rd ℣

Color of the day: Purple
Incense of the day: Jasmine

A Peony Spell for Protection

Peonies are blooming now in many regions. Not only are they beautiful, but they are also excellent at repelling evil forces. For this reason, they are frequently cut and brought into the home.

For this spell you'll need one to three cut peony stems placed in a vase of water. Set them near an exterior door. Then look at them and say:

Peonies, let the spirits of light stay.

Peonies, let the spirits of darkness be on their way.

Allow the peonies to sit undisturbed until the petals fall. Then gather the petals along with the vase and carry them outside. Compost the petals or toss them on the ground. Do the same with the stems. Then pour the water on the ground, but don't use it to water another plant. Wash out the vase to use for other purposes. Your home is now spiritually clean.

James Kambos

May 20
Friday

3rd ♑

☽ v/c 8:00 am

☽ → ♒ 8:53 am

☉ → ♊ 9:23 pm

Color of the day: Pink
Incense of the day: Rose

World Bee Day

Today is World Bee Day. Bees are of vital importance to our ecosystems and human food production, and wild bee populations have been in significant decline for over forty years. Year after year, bees bless us with the beauty of flowers and trees, the magic of herbs, the sweetness of honey, and the sustenance of fruit, nuts, and seeds. So today, bless the bees. First, close your eyes and place your hands in prayer pose. Take some deep breaths and connect with Mother Earth. Say:

Gaia, Great Goddess, please bless the bees. Surround them with the golden light of wellness and vitality. Help them multiply and thrive. Thank you.

Then plant one or more plants that support bees in your garden or an outdoor pot, or gift someone you know with such a plant (or seeds). Plants that support bees include borage, crocus, bee balm, goldenrod, calendula, and sunflower.

Tess Whitehurst

May 21
Saturday

3rd ♒

Color of the day: Blue
Incense of the day: Pine

Magical Quartz Battery

For this spell you'll need a piece of clear quartz, a plant pot or a spot in the garden, and a seed of any kind. As the seed germinates and blossoms into a plant, you'll be charging the quartz with the energy of growth.

Prepare the soil, then hold the seed and quartz in your hands, closing your eyes and coming into a light meditative state. Focus on the intention that the quartz will record the energy of the plant's divinely guided growth, allowing you to tap into this "battery" whenever you need to.

Then plant the seed and anchor the quartz in the soil nearby. Tend to the seed in the coming weeks, and as the plant grows, the crystal will be charged with this energy. When you want to use it, retrieve the crystal, empower any magical workings with its energy, then place it back in the soil to recharge.

Melissa Tipton

May 22
Sunday

3rd ♒

☽ v/c 3:19 am

☽ → ♓ 11:49 am

4th Quarter 2:43 pm

Color of the day: Amber
Incense of the day: Hyacinth

Double It!

Welcome to Gemini season! The celestial twins remind us that more can be better. What in your life needs to be doubled (without, of course, wreaking havoc in other areas of your life)? Do you need more funds? More time? More patience?

Go outdoors (Gemini is an air sign) and take in two (for the twins) deep breaths—in through your nose and out through your mouth. With each exhale, say or think this two-line incantation to bring double-good energy to that which needs multiplying:

Double, double—without any trouble!

Double my _____.

Fill in the blank with what you need.

Natalie Zaman

 May 23
Monday

4th ♓

Color of the day: Gray
Incense of the day: Clary sage

Victoria Day (Canada)

Successful Coins

Success and money are closely connected. Usually you need some money to start with, and success tends to bring money along with it. So each one can be used to attract the other.

For this spell you'll need a set of coins, including a penny, a nickel, a dime, a quarter, a half-dollar, and a dollar (preferably golden, but silver will do). You'll also need a gold-tone picture frame just big enough to hold the coins and a bit of black velvet for backing. Lay the velvet over the inside back of the frame. As you place each coin, starting with the penny, say:

From the small to the great,

Such success is my fate,

That it's drawn to my name,

And it fills up the frame.

After you finish placing the coins, put the front of the frame on and fasten it. Say the verse one last time. Then hang the frame where you want to attract wealth and success.

Elizabeth Barrette

May 24
Tuesday

4th ♓

☽ v/c 5:33 pm

☽ → ♈ 5:39 pm

Color of the day: Maroon
Incense of the day: Cedar

Peace and Prayer Flags

Following the example of Tibetan flags, you can make your own flags for prayer and peace. You'll need some natural fabric (cotton, linen, etc.) in 12-by-8-inch pieces. Finished flags will be about 8 inches wide and 10 to 11 inches long. Choose colors that have magical significance (e.g., white for peace, blue for calm, green for nature, and so forth), or just choose those that you love.

You'll need a thick rope or cord to stretch horizontally across a space; the flags will hang vertically along the cord. You'll need a means of sewing, gluing, or hot-fusing the top edge of each flag.

Cut out your flags. Fold over one narrow edge, creating a 1-inch pocket for the cord to run through. Secure the folded pocket by sewing, gluing, or using iron-on fusible webbing.

Use permanent ink to inscribe prayers, symbols, etc., on each flag. String the flags along the cord and display. Use them in spell, ritual, or meditation or simply for happiness.

Susan Pesznecker

▽ **May 25**
Wednesday

4th ♈

Color of the day: Brown
Incense of the day: Lavender

Wildflower Essence

The woods are bursting with wildflowers at this time of year. Trillium, dogtooth violet, and trout lilies abound in my area. Wildflowers are resilient, strong, willful, and beautiful. Get outside and find some. If you live in a city, you may find wildflowers in the unexpected wild lands of urban ravines, parks, and cemeteries. Don't pick the wildflowers that you find, but draw from their energy, knowing how much it took for them to push up through the snow, mud, and soil. Let each wildflower teach you about its essence. Take their magic to heart, holding onto a little of their spunk and resilience. Tap into wildflower ferocity, willfulness, and strength. Witness the beauty they bring to the world. In the days to come, "be" a wildflower—let your resilience, strength, willfulness, and beauty shine for all to see.

Dallas Jennifer Cobb

May 26
Thursday

4th ♈

☽ v/c 11:20 pm

Color of the day: White
Incense of the day: Myrrh

Draw Sweetness to You

The bathtub is my favorite cauldron—it's an ideal place for working magic, in my opinion. This bathtub magic is a twist on the traditional honey jar spell, which is generally used to sweeten someone's disposition toward you. In this case, the bath becomes the jar, and you become the focus to draw sweetness to you in general. The ingredients are pretty simple, and fresh is best if you can manage.

- Handful of rose petals
- Handful of honeysuckle blossoms
- 1 teaspoon honey

Sprinkle the flowers in the bathtub as you turn the water on, and deposit the honey near the tap so it dissolves more quickly. (If you don't want to clean up a mess of flowers when you're done, you can put them in a cotton mesh bag instead.) Get in the tub and soak for at least twenty minutes. Afterward, spread the flowers outside by your door.

Laura Tempest Zakroff

NOTES:

May 27
Friday

4th ♈

☽ → ♉ 2:22 am

Color of the day: Purple
Incense of the day: Violet

Tending Our Gardens

Is there a Pagan who does not have a garden, whether on a table by the window or outside in a sunny spot? If you've planted seeds and transplanted plants from friends or the local nursery, the end of May is high time to give your garden some extra attention: watering, weeding, trimming. While you're doing your gardening, recite old nursery rhymes to the plants. Here are two. Find more online and encourage your garden to grow and bloom.

Mistress Mary, quite contrary,

How does your garden grow?

With silver bells and cockle shells,

And pretty blossoms all in a row.

Round and round the garden

Like a teddy bear;

One step, two step,

Tickle you under there!

As you tend your earthly garden, also think about the metaphorical gardens in your life. These are your friendships in your mundane life, in circles and covens, or on social media. Tend these gardens, too. Start with a friendly email or an invitation to lunch, or post a nursery rhyme.

Barbara Ardinger

NOTES:

May 28
Saturday

4℉ ♉

Color of the day: Gray
Incense of the day: Ivy

Setting Boundaries

Today is a good time to renew the physical boundaries of your home or property. You will need a few small stones to set along the edges of the property. You can use smokey quartz, black obsidian, black tourmaline, or any protective stone you connect with. You will need to walk the boundaries of your property. As you do this, set the stones in the corners of your property line. You may bury them if they are outdoors, so they will not be disturbed. If you live in an apartment, you can simply place them near the doors or windows of your home where they will not be in the way. As you walk the boundaries, at each point where you are placing a stone, say:

Only those who are welcome may stay. All others must go away.

When the last stone has been placed, the ward is sealed and the property protected.

Charlynn Walls

 May 29
Sunday

4℉ ♉

☽ v/c 10:11 am
☽ → ♊ 1:23 pm

Color of the day: Orange
Incense of the day: Juniper

Garden Blessing Spell

When we prepare our garden every year, we like to bless it by invoking the blessings of its past, present, and future. For this spell you'll need some seeds from last year's garden, a handful of your garden's soil, and some new seeds or seedlings to plant.

Grab last year's seeds with your dominant hand and sprinkle them into your garden while saying:

May last year's abundance return.

A fine harvest we wish to earn.

Follow that by picking up a handful of your garden's soil and sprinkle it over your garden while saying:

The soil we bless of this time and place,

Harvest joy, come to our garden space.

Finally, sprinkle your new seeds while saying:

Growth and possibilities today we plant.

A bright future may the earth to us grant!

Ari & Jason Mankey

May 30
Monday

4th ♊

New Moon 7:30 am

Color of the day: Silver
Incense of the day: Hyssop

Memorial Day

Memorial Day Moment

In the United States, today is Memorial Day. On this day, we celebrate those who have served in the armed forces and made the ultimate sacrifice. Whether or not we approve of war, those who serve—and the families who love them—are worth remembering with honor.

There are also other warriors, those who fight for the environment, for the rights of the downtrodden, for justice and truth, and for those who cannot speak for themselves. Let us remember them too, and send our love and energy and gratitude to all those who put themselves in harm's way on behalf of others. Take a moment to be grateful and perhaps to consider ways you can become a warrior on behalf of the light.

Deborah Blake

May 31
Tuesday

1st ♊

☽ v/c 4:10 pm

Color of the day: Red
Incense of the day: Basil

Water Bowl Spell

Water bowls are altar items that represent the moon. They help connect you with lunar power and manifest that which you seek.

Set a large bowl on your altar and fill it with water. Sprinkle a handful of sea salt into the bowl and say:

Bowl of water sprinkled with salt,

I call upon the ocean's heart.

Place your hands on either side of the bowl and take a deep breath in. Feel the rocking waves of the ocean within you. Say:

With pure intent and crescent moon,

I ask ocean, moon, and water to gift me a boon.

Speak your wish aloud to the surface of the water. Anoint your third eye and temples with the water, then give thanks.

Leave the water bowl on your altar for the whole moon cycle, each day anointing your third eye and temples and giving thanks. Your boon should arrive by the end of the moon cycle.

Astrea Taylor

June

The month of June is a time that inspires warmth, love, passion, and deep appreciation of beauty. Agricultural festivals in old Europe acknowledge and celebrate the many flowers and fruits that become abundant at this time. It is no coincidence that these plants—such as roses, raspberries, strawberries, wildflowers, and those that feature red or pink flowers or fruit—are associated with the planet Venus and the goddess Aphrodite. June is also the traditional month for weddings, and the term *honeymoon* refers to the beverage mead, made from fermented honey, that was traditionally given to the bride and groom as an aphrodisiac.

June brings the start of summer, and for thousands of years the summer solstice has been a prominent festival in many cultures. This celestial festival signifies the beginning of warm weather and abundant growth yet also reminds us of its opposite calendar festival: the winter solstice. All hail the Holly King! Spells done in June are often connected to love, romance, growth, health, and abundance.

Peg Aloi

 **June 1**
Wednesday

1st ♊

☽ → ♋ 1:49 am

Color of the day: Yellow
Incense of the day: Honeysuckle

Water Purification

In just two days, Mercury goes direct. Today, purify yourself with the water element to reset your energy and let go of any stress or negativity that may have entered your energy field during this Mercury retrograde period. Light a white candle in your bathroom and draw a warm bath. Add one cup Epsom salt and one tablespoon sea salt and swirl the water in a clockwise direction to dissolve. (If you don't have a bathtub, skip the salt and turn on your shower.) Before getting in the bathtub (or shower), direct your palms toward the water. Say:

> *Great Goddess, Divine Mother, Lady of the Rivers and the Sea, fill this water with your light. Thank you.*

Envision the water surrounded and filled with a sphere of golden-white light. As you soak (or stand under the spray), feel old stories of disempowerment dissolving away as you call all your energy back to you and regain your sense of clarity and calm. Extinguish the candle when you're done.

Tess Whitehurst

 **June 2**
Thursday

1st ♋

Color of the day: Crimson
Incense of the day: Apricot

Safe Home Spell

For this spell to keep your home safe, gather these items:

- ◆ Salt
- ◆ Bits of obsidian
- ◆ Powdered garlic
- ◆ Powdered rosemary
- ◆ A small candle
- ◆ A match
- ◆ Some charged water

Leave your home through the front door and proceed clockwise to the northern side of the house. Face north and say:

> *Powers of earth, protect this house.*

Cast the salt onto the ground. Move to the home's east side.

(Note: Upon passing any corner of the building, bury one of the obsidian pieces, saying, "Protection HERE." Upon passing any door or window, scatter garlic powder around it, saying, "Protection HERE.")

On the east side of your home, face east and say:

> *Powers of air, protect this house.*

Cast the rosemary into the air. Move to the south side.

On the south side of your home, face south and say:

Powers of fire, protect this house.

Light the candle safely, wafting smoke into the air. Then bury the candle in the ground. Move to the west side.

On the west side of your home, face west and say:

Powers of water, protect this house.

Pour the water into the ground.

You have "warded the bounds" of your home.

Susan Pesznecker

NOTES:

June 3
Friday

1st ♋

☽ v/c 11:15 am

☽ → ♌ 2:38 pm

Color of the day: Coral
Incense of the day: Cypress

Oomancy (Egg Magick)

National Egg Day in the United States falls on June 3. This is an excellent time to work magick with eggs. You can divine with eggs!

Consider what you want to know and write down your question. Choose the egg from your fridge that calls to you for this purpose. You will need a small dish with some water to crack an egg into. Check to see if there are any abnormalities in the egg first. Take note of anything odd. Then break the yolk and swirl it around and look at the patterns within the yolk. What are the shapes that appear to you? Write down anything you notice from the patterns revealed to you. See how they apply to your original question and keep a record of it. You can then refer to your records to gauge the results of your prediction.

Charlynn Walls

 **June 4**
Saturday

1st ♌

Color of the day: Brown
Incense of the day: Rue

> Shavuot begins at sundown

Planting Seeds

The thing about gardening is that different seeds need to be planted at different times, depending on the conditions. Spinach and lettuce and peas can go into the ground as soon as it can be worked. Corn and squash like warmer soil. Tomato plants must wait until after the risk of frost is over.

The seeds we plant in our lives are like that too. Depending on the project and the goal, we sometimes have to wait for the time to be right and the conditions to be optimal for success. But it isn't always easy to tell when that time is. You can use this spell to help with an actual garden or to guide you in when to start an important endeavor:

> God and Goddess, tell me
> when the time is right,
>
> And the conditions are at their best,
>
> So the seeds I plant may
> come to fruition
>
> And bring me my request.

Deborah Blake

June 5
Sunday

1st ♌

☽ v/c 7:12 pm

Color of the day: Yellow
Incense of the day: Frankincense

Recreate Your Own Vestalia

Vestalia was a Roman festival that honored Vesta, the goddess of hearth and home. Her name comes from a Sanskrit root that means "shining one." Because landlords and mortgage companies have zero interest in shining goddesses, the sacred element of our home is usually missing until we create it ourselves.

At noon today, stand before your home altar with a candle of your favorite color. As you light the candle, invoke Vesta:

> Gentle Goddess, Shining One—
>
> Bless my home and hearth
>
> Today and every day.

After the candle has burned down safely, clean your home. Clean out the fridge, clean out your closets, give away clothes you no longer wear. Honor and celebrate Vesta by making your home shiny-clean. If you can, bake a loaf of bread. Invite friends for lunch. Ask them to bring food and candles and together create a new ritual to honor Vesta.

Barbara Ardinger

June 6
Monday

1st ♌

☽ → ♍ 2:22 am

Color of the day: White
Incense of the day: Neroli

Start Your Day Spell

Most of us start our day with some sort of beverage. For many of us, that drink is coffee. For others, it might be a glass of juice or water. No matter what it is, you can make it a bit more magickal and use it to start your day on the best foot possible. Before drinking your morning beverage of choice, take a moment to think about just why you drink it. Hold that reason in your mind, and see its powers helping you throughout your day. Then say this spell before drinking:

*Morning drink. revitalize
my spirit and mind,*

*Prepare me for the day
ahead; may it be kind.*

*Humble drink, and yet a
gift from the earth,*

*Work your magick as I
prepare to set forth.*

*May this day be one of
satisfaction and glee,*

*For this I thank the gods.
So mote it be!*

Ari & Jason Mankey

 June 7
Tuesday

1st ♍

2nd Quarter 10:48 am

Color of the day: Gray
Incense of the day: Ylang-ylang

Wear Gold for Prosperity

A little over five hundred years ago, King Henry VIII of England and King Francis I of France held the Field of the Cloth of Gold, an event wherein they showed off their wealth to each other. Does the apparel maketh the man? Sometimes.

Don some gold for prosperity. It's the element of wealth and confidence, and by wearing it you literally envelop yourself in prosperity. It does not need to be a piece of jewelry or have a metallic element to it—nor does it have to be visible! Bless the item before you put it on:

Gold near me,

Gold on me,

Gold for me!

Repeat this mantra throughout the day to attract prosperity and prosperous opportunities.

Natalie Zaman

June 8
Wednesday

2nd ♏

☽ v/c 8:09 am

☽ → ♎ 11:23 am

Color of the day: Topaz
Incense of the day: Lilac

Clear as a Bell

Use this spell to pave the way for clearer communication before conversations, work meetings, presentations, etc. You'll need two pieces of paper and a bell.

Start by writing the names or a descriptor of the two parties involved, one on each piece of paper. For example, you might write your name on one and "the audience of my presentation tonight" on the other. Set the papers in front of you, a few inches apart, and imagine a channel of clear communication energy flowing between them.

Ring the bell, dissolving any obstructions within this channel as you chant:

Communication, clear and bright,

Fill my words with love and light.

My message is received most true,

Divinely guided through and through!

After your talk, you can safely burn the papers with gratitude or recycle them after making a horizontal karate chop motion over each, intending that the link between paper and person(s) be dissolved with love.

Melissa Tipton

NOTES:

▽ June 9
Thursday

2nd ♎

Color of the day: Purple
Incense of the day: Balsam

Outdoor Magic

June is Great Outdoors Month, and a perfect time to get outside and enjoy nature. Go to a natural setting, rural or urban, and spend some time exploring. Find natural totems representing the four elements, such as a feather or leaf representing air, sunlight or lamplight to represent fire, some water, and a stone representing earth. Sit on the earth and place your air totem in the east. Say:

Air of the east inspires me.
I breathe in new life.

And breathe.

In the south, let your face turn toward the sun or lamplight. Say:

Fire of the south, warm me.
Warm my hands, heart, head, and
health so that I am nourished.

In the west, lay the water, saying:

West and water, intuition and
feeling, help me flow and heal.

In the north, lay the earth totem, saying:

Mother Earth supports me. I am secure
and stable. I am at home outdoors.

Dallas Jennifer Cobb

① June 10
Friday

2nd ♎

☽ v/c 1:36 pm
☽ → ♏ 4:41 pm

Color of the day: Pink
Incense of the day: Orchid

Empowering Sun Tea Spell

Today is National Iced Tea Day, and sun tea is a wonderful way to enjoy it because the sun's energy is used to brew the tea instead of electricity or gas. The sun nourishes every part of our earth, and sun tea can be drunk for empowerment and positive energy.

This spell uses tea (such as black tea or hibiscus), a clear glass pitcher of water with a lid, sunshine, and a cup of ice. Drop the tea in the pitcher of water, replace the lid, and set it in direct sunlight. Gaze at the light-filled pitcher and say:

Great star, I ask that you

Infuse this water

With your brilliance, empowerment,

And uplifting qualities.

After two to three hours, pour the tea over ice and enjoy the taste of the sun's bright energy. Sun tea can also be used in your magic in place of water whenever you want to add solar energy to your works.

Astrea Taylor

June 11
Saturday

2nd ♏

Color of the day: Blue
Incense of the day: Pine

A Garden Blessing

As gardens are really beginning to grow now, it's a good time to bless your garden with this simple ritual. You'll need one shiny new penny. Begin by standing in your garden at sunrise as you hold your penny. Face east. Breathe deeply as you ground and center. Whisper to yourself:

Divine Power, bless this garden.
Bless you and the four cardinal
directions that provide me with the
bounty and beauty from this garden.

Then thank the guardians of each direction, starting with the east. Simply say:

I thank the guardians of the east
for protecting my garden.

Repeat this for each direction as you turn to face each one in this order: south, west, and north. Now, facing east again, look up and say:

Thank you, Father Sky.

Look down and say:

Thank you, Mother Earth.

Then return to an everyday state of mind. End by pressing the penny into the soil as an offering.

James Kambos

June 12
Sunday

2nd ♏

☽ v/c 5:40 pm

☽ → ♐ 6:31 pm

Color of the day: Gold
Incense of the day: Almond

Love, Take Root

Today is National Red Rose Day in the US. The red rose symbolizes love and romance in the language of flowers and is also the birth flower for the month of June. Today is also Loving Day, which commemorates the 1967 US Supreme Court ruling disbanding all laws that made mixed-race marriages illegal. Therefore it's an ideal day for this spell.

Consider every plant you put in your garden to be the beginning of a magical relationship. By planting a red rose, you are helping foster love of all kinds in your home and neighborhood. After selecting a spot where the rose will flourish, prepare the ground and plant the rose. Next, water and bless the earth and rose with these words:

O beautiful rose red,

To this home, love is led.

Take root, blossom, and grow.

Starting now, love will flow.

Remember to take care of the plant regularly and refresh the chant.

Laura Tempest Zakroff

June 13
Monday

2nd ♐

Color of the day: Silver
Incense of the day: Narcissus

A Spell for Academic Study

We magickal folk are constantly learning. We are forever in the process of experientially learning about the world around us and our place in the grand scheme of things. Many of us also take classes, courses, workshops, and other structures of study that require our utmost focus in order to excel.

If you are studying material for an exam, a course, an esoteric order, or a coven, consider making a sachet containing any of the herbs spearmint, rosemary, eyebright, dill, or jasmine. As you mix the herbs or grind them with a mortar and pestle, repeat these words:

Herbs of focus, herbs of wisdom,
give me knowledge, give me vision.

Place the herbs in the sachet (any color but black will do for the sachet, and orange is the ideal) and draw the alchemical symbol for Mercury (☿) on the bag with a permanent marker or ink. Keep this bag near you while studying to boost successful study.

Raven Digitalis

June 14
Tuesday

2nd ♐

Full Moon 7:52 am

☽ v/c 10:58 am

☽ → ♑ 6:14 pm

Color of the day: Scarlet
Incense of the day: Cinnamon

Flag Day

Flag Day Affirmation

Freedom and justice for all is a promising concept; its tenets are embodied in our flag. Today is Flag Day and a supermoon. Spells done today are supercharged.

The colors of the US flag are symbolic:

- *Red:* Hardiness and valor
- *White:* Innocence and purity
- *Blue:* Perseverance, justice, and vigilance

For this spell, candlelight will be used to symbolize the fire element. You will need:

- A reusable bag
- A sheet of paper
- A sharp pencil
- Scissors
- 1 large white pillar candle
- 2 medium-size pillar candles, one red and one blue

- A fireproof plate
- Matches or a lighter

Ponder the meaning of freedom and justice as you go outside at dusk with your bag containing all the spell items. Sit respectfully on Mother Earth.

Take your piece of paper from the bag and write down your thoughts on freedom and justice. Then cut the paper into strips.

Now create a candle plate, with the white candle in the center of the fireproof plate and the red and blue candles on the sides.

Slide your paper strips underneath the plate. Light the candles.

Say this affirmation three times, gazing into the lit wicks:

May my words produce strong action.

May my thoughts become deeds.

So mote it be!

Reflect on the spell and the flames until you are confident the affirmation has taken hold.

Snuff out the candles with wet fingers of your dominant hand.

Pack up your materials.

Stephanie Rose Bird

June 15
Wednesday

3rd ♑

Color of the day: Brown
Incense of the day: Bay laurel

Recovering Memory

Memory is spurious, and the following magical approach, relying on the practice of freewriting, can boost recall.

You'll need a candle, rosemary essential oil, paper, a pen or pencil, and a memento linked to the memory in question, such as a photograph, book, personal item, etc.

Anoint the candle with the oil, and add several drops of the oil to the candlewick and the wick well. Light the candle safely. Place the memento before you, and ready your writing tools. Repeat:

Pen and paper, rosemary,

May my memories return to me.

Holding the memento, close your eyes, breathe in the rosemary scent, and let the memory fill your mind. After a moment, open your eyes, set the item down, and start writing. Write whatever comes to mind, and write without stopping. Don't worry about corrections—just write, allowing it to be rough and unformed. Add doodles if you wish. Write for ten to fifteen minutes. Extinguish the candle.

Freewriting helps recover retained, forgotten memories. You may be surprised at what you remember.

Susan Pesznecker

NOTES:

June 16
Thursday

3rd ♑

☽ v/c 2:41 pm

☽ → ♒ 5:44 pm

Color of the day: Turquoise
Incense of the day: Myrrh

Waters of the Night

According to Egyptian lore, this is the Night of a Tear Drop. When Isis shed a tear for her lost love Osiris, the goddess Satis caught it and used it to make the Nile River flood. This flood replenished the fields, bringing good out of sorrow.

In most places, water comes from rain rather than a flooding river, but the concept still carries over. Sometimes it's good to sit with a feeling and just let it be what it is. Tonight, go outside in a dark and quiet place. Think of something in your life that makes you sad. When the tears begin, say:

As the tears of Isis

Made the Nile rise,

May the rains of summer

Flow from my eyes.

Let your tears fall on dusty ground, then repeat the verse. Finally, let go of the sorrow, like a storm passing. In the morning, the sun will rise and bring cheerful feelings once more.

Elizabeth Barrette

June 17
Friday

3rd ♒

Color of the day: White
Incense of the day: Mint

Refresh Your Altar

As we approach the day of the summer solstice, you might want to consider taking some time to refresh your altar (or to create one, if you haven't yet). Think of it as a bit of Midsummer spiritual housecleaning, a way to prepare yourself for the magical workings of the second half of the year.

Working mindfully and with focus, remove everything already on the altar, and clean and dust as necessary. You can either return all of the objects to their original spot or perhaps change things up to reflect the season or new magical goals. You can finish up with an offering of fresh flowers, or perhaps a small glass of mead or milk for the faeries, if it is safe to do so. Take a moment to send out appreciation for the altar, the day, and the presence of the gods in your life.

Deborah Blake

June 18
Saturday

 June 19
Sunday

3rd ♒

☽ v/c 2:50 pm

☽ → ♓ 7:01 pm

Color of the day: Black
Incense of the day: Sage

Crystal Grid

Today, create a crystal grid to fine-tune the energy in your home. You can use crystals you already have or acquire new ones for this purpose. First, clean your home and cleanse the energy with a chime or sage smoke. Then choose one stone to act as a center point and anchor for the grid. Hold it in your hand as you mentally charge it with the intention to establish sacred space and harmonious energy in your home. Place that stone on a flat surface where you'd like to build your grid (such as a countertop or table), and position the remaining crystals around it. You can simply surround the center crystal with four, six, or eight stones, or you can elaborate on the radial pattern by arranging several more layers around the center. You can also get creative and add other natural items to the mandala-shaped grid, such as fresh leaves or blossoms, star anise, or coffee beans.

Tess Whitehurst

3rd ♓

Color of the day: Orange
Incense of the day: Heliotrope

Father's Day – Juneteenth

Juneteenth Spell for Father's Day

Juneteenth, celebrated today, commemorates the end of slavery in the United States. This year the holiday falls on the same day as Father's Day, which is celebrated every third Sunday of June. On the conjunction of these two holidays, we can't help but think of all the fathers who were taken from their children as a result of racial injustices such as slavery, lynchings, and police brutality.

Set up a small candle on your altar (or wherever you do your magickal work) and say:

I light this candle that all fathers may find a way back to their children. May souls be reunited, wrongs righted, and justice found. Let love be the law and hate cast aside, so that all may live a life filled with opportunities.

As you light your candle, reflect on what you can do to make these words a reality. Extinguish the candle.

Ari & Jason Mankey

June 20
Monday

3rd ♓

☽ v/c 11:11 pm

4th Quarter 11:11 pm

☽ → ♈ 11:37 pm

Color of the day: Lavender
Incense of the day: Clary sage

Who's Your Muse?

The daughters of Memory, the nine Greek muses, are as follows:

Clio: "fame-giver"

Euterpe: "joy-giver"

Thalia: "the festive"

Melpomene: "singing"

Terpsichore: "lover of dancing"

Erato: "awakener of desire"

Polyhymnia: "many hymns"

Urania: "heavenly"

Calliope: "beautiful voiced"

We honor the muses whenever we visit their home, the museum.

Poets, playwrights, and artists have always invoked their favorite muses. So why can't ordinary people like us invoke them, too? Why can't we appeal to the muse who most inspires us? Which muse will help us be better than we are, be more talented?

Consider what you enjoy, what you're good at, what you want to do better. Read more about the muses and figure out who would best inspire you. When you're ready, cast your circle and invoke your muse:

_____ *(Name of muse), I ask
you to be present in my life.*

Help me find mentors and teachers.

*Remind me to practice what I learn
And to be faithful to you.*

*Gentle _____ (Name of muse),
inspire me to be the best I can be.*

Barbara Ardinger

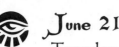

 June 21
Tuesday

4ᵗʰ ♈

☉ → ♋ 5:14 am

Color of the day: Red
Incense of the day: Geranium

Litha – Summer Solstice

Sacred Prayer

Here is a prayer for the summer solstice. Feel free to reword it as you wish.

I welcome the east, where energy rises; call in the south, where the light reaches; gather the west, where we seek sacred rest; and greet the north, where we sink into our roots. Hail above, where our planetary parents Sun and Moon reside, and below, where all that has come before informs us.

Rise. Reach. Rest. Roots.
Above and below.

I place my hands on my heart and know that as I stand in the bright light of the summer solstice, I celebrate mother and father, above and below, day and night, sun and moon. All of these live within me.

And as the sun stops and changes direction, I too am called to shift my trajectory, turning away from what no longer works, releasing what no longer serves, letting go of ancestral trauma and inherited patterns.

Welcoming the radiant light of my sacred parents, I stand solidly on Earth and imagine new ways of being.

Blessed be.

Dallas Jennifer Cobb

NOTES:

June 22
Wednesday

4th ♈

Color of the day: White
Incense of the day: Marjoram

Paying the Ferryman

On this day in 1978, Pluto's moon Charon was discovered, so this is a good time to honor that archetype. In Greek and Roman mythology, Charon is the ferryman of the dead to whom souls paid a coin for passage into the next life.

What's next for you? Find a penny—with this year's date on it, if possible—and cleanse it with salt and water. If you can, pass it through the smoke of jasmine incense (which is good for dreaming). Place the coin under your bed (or between your mattress and box spring or in your pillowcase) with these words:

I've paid the toll. Show me what's next.

Keep a journal by your bed so you can record what Charon reveals to you in your dreams.

Natalie Zaman

 June 23
Thursday

4th ♈

☽ v/c 4:02 am
☽ → ♉ 7:58 am

Color of the day: Purple
Incense of the day: Clove

Shield of the Sun

This spell taps into the power of the sun, which is in the sign of Cancer today, to create loving boundaries that provide a safe space for emotional and ancestral healing to unfold. You can perform the spell at high noon, when the sun is at its full power, but any time during daylight hours is fine.

Sitting where you can feel the warmth of the sun on your skin, come into a light meditative state. Envision your aura around you, and see and feel the rays of the sun cleansing your energy field. Visualize the outermost layer of your aura glowing strong and bright, empowered with the sun's rays, as you chant:

My aura shines with healing light,

And Cancer guards me with her might.

Safe from harm in sun's embrace,

I'm whole,

I'm healed,

In sacred space.

Melissa Tipton

June 24
Friday

4th ♉

Color of the day: Rose
Incense of the day: Thyme

homes for house Spirits

Cultures from around the world acknowledge the presence of house spirits. Though they are called by different names, there's a common theme throughout: if you want things in your home to be copacetic, then respecting the house spirits is crucial. If this is a new idea to you, it may help to build or provide a tiny home or space just for the spirits where you can interact with them. Possibilities include a small birdhouse, a little curio cabinet, or a snail shell—nothing with locks or seals, so they can come and go as they please. Decorate as you feel inspired, and place it near the center of your home, ideally tucked away, semi-private (in a corner, on a shelf, on top of a mantel, etc.). Announce to them:

Spirits of this home,
creatures of this place,

I acknowledge your
presence in this space.

Just for you, this special
space I have made.

Please do protect and bless
this house in trade.

Be sure to keep the area around the spirit home clean and respected, and if you feel called to make additional offerings, you can do so at this spirit home.

Laura Tempest Zakroff

NOTES:

June 25
Saturday

4th ♉

☽ v/c 3:02 pm

☽ → ♊ 7:13 pm

Color of the day: Gray
Incense of the day: Sandalwood

A Gazing Globe Spell

Originally, garden gazing globes had magical significance. They were placed in the garden to repel the evil eye or to reflect back the envious stare of a passerby. This spell will help you magically charge your gazing globe.

You'll need some bottled spring water and a soft cloth. Moisten the cloth with the water. Gently wipe your gazing globe with the damp cloth as you speak this charm:

I bless you, gazing globe,
return all evil glares.

Protect my home, send back
all envious stares.

Try to place your globe so it can be seen from the street. Renew your magical charge once a year or more if you feel the need.

James Kambos

 **June 26**
Sunday

4th ♊

Color of the day: Amber
Incense of the day: Marigold

Tarot for Connecting with Source Energy

Whenever we connect with source energy, we can tap into a deeper meaning in life that transcends the day-to-day. "Source" can mean our higher selves, the gods, ancestors, spirit, or wisdom. This tarot reading gives you insights on connecting with it.

Hold a deck of tarot cards to your heart for a few breaths. Shuffle them, then choose five cards from the center.

Card 1: Where you are now

Card 2: How you get confused or disconnected

Card 3: What you do when you get confused/disconnected

Card 4: What's holding you back from connecting with source

Card 5: What you have no control over and need to let go of

Write down the messages you receive from your reading in your Book of Shadows or journal. Choose one symbol that encompasses the most important insight. Draw it in seven places where you'll see it every day and be reminded of it. If you have a dry-erase marker, mirrors and windows are especially great places. Whenever you see the symbol, honor its message.

Astrea Taylor

NOTES:

 June 27
Monday

4th ♊

☽ v/c 10:38 pm

Color of the day: Ivory
Incense of the day: Hyssop

A Protection Charm for Empaths

Empathy is the glue that binds us together as a society and propels the evolution of our species. Although empathy is the greatest gift we have as humans, it can sometimes hurt when turned on high for too long.

In addition to reading my book on the subject, *Esoteric Empathy* (yeah, shameless self-promotion), empaths can create a charm for when things seem altogether too much or when you are preparing to enter a potentially challenging social situation.

Find or create a necklace of black tourmaline. Alternatively, you can simply buy a small piece of black tourmaline and keep it in your pocket when needed.

To enchant the tourmaline, surround it in a bowl of sea salt and the herb yarrow and leave it there overnight. Repeat the following verse ten times:

> *This stone is blessed and guards my emotions; I am in harmony with my life's devotions.*

Raven Digitalis

June 28
Tuesday

4th ♊
☽ → ♋ 7:53 am
New Moon 10:52 pm
Color of the day: Black
Incense of the day: Ginger

Breaking Through

The new moon is a time of breaking out and starting anew. It is the darkest point in the lunar cycle before moving into the illumination of the light. If you are looking to start an endeavor in your life, you can use this energy to break through to the next level.

Find a quiet spot in your home or property. You will need a piece of paper, a writing utensil, and a candle. Write down what you are wanting to break through to, and place that piece of paper under the candle. Now turn off all the lights and see yourself emerging from where you are into the next stage of your evolution. Once you can visualize where you need to be, light the candle to symbolize your breaking through to a new you. Extinguish the candle when done.

Charlynn Walls

June 29
Wednesday

1st ♋
Color of the day: Yellow
Incense of the day: Lavender

harvesting herbs

In East Anglia, this is Herb Harvesting Day. According to ancient tradition, today is the best day of the year to harvest herbs meant for healing. It's a good time to pick herbs for magical or culinary uses too.

First, plan to pick herbs around midmorning. Wait until the morning dew has evaporated and everything is dry. By noon, though, the sun begins to affect the essential oils in the herbs. So they are strongest at midmorning.

Use garden scissors to cut the stems. In some cases, like with rosemary or thyme, it works best to cut sprigs and strip the leaves off later. Others such as basil or sage can be picked by the leaf. Place the herbs in a basket to keep them safe while you pick more. Give thanks to the plants and encourage them to keep growing.

Indoors, bundle sprigs with string and hang in a warm, dark place to dry. Individual leaves are best dried flat on screens. When fully dry, store them in labeled jars.

Elizabeth Barrette

June 30
Thursday

1st ♋

☽ v/c 4:14 pm

☽ → ♌ 8:40 pm

Color of the day: White
Incense of the day: Mulberry

Nonbinary Pride Meditation

It's the end of Pride Month. Let's balance our energies with the help of Erinle, the Yoruba orisha and patron of the LGBTQIA+ community. This orisha, like many nonbinary people, doesn't fit neatly into any one gender category.

Erinle is a hunter who resides in many places: forests, farms, and waters. This complex orisha is the perfect choice to engage with the energies of a beautifully diverse community. Let's draw the orisha to us with gorgeous coral, turquoise, and/or indigo silk or satin cloth. Set a piece of fabric of this type on a table to begin. In a crystal or glass bowl, drop the following essential oils:

21 drops frankincense

21 drops myrrh

14 drops vetiver

7 drops patchouli

14 drops lavender

Swirl to mix or use a glass stirrer, and place the bowl on the cloth. Put on some relaxing music for an hour.

Touch your pulse points with the oils. Lie on a yoga mat and meditate. See what Erinle has to show and say to you.

Stephanie Rose Bird

NOTES:

July

In 46 BCE, when Julius Caesar decided to reform the Roman lunar calendar, the names of the months were numbers. He moved the first of the year back to January, and, being the egoist he was, he renamed the fifth month (the month of his birth) for himself: Iulius (Julius, today's July). He also gave it a thirty-first day. (Then he named the next month after his heir, Augustus.)

July (the month of my birth, too) is high summer. In many places, it's the hottest month of the year. It's the month in which everything blooms until the heat of the sun makes flowers—and people—wilt and nearly melt.

What do I remember from my childhood Julys? Rereading my favorite books. Dragging the big old washtub out on the side lawn, filling it with cold water, and splashing all afternoon. Helping my father tend his flowers—roses, columbines, tulips, and hydrangeas. Climbing to the very top of our neighbor's huge weeping willow tree. Chasing fireflies before bedtime and putting them in jars to glitter and wink throughout the night. Sleeping in the screened porch with all the windows open to catch every possible breeze. What are your favorite July memories?

Barbara Ardinger

July 1
Friday

1st ♌

Color of the day: Pink
Incense of the day: Orchid

Canada Day

National Pride Spell

I am Canadian and I love my country. On July 1, Canada celebrates independence and our ongoing growth and development as a nation. Wherever and whoever you are, celebrate with us Canadians today. Celebrate your national pride.

Gather a paper, a pen, and a small piece of ribbon or string. Write down ten things you love about your country. I love Canadian manners, and politeness; socialized medicine and education; regional diversity and how we embrace newcomers; racial diversity, equity, and respect; and our varied natural geography.

Now roll up your list, saying:

The best of my country is the best of me. I celebrate my country and diversity. I hold this strength and wealth within me. So mote it be.

Tie the ribbon around the roll and place it on your altar. Your national pride energy is collected in one place and will aid you in working powerful magic.

Dallas Jennifer Cobb

July 2
Saturday

1st ♌

Color of the day: Indigo
Incense of the day: Patchouli

Approaching Independence

As we approach Independence Day, identify something in your life that makes you feel like you may be a captive or at least kind of tied up. From what are you yearning to be free?

In the 1972 film *1776*, Jefferson, Franklin, and Adams sing "The Egg." This is when they decide the eagle will be the new nation's national bird. Create an altar today featuring a symbol of what is holding you captive. Find an illustration in a magazine or online or draw what you seek to be free from. As you set out your elemental symbols, see each elemental power taking some action to drive away that which is holding you captive. Light a blue candle and visualize an eagle swooping toward you. It's coming to free you. Ask the eagle for help:

Great eagle, bird of freedom,

Bring me freedom from _____.

Carry it away, out of my aura, out of my life.

As you fly, let me breathe freely and live!

Extinguish the candle.

Barbara Ardinger

July 3
Sunday

1st ♌

☽ v/c 5:59 am

☽ → ♍ 8:31 am

Color of the day: Orange
Incense of the day: Hyacinth

Elixir of Inspiration

July 3 is when the Festival of Cerridwen was observed. Cerridwen is a Welsh goddess who kept the cauldron of rebirth, transformation, and inspiration. We can work with Cerridwen today to harness that inspiration for ourselves.

Pour some water into your own cauldron or vessel. You can add items sacred to Cerridwen, including grain, oak, sage, sandalwood, and apple. Stir in a clockwise motion. Once the mixture has been combined, apply three drops of your elixir to your thumb to represent the three drops of Awen that fell on Gwion when he was gifted with inspiration. Chant:

Inspiration from drops of three.
Past, present, and future,
awaken the power within me.

The transformative and creative powers will now begin working with you.

Charlynn Walls

NOTES:

July 4
Monday

1st ♏

Color of the day: Silver
Incense of the day: Lily

Independence Day

A Spell of Independence

For those of us in the Unites States, Independence Day is an ideal time to consider the things that make us independent as a country and as individuals. Although no country is perfect, we are afforded great freedom to live an authentic life.

Light a white candle and "pull" the flame into each of your body's seven chakras. Quickly and safely pinch the flame with your right hand, and draw this energy into the chakra. Say the following at each chakra point:

1. *Base:* "My body is sovereign. I am in control."

2. *Navel:* "My sexuality is sacred. I determine its expression."

3. *Solar plexus:* "My soul creates my experience. I choose my path."

4. *Heart:* "My kindness is my nature. I declare empathy for all."

5. *Throat:* "My expressions are authentic. I am inspired to inspire."

6. *Brow:* "My visions are clear. I am a psychic being."

7. *Crown:* "My connection to Spirit is pure. I am me and I am free!"

Extinguish the candle when done.

Raven Digitalis

NOTES:

July 5
Tuesday

1st ♏

☽ v/c 2:04 pm

☽ → ♎ 6:25 pm

Color of the day: Scarlet
Incense of the day: Bayberry

A Thunderstorm Banishing Spell

This spell uses the awesome power of a thunderstorm to banish an issue from your life. You'll need a six-inch terracotta flowerpot saucer and some garden or potting soil. As a thunderstorm approaches, fill the saucer with the soil. Smooth out the soil. With your finger, a pencil, or a stick, write a word describing your problem in the soil, or draw a symbol or image of it. For example, if you're having money worries, you could write "money" or draw a dollar sign. When done, place the saucer and soil outside. Go inside to wait out the storm and think about the rain cleansing the problem from your life.

When the storm passes, go out and check the soil. The word or image should be rinsed away. Scatter the soil on the ground. End by rinsing out the saucer. You may use it again for magic. Your problem should begin to diminish.

James Kambos

 July 6
Wednesday

1st ♎

2nd Quarter 10:14 pm

Color of the day: Brown
Incense of the day: Marjoram

Bind Your Distractions

First quarter moons can really test new moon intentions. This spell to bind distractions is useful for staying the course. All you need is a candle, a lighter, a medium-sized piece of paper, a pen, a twist tie, tea tree oil, clove oil, and a ceramic bowl.

Light the candle and think of how annoying your distractions are. Write them down on the paper, then roll the paper into a tight scroll and secure it with the twist tie. Say:

I bind my distractions with wire!

Carefully catch one end of the scroll on fire, stub it out in the bowl, and then drop it into the bowl. Say:

I bind my distractions with fire!

When the embers are completely out, put three drops of each essential oil onto the scroll. Say:

I bind my distractions with clove and tea tree!

The things on this list have no power over me!

Keep the scroll in a safe place and extinguish the candle.

Astrea Taylor

July 7
Thursday

2nd ♎

☽ v/c 9:04 pm

Color of the day: Crimson
Incense of the day: Apricot

Amethyst Unblocking

If you feel stuck in a certain life area, this spell will help you transform that block into positive momentum and flow. First, write a positive affirmation on a small slip of paper. Choose an affirmation that describes exactly how you want to feel in this life area, in the present tense. For example, you might write, "My finances are flowing," "I am in love with someone wonderful who loves me back," or "I am experiencing wonderful success in my career."

Empower a small amethyst in bright sunlight for a few minutes. Then place the affirmation on your altar so the words are facing up. While holding the amethyst, go to your front door, open it all the way, stand in the threshold, and speak aloud the affirmation you wrote. Place the amethyst on top of the affirmation on your altar. After twenty-eight days, release the amethyst in a moving body of water and recycle the paper.

Tess Whitehurst

July 8
Friday

2nd ♎

☽ → ♏ 1:15 am

Color of the day: Rose
Incense of the day: Alder

Prosperity Magic

Summer is a great time to work prosperity magic, since the natural world around us is filled with energy for growth and abundance. Here is a simple spell for prosperity that you can do outside if you have a yard, or inside in a potted plant if you don't have a garden. Take five coins—it doesn't matter what they are, as long as they are new and shiny. Pennies or dimes work well, although you can use something fancy like a half-dollar or dollar coin. Hold them in your hands and visualize them multiplying, becoming larger and larger piles of money. Plant the coins in the dirt and visualize the sun infusing them with power and energy, then say:

Money, money, grow for me,

Bring me bright prosperity.

Deborah Blake

July 9
Saturday

2nd ♏

Color of the day: Blue
Incense of the day: Magnolia

Uniting the Lovers Within

The Lovers card of the tarot has rich meaning, one being the union of the conscious and unconscious selves, which gives rise to the transcendent function, often symbolized by an angel watching over the couple. When these two aspects of the self are brought into partnership, we are gifted with useful insights and divine inspiration.

Set aside the Lovers card from your deck of choice, then use the following incantation before shuffling the cards:

Deep within my heart,

The Lovers hold the key

To uniting my full self

In perfect harmony.

Teach me, Lovers.

Draw three cards: the first is the desire of your conscious self, the second is the desire of your unconscious self, and the third is the result of honoring both of these inner yearnings through your daily choices.

Melissa Tipton

NOTES:

July 10
Sunday

2nd ♏

☽ v/c 12:34 am

☽ → ♐ 4:34 am

Color of the day: Yellow
Incense of the day: Frankincense

Staying Connected

U se this charm to stay connected with your loved ones.
Ideally, those wishing to be connected
should create the bracelets together.
Otherwise, bracelets may be sent to
the other(s).

Each person will cut 12-inch
lengths of cotton thread or embroidery floss in a favorite color, one
length for each bracelet. Imagine
person A chooses blue, person B red,
and person C purple. Each person
would cut three lengths of thread in
their color. Each bracelet will include
a length from each person. With the
above example, each bracelet would
have blue, red, and purple strands.

Form a bracelet by twisting or
braiding the strands together. Tie
a figure-eight knot in the middle of
each: a sign of the infinite nature of
friendship.

Tie bracelets to wrists with square
knots. As each knot is tied, say:

Friends together, friends forever.

Each time you look at your bracelet,
imagine your friend(s). When the

bracelet falls off, write a letter to your
friend(s), recalling shared memories.

Susan Pesznecker

NOTES:

July 11
Monday

2nd ♐

☽ v/c 9:42 pm

Color of the day: Ivory
Incense of the day: Narcissus

Bloodstone for Energy

Bloodstone is a type of jasper crystal. It's useful for a variety of reasons, being a stone that both contains healing energy and helps deflect negativity. Over the years we've found that its healing powers are useful for bestowing extra energy. This is especially helpful to us in the summer when we are on vacation or going on an extended hike.

Before going on a long day of walking or engaging in any vigorous activity, place a small piece of bloodstone in your pocket or purse. When you feel yourself starting to get tired, take out the bloodstone and place it in your dominant hand. Squeeze the bloodstone and feel the energy it gives off, letting that energy flow into your hand and move throughout your body. Take three deep breaths while holding the stone and feeling its energy. You should now notice yourself feeling less tired, with your body prepared for new adventures.

Ari & Jason Mankey

 July 12
Tuesday

2nd ♐

☽ → ♑ 5:01 am

Color of the day: Maroon
Incense of the day: Basil

Hestia's Sweet Simplicity

Hestia is a Greek hearth goddess, and her domain is domesticity. Since it's National Simplicity Day, let's engage Hestia's energy to cleanse our altars. Altars need freshening up. Candlewicks get too long, stuck in dried wax, or encrusted in herbal dressings. You get the picture. Your altar craves some goddess-fueled TLC.

Carefully dismantle your altar. Clear its components in the manner most fitting to your spiritual path. You might smudge them or spritz them with Hoyt's Cologne, rainwater, spring water, lightning water, vodka, vinegar, or rose water. Cleanse chalices and shot glasses for libations and offerings. Handwash cloths on your altar using a soapwort infusion or gentle floral water rinse, then hang them outside to recharge. Wipe down candles and trim wicks. Bring special objects such as athames and besoms outside for clearing in the sun and air. Sun, sea salt and snow are dependable, simple, and natural cleansers from Mother Earth. Reassemble the altar and thank Hestia for her help.

Stephanie Rose Bird

July 13
Wednesday

2nd ♑
☽ **Full Moon** 2:38 pm

Color of the day: Topaz
Incense of the day: Lilac

Travel Button Altar

Buttons have always felt magical to me. I loved sorting through my grandmother's button tin as a child, and every button jar I see at a yard sale feels like a vessel of buried treasure. If you think about it, the job of a button is to hold things together, so you can work sympathetic magic with them in that way. They can also resemble hag or witch stones when they have holes through their center, giving protection and aiding in divination. They make a terrific travel altar if you sew them onto a handkerchief or similar small piece of fabric. Consider the following correlations:

- A white, clear, or yellow button for the element of air
- A red or orange or glass button for the element of fire
- A blue button or one made out of shell for the element of water
- A green or wooden button for the element of earth
- A silver or gold button for spirit

Laura Tempest Zakroff

July 14
Thursday

3rd ♑
☽ v/c 12:17 am
☽ → ♒ 4:13 am

Color of the day: Green
Incense of the day: Nutmeg

Road to Success Candle

For this spell you will need a green taper candle and a sheet of black beeswax. If you don't have beeswax, you can use black thread or embroidery floss. Cut the beeswax into long strips of equal widths and wind them (or the thread) around the taper or pillar to form a "road" that spirals around the candle. Press the beeswax strips or thread gently but firmly onto the taper. (You can also use a hair dryer to heat up the wax a bit so the thread or beeswax strips adhere better.) Once the road is set, dress the candle with a citrus essential oil if you have it. (Citrus oils such as orange, lemon, and bergamot will add uplifting energy to this work.) As you create the road and dress the candle, say:

Twist and turn,
The road will wind.
But be assured,
Success is mine!

Burn the candle in a holder or heat-proof dish when you need it (e.g., before a job interview or test, when making a big decision). Don't leave the candle burning unattended, and make sure all flames are fully extinguished when you're done.

Natalie Zaman

NOTES:

♥ July 15
Friday

3rd ♒

Color of the day: Purple
Incense of the day: Cypress

The heart's Mirror

The heart is the seat of the self. It holds emotions and virtues. It is the place to look when you want to discover yourself—your wants and needs, your potential and your purpose. For this spell you will need a mirror that you can open and close, like a compact case or a travel mirror. Wash it in water with a little salt to purify it, then in plain water, and wipe it dry. Look in the mirror and visualize your true self. Then say:

Mirror of the self,

Mirror of my heart,

Show the truth within

And reflect my Art.

Let the looking glass

Bless the path I take

As I live my life,

And each choice I make.

This will help you see who you really are. When you have an important decision, take out the mirror and look in it, imagining yourself on each possible path, and compare that to your true self. Keep the mirror closed when not in use.

Elizabeth Barrette

🜚 July 16
Saturday

3rd ♒

☽ v/c 12:36 am

☽ → ♓ 4:18 am

Color of the day: Indigo
Incense of the day: Ivy

Banishing Ritual

To banish means to prohibit, abolish, or eliminate. In magic, to banish something means getting it out of your life and your energy field for good. Banish a situation, condition, or relationship today by writing a simple word or phrase that represents what you want to banish on a small piece of paper. Place it on your altar. Say:

> Great Goddess, as you know, it is time for this to go. Thank you for helping me banish it from my life, now and in all directions of time.

Now, leaving the paper flat on your altar, spin it counterclockwise three times, feeling that you are unwinding its power over you. Next, either shred it with scissors or put it through a paper shredder. Place the shreds in a cauldron or pot and safely burn them. Bid your final farewell by releasing the ashes in a moving body of water or flushing them down the toilet. Give thanks to the Goddess and happily move on with your life.

Tess Whitehurst

♡ July 17
Sunday

3rd ♓

Color of the day: Gold
Incense of the day: Heliotrope

Strawberry Blessings

While the end of June is known for the first rush of local strawberries, in many areas the berries are still widely available in mid-July. Associated with purity and passion, perfection and righteousness, strawberries are the perfect food to use for blessings. Not just spiritually powerful, strawberries are filled with healthy antioxidants.

Whether alone or with family or friends, create a strawberry blessing dessert. I love strawberries with sponge cake and a topping of Greek yogurt, but you can eat them with scones and whipped cream or shortbread and clotted cream as well. As you wash the berries, intone purity. As you cut the berries, notice how perfectly red and juicy they are, and how they are passionately heart-shaped. When you serve the berries, hold the blessings of purity, passion, perfection, and righteousness in mind so that all who eat this divine dessert are blessed and filled with sweetness.

Dallas Jennifer Cobb

⊕ July 18
Monday

3rd ♓

☽ v/c 2:43 am

☽ → ♈ 7:17 am

Color of the day: White
Incense of the day: Neroli

Prophecy

The ancient world had ten sibyls, who were prophetesses. The Cumaean Sibyl wrote her prophecies on leaves that she placed at the mouth of her cave. If no one came to pick them up, she let the wind scatter them.

A hot summer day is a good time to try some prophecy. Take advantage of "the heat of inspiration." First, cut 22 leaf shapes, one for each major arcana card in the tarot, out of colored paper and number them. Next, take your leaves, some colored pencils, and your favorite tarot pack and go outside and find a shady spot. Look at the Fool card and consider what you and he, working together, can predict. When the prophecy comes to you, write it on your first leaf. Repeat this with the rest of the cards and leaves. Write clearly. Add drawings. When the wind comes up, go to a windy place and imitate the Cumaean Sibyl. Pray that your prophecies will come true.

Barbara Ardinger

July 19
Tuesday

3rd ♈

Color of the day: Black
Incense of the day: Ginger

A Ritual of Thanks

During July, the earth begins to bless us with its bounty. This ritual gives thanks for our food supply. Begin the ritual at sunset. Drape your altar in rich purple or green fabric. Upon the altar place one glass of red wine or purple grape juice. Face west, then ground and center. Speak these words:

*Slowly the sun's power
begins to decline.*

*Still we're blessed with the fruit
of the orchard from the vine.*

*Great Mother, thank you for
your gifts from the land.*

*Farmers, thank you for all that
comes from your calloused hands.*

Now raise your beverage in a toast and take a sip. Truly stop and think about where our food comes from. Next, carry the rest of your beverage outside. Respectfully pour it upon the earth in a show of thanks. Finally, when you can, purchase something from a farmers' market to support your local growers.

James Kambos

 July 20
Wednesday

3rd ♈

☽ v/c 10:19 am

4th Quarter 10:19 am

☽ → ♉ 2:23 pm

Color of the day: Yellow
Incense of the day: Honeysuckle

**A Witch's Potion
to Bless the House**

A fun way to bless your room, home, or property is to pull out the ol' cauldron for some boilin' and bubblin'. Since we are modern Witches, a pot on the stove will suffice! Bring some water to a boil (however much you'd like) and set aside a handful of sea salt along with the herbs you most associate with blessing and energetic protection. Because there are so many, I will leave the herbal concoction up to you!

Once the water has boiled, add the herbs and place your hands safely in the vicinity of the pot while saying:

Boiling and brewing, this potion's alight. Blessed and protected for all days and all nights.

Simmer for thirteen minutes. Once cooled, strain the herbs and asperge (sprinkle) the potion all around your room, house, and/or property. Leave the strained herbs outdoors to finish working their magick.

Raven Digitalis

▽ **July 21**
Thursday

4th ♉

Color of the day: Turquoise
Incense of the day: Myrrh

Offering for Spirits of the Land

With the moon in Taurus today, we may find ourselves drawn to the element of earth. One of my favorite things to do is to make an offering to the spirits of the land. They're always present in natural areas, and they love receiving something beautiful.

Before leaving home, grab something natural that you feel the spirits would appreciate, such as a stone or a natural object like a pinecone. Go outside and walk to a natural area. When you arrive at a place that feels right, align with the energy and set the offering on the ground. Say:

Spirits of earth,

I leave this for you,

In gratitude for all you do.

Leave the offering and make your way home again. When you wish to connect with the element of earth in your magic, you can call to mind the energy of that place and the offering.

Astrea Taylor

July 22
Friday

4th ♉
☉ → ♌ 4:07 pm
☽ v/c 7:45 pm

Color of the day: White
Incense of the day: Vanilla

Finding Lost Objects

Every now and then we all lose something that is meaningful to us. Today we can call upon our faerie allies to help us find what is lost. The Faerie occupy an in-between realm and often have a unique vantage point. Where we may overlook something, you can bet that the Fae will not. For this spell you can simply stand outside in an area that is a little wilder than the other surroundings. If you live in an apartment, you will want to open a window. Speak directly to those in the other realm:

Faerie kind, hear my plea. Help return what is missing to me.

Once you have spoken to the Fae, have an offering for them ready to show your appreciation. A traditional offering is that of milk and honey. You can pour this into the wild area after the spell. If you are in an apartment, you can leave the offering in a small dish where it will not be disturbed. You can and should repeat the offering once the object is found.

Charlynn Walls

July 23
Saturday

4th ♉
☽ → ♊ 1:11 am

Color of the day: Brown
Incense of the day: Rue

Connecting with Earth

The four elements of earth, air, fire, and water are an important part of a Witchcraft practice. We tend to take these elements for granted, but it's a good idea to take a moment occasionally to consciously connect with them.

The summer provides many great opportunities to connect with the element of earth. If you are a gardener, you can put your hands in the dirt and say thank you. Or you can take a walk outside, being extra aware of when your feet meet the land. Or simply sit on the grass and feel how grounding it is to be in touch with the earth. If you like, you can say these words:

I reach out to you, element of earth,

And thank you for grounding me,

For providing solid footing for my life,

And for all the growth that springs from your soil.

I am the earth, and the earth is me.

Deborah Blake

July 24
Sunday

4th ♊

Color of the day: Amber
Incense of the day: Marigold

Sacred Smoke

Burning incense is a great way to tap into the power of the air element, and making a homemade batch allows you to connect with this energy on a deeper level. You'll need:

- 2 tablespoons sandalwood powder
- 1 teaspoon frankincense resin (can be purchased in powder form or ground by hand with a mortar and pestle)
- ¼ teaspoon guar gum
- Water

Combine the first three ingredients in a small bowl, then add a teaspoon of water at a time, mixing thoroughly. I typically use just shy of 3 teaspoons. Pinch off small chunks of dough and shape them into little cones with your fingers. Let dry completely (this can take up to a week).

Hover your palms above the incense as you chant:

I call upon the power of air!

Please charge this incense with the energy of change, clarity, and wisdom.

So mote it be!

Melissa Tipton

July 25
Monday

4th ♊

☽ v/c 4:14 am

☽ → ♋ 1:54 pm

Color of the day: Lavender
Incense of the day: Rosemary

A Charm for Safe Travel

With this charm in your pocket, your travels will be easier and safer. Add the following to a small drawstring bag or zippered pouch:

- A smidgen of dirt from just outside your front door, wrapped in plastic wrap, to guide your footsteps home again
- A penny or other coin offering (Leave this at your destination as payment for passage. You can also flip the coin as a divination tool.)
- Tiger eye, fluorite, and/or rosemary for protection
- Obsidian for binding you to your home
- Dried lemon peel for good health
- Salt or dried lavender for purifying your destination
- A chamomile or mint tea bag for calm and relaxation
- A small personal item to tie you to the bag and keep it close

• Commonsense items, such as loved ones' names and contact information, headache medication, an eye mask for rest, etc.

Before traveling, bless the bag and items and leave on your altar for a period equal to the length of the trip.
  Happy travels!

Susan Pesznecker

NOTES:

 July 26
Tuesday

4th ♋

Color of the day: Red
Incense of the day: Cedar

Banishing Pentagram at the Beach

All that's required for this spell is a sandy shore, some waves, and the tide. At the shoreline, draw a banishing pentagram in the sand. As you draw it, think of something you would like to remove from your life (such as a bad habit or a relationship), letting all of the energy within you associated with that thing or person drain into the sand and the pentagram.

When you are done drawing the pentagram, ask the water to take away whatever you are banishing:

Cleansing waters, take this burden away from me. Wash over what I wish to get rid of and leave me fresh and renewed. So mote it be!

As the tide comes in, your pentagram will fade away, taking away that which you wish to be rid of.

Ari & Jason Mankey

July 27
Wednesday

4th ♋
☽ v/c 8:54 pm

Color of the day: Brown
Incense of the day: Bay laurel

Magical Walk

Today is Take Your Houseplant For a Walk Day and Take Your Pants for a Walk Day. While both of these sound rather silly, they are geared toward getting folks to go outside and move their body.

You are certainly welcome to give your house or office plant a change of view or show off a favorite pair of pants today, but for Witches and magical folk, I recommend making it a daily practice to get outside and observe the world around you.

Far too often we're more concerned about where we're going and getting there as fast as possible or checking our phones. If we pay more attention to the world around us, we're able to connect more deeply. I like to say that 80 percent of Witchcraft is observation. Give yourself a weekly challenge. Here are some ideas:

- What color is the sky? What do the clouds look like today?

- Identify one plant you see (a tree, herb, etc.).

- What animals do you notice?

- Note different windows or doorways.

Laura Tempest Zakroff

NOTES:

July 28
Thursday

4th ♋

☽ → ♌ 2:36 am

New Moon 1:55 pm

Color of the day: White
Incense of the day: Balsam

Find Your Fame

Yearning to be respected and admired is intrinsic to the human psyche. Today, work magic to manifest that desire. First, clarify one thing you're passionate about that you'd also like to be known for, either in your community or in your world. Maybe you'd like to be a trusted doctor, a legendary drummer, or the bartender who makes the best margaritas in town. Next, choose a deity, character, or famous person who exemplifies the qualities or skills you'd like to be known for. Find or print out an image of that being, frame it, and place it near a red candle. Light the candle as you gaze at the image. As you inhale, internalize the vibration and essence of the fame you desire. As you exhale, feel that you are generously gifting the world with your unique talents and gifts. Repeat for a few breaths. Extinguish the candle. Vow to work hard to provide value and service to the world, and expect to receive loving recognition in return.

Tess Whitehurst

▽ July 29
Friday

1st ♌

Color of the day: Coral
Incense of the day: Violet

Islamic New Year begins at sundown

Lessons of the Tiger

Today is International Tiger Day. Let's celebrate and recognize one of the most commanding creatures among us. Tigers have much to teach us, for they are determined, persistent, strategic, stealthy, and deliberate. They may seem relaxed, but when the moment comes, they always have enough energy to take on the tasks necessary for survival.

Tigers smell musky and of the earth. Take on some of this characteristic today by wearing a musk cologne or essential oil such as vetiver, myrrh, patchouli, or ruh khus. Dab cologne or oil on your third eye (the center of your forehead just above your eyebrows). Take a few deep breaths so the oil permeates your senses. Sit in a comfortable position for ten to fifteen minutes. During this time, do the following:

- Put on some nature sounds music.
- Close your eyes, focusing on your third eye as you visualize a tiger in its natural environment.

- Relax and stay comfortable, breathing deeply to take in the aromatic messages of the oils.
- Go on the magickal journey designed just for you, as you follow the tiger.

Stephanie Rose Bird

NOTES:

July 30
Saturday

1st ♈ ♌

☽ v/c 12:29 am

☽ → ♍ 2:11 pm

Color of the day: Gray
Incense of the day: Sage

Thanks to Friends

Today is International Day of Friendship. Everyone benefits from friends. They keep us company and lend a helping hand when we need it. Without close relationships, health tends to suffer. In fact, loneliness is as bad as obesity or smoking when it comes to causing health problems.

Take some time today to express your gratitude for the friends in your life. For this spell you will need a small bouquet of flowers that represent friendship. Sunflower, iris, or geranium work well and are readily available in stores. Ivy, another symbol of friendship, makes good greenery. Put the flowers in a vase on your altar. Then say:

Flowers of friendship, free of strife,

Brighten the garden of my life.

For each good friend within the ranks,

I bow my head and I give thanks.

Name your friends—the more the better—and state why you feel grateful for them. When you finish, say the verse again. Then go do something nice for your friends to show your gratitude.

Elizabeth Barrette

NOTES:

July 31
Sunday

1st ♍

Color of the day: Gold
Incense of the day: Eucalyptus

Where Shall I Wander?

Sometimes you just need to get away—but where? First deal with the mundane details. Think about where you can go, physically, financially, etc. Then print out a map that encompasses all the possible areas, and set it on a table or place it on the floor—upside down so that you cannot see the various destinations.

Take a piece of tourmaline. (It's protective, and you want to get to your destination safely. If you don't have tourmaline, use another protective stone, like turquoise, or a penny.) Gently toss the tourmaline onto the surface of the upside-down map with these words:

Wither shall I wander,

Where shall I go,

To lift my heart

And heal my soul?

Make a pin prick on the map where the tourmaline lands, and repeat two more times. Flip the map over and your destination will be revealed.

Natalie Zaman

August

Summer is at its height of power when August rolls in, bringing with it the first of the harvest festivals, Lughnasadh (or Lammas), on the first of the month. Lughnasadh is a festival of strength and abundance, a reflection of August itself. Lugh and the Corn God are highly celebrated during this month and are particularly good to work with in spells or rituals for abundance, prosperity, agriculture, marriage, or strength. The Earth Mother in her many forms is ripening and overflowing with abundance. While we often see the first harvest as being associated with corn, there is much more that has been harvested by this point. We must remember not to overlook anything or take anything for granted in our lives, and the harvest is an excellent reminder of that. It is a time to begin focusing on expressing appreciation and giving thanks for all that we have.

The full moon this month is most often called the Corn Moon, but also goes by the Wyrt Moon, Barley Moon, or Harvest Moon. The stones carnelian, fire agate, cat's eye, and jasper will add extra power to your spells and rituals at this time. Use the herbs chamomile, St. John's wort, bay, angelica, fennel, rue, barley, wheat, marigold, or sunflowers in your spells. The colors for August are yellow, gold, and the rich green of the grass and leaves.

Kerri Connor

▽ August 1
Monday

1st ♏

☽ v/c 6:29 pm

Color of the day: Gray
Incense of the day: Lily

Lammas

A Lammas Corn Ritual

It's Lammas, the first of the harvest sabbats, celebrating corn and Lugh, an ancient harvest god. Grains are honored during this sabbat, but especially corn.

Begin this ritual at sunrise. Cover your altar in yellow fabric. In the center, place one yellow candle. In front of the candle, lay one ear of corn with the husk removed. Safely light the candle. Meditate on how grains such as corn, the Mother of Seeds, have fed civilization since before recorded history. Then speak these words:

In the stars, the lion reigns.

On Earth, mighty Lugh
rules the grains.

Praise the harvest, praise the corn.

Thank you, Lord and Lady,
for this Lammas morn!

Snuff out the candle safely. Then with care, as if carrying a child, carry the ear of corn to a quiet place outside. Holding the corn, visualize all people on Earth being nourished and fed. Then gently lay the corn on the ground, so it may be shared with our wild friends, such as the squirrels.

James Kambos

NOTES:

August 2
Tuesday

NOTES:

1st ♍

☽ → ♎ 12:06 am

Color of the day: White
Incense of the day: Basil

Vigil Fire

While the summer nights are still warm, it's a good time for vigil fires, which have long been held for ceremonial purposes.

Begin with planning. What is the purpose of your vigil fire? Where will you have the fire? Will you hold vigil for an hour or two or an entire night? Or something else? Will you stay awake or sleep by the fire? What will you do during the vigil?

Consider your comfort: warmth, food, drink, and a light source.

Consider fire safety, and be sure someone knows where you are and when you'll return.

Build the fire in a safe location. A log cabin–style fire with wood that can be pushed in from the sides will last for hours.

Hold your vigil at fireside, periodically repeating this chant:

Sitting with the vigil fire, watching embers through the night.

Powers of vigil, rite and ritual, shine in me like firelight.

Susan Pesznecker

August 3
Wednesday

1st ♎

Color of the day: Yellow
Incense of the day: Lavender

A Wednesday Rite for Now

Wednesday is referred to as hump day, inferring that we've made it halfway through the week. This vision requires looking backward and forward. How about a rite about being in this moment?

Wednesday is the day of wisdom and messages, and with its association to the color green, you may find prosperity flowing your way. This is also a day of the lungs, making it perfect for aromatherapy-enhanced work.

Gather these items:

• Clary sage essential oil

• Matches or a lighter

• A green candle

• A firesafe candleholder

• Pen and paper

Dab your pulse points and third eye (the center of your forehead just above your eyebrows) with clary sage. Light the candle and affix it to the holder.

Walk while reciting the following:

I am here in the now, ready to receive.

Stand back, Odin, no time today to be deceived.

I listen and wait.

As I walk and listen,

I will learn more about the meaning of this date.

Repeat this verse at least twice more.

Sit down and reflect on your journey through your home. What messages have the spirits sent to you? Jot down your thoughts. Extinguish the candle.

Stephanie Rose Bird

NOTES:

August 4
Thursday

1st ♎

☽ v/c 2:20 am

☽ → ♏ 7:47 am

Color of the day: Purple
Incense of the day: Carnation

Seeking Wisdom

Today is the Double Seventh Festival in China. It is traditionally a time when Chinese girls go to local temples in order to seek wisdom. We can also seek out wisdom today. We need only tap into the energies of the day. Since we are doing our magickal work on a Thursday, we can work with Jupiter and use the colors blue or purple. Use a candle in one of those colors or in white. If it is a white candle, use a blue or purple marker to write the word *wisdom* on it. Light your candle and ask for Jupiter to grant wisdom to you:

*Jupiter, I call to you. Allow me
a deeper understanding of the
world of myself so I can better
understand the world around me.*

Allow the candle to burn completely out so that the magick can take effect. Once it is extinguished, bury any remaining candle wax outside.

Charlynn Walls

August 5
Friday

1st ♏

2nd Quarter 7:07 am

Color of the day: Rose
Incense of the day: Thyme

The Spirit of Money

Many of us have absorbed toxic messages about money, and going directly to the source—the spirit of Money—can be a powerful way of breaking free from destructive patterns.

Light a green candle on a heatproof surface, gaze softly at the flame, then close your eyes, coming into a meditative state. Call upon the spirit of Money. If you have a specific concern, you can ask how to heal this issue. Or request more general guidance on how to improve your relationship to Money. When done, snuff out the candle with gratitude.

Money is closely tied to the energy of exchange and flow, so it's quite common for Money to advise action that requires you to put energy in motion. This could be anything from donating old clothes, surprising a friend with home-baked goodies, or gratefully receiving a compliment.

If you feel called, continue seeking Money's guidance to maintain this open channel of giving and receiving.

Melissa Tipton

August 6
Saturday

2nd ♏

☽ v/c 7:24 am

☽ → ♐ 12:39 pm

Color of the day: Blue
Incense of the day: Patchouli

Restful Sleep Spell

Long days and too much to do can make falling asleep during the summer a real struggle. Luckily a little magick can go a long way toward getting a full night's sleep. For this spell you'll need a small piece of moonstone. Once you get into bed, hold the moonstone in your dominant hand and say:

> I now breathe away the
> remains of the day,
>
> In blissful sleep and
> contentment I will lay.
>
> May the piece of moon I
> hold in my hand
>
> Take me to peaceful slumber's lands.

Take three deep breaths. As you exhale each time, imagine all the worries of the day being removed from your body and pushed away. When you are done, place the moonstone under your pillow so that its power can aid your sleep and protect you from any bad dreams.

Ari & Jason Mankey

August 7
Sunday

2nd ♐

Color of the day: Yellow
Incense of the day: Juniper

Questions and Answers

Sometimes it's handy to be able to get a quick answer to a pressing question. If you don't have the time (or the inclination) to do a major tarot reading, here are a few fast ways to get simple answers—usually along the lines of "yes," "no," or "sorry, no answer."

Make sure your question is clear in your head; for instance, "Should I take this trip?" Then pull one tarot card, or one card from an oracle deck that lends itself to that kind of use. If the answer isn't obvious (the Chariot would be "yes" and the Tower would be "no"), listen to your gut. You can also pull one rune stone (Raidho would be "yes" and Isa would be "no"). Or you can use a pendulum, which is best for simple answers. If you want, say:

> Divination, tell me true,
> what it is that I should do.

Deborah Blake

August 8
Monday

2nd ♐

☽ v/c 6:30 am

☽ → ♑ 2:39 pm

Color of the day: Ivory
Incense of the day: Hyssop

Transforming Water

I live in a lakeside village, swim a lot, and enjoy backcountry kayaking and camping. Potable water is an issue when camping. I no longer take water for granted. When I purify water for backcountry consumption, I always pause to thank and bless the element of water.

Nibi Wabo, the First Nations water blessing ceremony usually done on a February new moon, reminds us to give thanks to water in ceremony. When you brush your teeth, give thanks. When you drink tea or coffee, give thanks. When you shower, bathe, or wash your hands, give thanks. Use these Ho'oponopono words (an ancient Hawaiian practice for forgiveness, reconciliation, and making relationships right) to bless water. Each time you use water, say:

> I'm sorry, Forgive me,
> Thank you, I love you.

Your gratitude raises the vibration of water in a healthy way and acknowledges the gift of this element.

Dallas Jennifer Cobb

 August 9
Tuesday

2nd ♑

Color of the day: Maroon
Incense of the day: Cedar

Much Melon Magic

Take the time today to savor a ripe melon, whether it comes from your garden or the nearby farmers' market. Watermelon and honeydew are among the easiest to find pretty much anywhere, but there are many varieties from around the world to try. Melons make the perfect summer salad or dessert with added health benefits. Not only can you enjoy some delicious melon, but there's an added bonus as well: collect the seeds and use them in magical workings to bring abundance, fertility, and prosperity.

Be sure to wash the melon seeds thoroughly and then set them out to dry on some towels. Once dry, store them in a glass jar in a cool place. You can include the seeds in satchels, jars, and other ingredient-based magical workings. Some varieties of melon produce seeds that are large and sturdy enough that you can draw symbols, words, or sigils on them with a fine-point marker.

Laura Tempest Zakroff

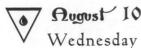

▽ August 10
Wednesday

2nd ♑

☽ v/c 12:39 pm

☽ → ♒ 2:45 pm

Color of the day: White

Incense of the day: Marjoram

A Seashell Sea Spell

There aren't many better representations of the ocean than seashells. Easy to acquire, they carry the mighty energy of the endless sea. The ocean, of course, also aligns with the Great Goddess energy, numerous deities, and the tides of emotion within ourselves.

Being a fan of both Hoodoo and the traditions of the African diaspora, I personally favor cowrie shells, but any type of shell may be used.

All of life evolved from the ocean. Additionally, we are always evolving personally in this lifetime, on every level: physically, emotionally, cognitively, spiritually, and so on.

Place one seashell (or more, if you wish to gift them to friends) in a cup with sea salt. As you fill the cup halfway with water, enchant the shell by saying the following nine times:

As the tides do turn and the
earth revolves, this shell is
enchanted so that I may evolve!

Raven Digitalis

☽ August 11
Thursday

2nd ♒

Full Moon 9:36 pm

Color of the day: Turquoise

Incense of the day: Clove

Full Moon Divination

Tonight is the full moon, conveniently occurring at a time when most people can catch it. This lunar phase lends power to many magical workings. One of those is divination. You can see things by the light of the full moon that are difficult or impossible to spot at any other time.

For this spell you will need a bowl or a chalice that is black (or at least dark) on the inside. This makes it more reflective and aids in scrying. Fill the bowl with water and add a pinch of salt, preferably sea salt. Go outside where you can see the full moon. Move around until you can catch its reflection on the surface of the water. Then say:

Full moon, shining round and bright,

Give to me the inner sight.

What is past or yet to be,

Let it now appear to me.

Gaze into the bowl, and you should glimpse images of the past or of future possibilities of use to you. Afterward, pour the water on the ground.

Elizabeth Barrette

August **12**
Friday

3rd ♒

☽ v/c 7:07 am

☽ → ♓ 2:44 pm

Color of the day: Purple
Incense of the day: Rose

Incense Blessing

If you're like many magical practitioners, you have a good amount of incense lying around. Even if you only have a little (or if you'd like to purchase some for this purpose), bless your incense today to refresh its magic.

First, round up all your incense: sticks, cones, or powder. Spread a white cloth outdoors in full sunlight. (If there's no sunlight in your area today, you can do this indoors. In this case, safely light four white candles at the four corners of the white cloth.) Place all your incense on the cloth, leaving it in its packaging or containers. Direct your palms toward the incense. Say:

Earth, air, water, fire, and spirit, Goddess and God, please bless these sacred scents.

Reawaken their magic. Infuse them with light. Align them with your power.

Thank you and blessed be.

Let the incense soak up the light for a minute or two more, then return it to its rightful place in your magical supply box (or wherever you keep it). Extinguish the candles if you used them.

Tess Whitehurst

NOTES:

August 13
Saturday

3rd ♓

Color of the day: Black
Incense of the day: Ivy

Staple Spell

Staples are magic! Most staples are made of zinc and steel. Zinc can be used for protection and invisibility, and steel for endurance—a perfect shield!

What information do you want to keep safe? Write it down on a piece of paper, then fold the paper in half and then in half again (four quarters, four for stability). Staple it all around as you say these words:

What's written within

Is only for me.

All others stay out.

So mote it be!

Burn the paper safely in a fireproof dish. When the embers have died and the ashes are cool, bury them and the staples to hide your secrets from prying eyes.

Natalie Zaman

August 14
Sunday

3rd ♓

☽ v/c 11:11 am

☽ → ♈ 4:43 pm

Color of the day: Orange
Incense of the day: Marigold

Banish Useless Anger

There are times for righteous anger, but sometimes anger is unfounded or its time has passed. Lingering anger can be banished with this spell, which requires a bowl, a glass of water, and ten matches.

Pour half the water into the bowl before you, then hold a match. Get in touch with your anger. Remember what stoked this emotion.

When you really feel the anger, strike the match and watch it burn, bright and hot. Drop it into the bowl before it burns your fingers.

Repeat this with the other nine matches, calling your anger to the surface and dropping the match.

When you're done, look at the spent matches before you. See how much energy was spent on this anger and what a waste it was. Those matches could have been used for other projects like lighting spell candles or celebratory bonfires.

Drink the water in the glass. Imagine that it instills peace and love in all the places where anger once resided.

Astrea Taylor

NOTES:

August 15
Monday

3rd ♈

Color of the day: Lavender
Incense of the day: Clary sage

Visiting Your Inner Temple

One meaning of the Greek word *temenos* is a sacred space dedicated to the gods, and in magical practice, it's quite common to delineate this space by casting a circle. This meditation supercharges your circle casting by connecting to the archetype of the temenos, tapping into the energetic current of all beings who have created sacred space throughout the ages.

Come into a meditative state, and see a door in your mind's eye. Know that beyond this door awaits your perfect sacred space. Step through with intention, and allow yourself to explore, soaking in the potent energy of this place and allowing it to gather at your heart. Give thanks and return through the door of your mind.

The next time you cast a circle, see this energy awakening in your heart and let it flow through your hand or wand, recreating the power of the sacred space from your meditative journey.

Melissa Tipton

August 16
Tuesday

3rd ♈

☽ v/c 4:18 pm

☽ → ♉ 10:22 pm

Color of the day: Black

Incense of the day: Geranium

A Personal Harvest Spell

Centuries ago, August afternoons were filled with the soft swooshing sound of the scythe blade as farmers swung it to harvest fields of grain. This spell is inspired by that long-lost tradition. It will help you cut out what you don't need in your life and keep what you do need. You'll need some 3-by-5-inch index cards, a pen, and a pair of scissors. Begin by writing down on the cards anything you might want to be rid of—one thought on each card. It could be a habit, a relationship, or physical clutter. Then speak these Words of Power:

What do I let go of, what do I keep?

What do I store, save, and reap?

It's time for my personal harvest.

Let me keep only what's best.

Now go through the cards. Be honest and select what you don't need. Set those cards aside, then cut them in half. End by recycling or throwing away the cards you've cut in half. Your personal harvest is done.

James Kambos

August 17
Wednesday

3rd ♉

Color of the day: Brown

Incense of the day: Honeysuckle

Festival of Diana

Around this time of year, the ancient Romans celebrated the feast of Diana. Diana is a lunar goddess as well as a goddess of the hunt. Her feast was used in part to ask for her help with the harvest, and it marked a day of rest for women and slaves. The festival was also called the Festival of Torches.

While the holiday itself has already passed, this is a good time to invoke the goddess, perhaps by lighting a candle in her honor in a firesafe container. You can ask for her help with your own harvest, or use this time to take an hour or two of much-earned rest for yourself. Light the candle and say:

Diana, I call your name

And light this torch in your honor.

May your blessings shine upon my life

As this light shines out into the night.

Snuff out the candle when you're done.

Deborah Blake

August 18
Thursday

3rd ♉

Color of the day: Green
Incense of the day: Jasmine

Mutabilitie

In his poem "The Faerie Queene," Edmund Spenser presents an Elizabethan take on pagan mythology as a masque (a play). First to appear on the stage is Mutabilitie, who "reigns in all things and to whom all things are subject." As the four elements enter, we learn that Vesta and Vulcan rule fire, Ops rules earth, Juno rules "ayre," and Neptune rules the seas.

Mutability is the quality of being changeable, like caterpillars on their way to becoming butterflies. As Spenser wrote, all things are subject to change. What do you want to change?

Call your coven or circle together and talk about mutability (or do this on your own). When (or if) you reach consensus, cast your circle with the deities Spenser names in the elemental corners. Speak aloud what you want to change, individually or working as a group. Now invoke Mutabilitie herself:

Great Mutabilitie, powerful and eternal,

Be present and bless us today.

Bless our intention to change _____,

And teach us how to work toward that change.

So mote it be!

Barbara Ardinger

NOTES:

August 19
Friday

3rd ♂
4th Quarter 12:36 am
☽ v/c 7:06 am
☽ → ♊ 8:06 am

Color of the day: White
Incense of the day: Mint

A Pantry of Magical Waters

Water is an essential part of the magical tool kit. With some planning, you can create an all-purpose pantry of magical waters.

You'll need some small lidded jars (four-ounce canning jars are perfect), masking tape or labels, and a permanent marker. Label and date each sample of water you collect.

Start by collecting water from any body of water you visit. The real and remembered links to that place will be powerful.

Collect rainwater, hail, sleet, snow, or ice to use when a stormy influence is needed. Store snow and hail in the freezer.

Collect morning dew for rituals of initiation, growth, and abundance.

Collect water on the sabbats.

Collect holy water from sacred sites, or bless water using your own sacred ceremony.

For moon magic, charge water under the full or dark moon or through a full moon phase.

For solar magic, charge water under the midday sun or from sunrise to sunset.

Add gems, crystals, plants, or objects to waters to create or boost a specific magical effect.

Susan Pesznecker

NOTES:

August 20
Saturday

4th ♊

Color of the day: Indigo
Incense of the day: Pine

Cutting Ties

Saturdays are a good time to work banishing magick. If you need to cut a tie with a person, a poor habit, or a job, now would be the time to do so. Take three pieces of black or purple thread, string, or cord and hold them in your hands. Weave the pieces together into a braid symbolizing your physical, mental, and emotional ties to the person (or issue). Once the braid has been created, visualize yourself as separate from the person you want to move away from. See in your mind all the ways you are connected and how you can separate yourself from them. You can then either disentangle the strands or cut them apart. Once the strands are separated from one another, you are free of the person (or issue) as well.

Charlynn Walls

August 21
Sunday

4th ♊

☽ v/c 6:06 pm
☽ → ♋ 8:29 pm

Color of the day: Gold
Incense of the day: Heliotrope

Successful Endeavors Spell

Before beginning any important new endeavor, write down what you want to achieve on a small piece of paper. While holding that paper in your dominant hand, look into a mirror and say:

*I will achieve all I wish
for in this endeavor.*

*Nothing out there can
stop me whatsoever.*

All obstacles in front of me will fall.

Only my success is what will befall.

*I can and will overcome
anything in my way.*

*What I will shall happen
for me on this day!*

When you are done saying these words, you should feel confident and secure. If not, say them again, and know that you will succeed! When you are done, keep what you have written in your pocket until you have achieved your goal.

Ari & Jason Mankey

August 22
Monday

4th ♋

☉ → ♍ 11:16 **pm**

Color of the day: Silver
Incense of the day: Neroli

Tooth Fairy Incantation

There's someone familiar in our lives with whom we have a give-and-take—it's the Tooth Fairy. As children, we almost looked forward to losing a tooth. Why? Well, the tooth fairy grants wishes and compensates us with money, of course! We envision the Tooth Fairy according to our generation or place of origin. Whether you see her as a mouse god or a sweet or scary fairy, today's the day to reflect on her work.

Do you ever think of the Tooth Fairy and wonder what she does with all those teeth? Teeth, after all, are tough and difficult to degrade. It's eerie to think about it, but today is the day for such things. Your teeth are still somewhere.

Here is an incantation and gratitude blessing to share with your forgotten friend:

Tooth Fairy, Tooth Fairy,

I'm calling out to you.

I want you to know I appreciate what you do.

Gratitude and honor are behind my call.

Granting wishes, giving coins and bills,

I thank you for it all!

Stephanie Rose Bird

NOTES:

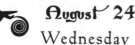

August 23
Tuesday

4th ♋

Color of the day: Scarlet
Incense of the day: Bayberry

Ready to Begin Again

Each of us has significant days in our lives. Days we mark every year. Good days and bad days. Days when things happened that changed us and our lives forever. August 22 is one of those days for me. In 1990 my life changed forever, in a moment. Over the years I still remember the trauma and the resulting pain, but I have come to think of August 23 as the day to begin again.

Regardless of what happens to us in life, good or bad, we must develop strategies to survive. We must learn to ground, release, breathe, and be ready to begin again.

Ground. Connect with the strong, resilient, and forgiving nature of Earth.

Release. Let Earth absorb your anger, fear, shame, or terror.

Breathe in new energy, feeling the vibration of the earth attune you.

And now you are ready to begin again. So begin.

Dallas Jennifer Cobb

August 24
Wednesday

4th ♋

☽ v/c 5:40 am
☽ → ♌ 9:09 am

Color of the day: Topaz
Incense of the day: Lilac

Fairy Cards

Fairies are nature spirits who can be very helpful if approached in the right way. Because many of them fly, they relate to communication and the element of air. This makes them useful assistants when you want to reach someone. A quirk of fairies is that they expect to be paid but never thanked. For this spell you will need a stack of postcards or notecards printed with fairies. Hold them in your hands and say:

Little People of the air,

Watch above my message fair.

Sent by night or sent by day,

See it safely on its way.

These cards are now blessed and protected. Use them when you need a little extra privacy and reliability.

Finally, make an offering to the fairies. Spread butter or honey on a piece of bread and leave it outside. Don't name them directly, only indirectly: "For the Little People" or "For my fair friends" are popular examples.

Elizabeth Barrette

August 25
Thursday

4th ♌

Color of the day: Crimson
Incense of the day: Apricot

Mercurial Communication

We are social creatures. As Witches, we have a particular obligation to be self-aware when communicating via any medium, whether it's in person, phone, text, social media, and so on. We, of all people, should be aware of the power we wield in the universe and the echoing influence we have in the world around us.

If you need to hone your communication skills or even add a magickal boost for a social event, turn to the planet Mercury, who oversees communication, among many other important aspects of life.

Using either a washable marker or natural ink, draw the alchemical symbol for Mercury (☿) on your body. The "horns" should go from nipple to nipple, with the circle at your solar plexus and the bottom crisscrossing your belly button.

Say any prayers to Mercury that you wish, and know that you are blessed by his energy today and ever onward!

Raven Digitalis

August 26
Friday

4th ♌

☽ v/c 2:55 am
☽ → ♏ 8:25 pm

Color of the day: Pink
Incense of the day: Yarrow

Thimble Protection Magic

A thimble is a metal cap with a closed end used in sewing to help push in the needle while protecting the finger. It's simple, utilitarian, and ubiquitous, which makes it perfect for spellcraft.

My grandmother was a talented seamstress who liked to collect decorative thimbles from the different places she visited. I have a few beautiful ones on my altar to remind me of her and to act as a connection to those places. But they're also useful for tapping into protective qualities.

On a strip of paper that can fit snugly inside the thimble, write down what you wish to protect. Roll up the paper and insert it inside of the thimble so it can't easily slide out. If you want to make sure the paper can't be read, thread a bead or small button on some red thread, then tuck it up inside. Place the thimble on your altar (open side facing down) or a similar safe place where it won't be disturbed.

Laura Tempest Zakroff

August 27
Saturday

4th ♏

New Moon 4:17 am

Color of the day: Brown
Incense of the day: Sandalwood

Barefoot Grounding Ritual

Tap into the earthy energy of today's new moon in Virgo to ground, center, and rebalance. If you are able, perform this ritual at the time of the new moon (4:17 a.m. EST), but any time of the day will do.

Stand outside on natural ground (grass or dirt rather than pavement if possible). If you are unable to stand, sit with your bare feet touching the ground. Close your eyes to experience the darkness of the new moon. As you breathe deeply, in through the nose and out through the mouth, feel the solidity of the earth seep up through the soles of your feet. With each breath, say aloud or to yourself:

New moon above,

Old earth below,

Your potential and endurance

To me bestow.

Natalie Zaman

August 28
Sunday

1st ♍
☽ v/c 11:08 pm

Color of the day: Amber
Incense of the day: Almond

Morning Cup Blessing

Legends of magical drinking cups that bestow powers upon the drinkers have been told for millennia. This spell is intended for your morning beverage cup to give you more energy and awareness. It requires a mug or cup and a chopstick.

Place the empty cup on your altar, with the handle pointing north. After reciting each of the following lines, use the chopstick to strike the cup in the corresponding direction, and let the sound ring out.

Spirits of the east, sing to me.
Lend your insights to this cup.

Spirits of the south, sing to me.
Lend your alertness to this cup.

Spirits of the west, sing to me.
Lend your heart to this cup.

Spirits of the north, sing to me.
Lend your power to this cup.

Recite the next line as you trace the chopstick over the lip of the cup:

The circle is cast, and so shall it be,
To give me morning productivity.

Give thanks whenever you use the cup.

Astrea Taylor

August 29
Monday

1st ♍
☽ → ♎ 5:45 am

Color of the day: Gray
Incense of the day: Rosemary

Charlie Parker's Birthday

On this date in 1920, jazz saxophonist Charlie Parker, also known as Bird, was born. In addition to being a virtuoso, Charlie Parker changed jazz (and music in general) as we know it by bringing in wilder, more complex and unexpected elements. As if that weren't enough, his music inspired an entire generation of artists of all varieties, which in turn brought more freedom to creative expression and more boldness in rebelling against artistic and cultural norms.

Today, tap into Charlie Parker's transformational creative power. Light him a candle, play his music, close your eyes, breathe, and listen deeply. Consciously connect with his unique genius. As you let your attention rest on music, bring to mind any goal, project, challenge, or situation that feels stuck or that might benefit from a new perspective or a revolutionary way of doing things. Consider the issue with a sense of curiosity and play. Keep a journal and pen nearby so you can jot down anything that comes to you. Extinguish the candle.

Tess Whitehurst

August 30
Tuesday

1st ♎︎

Color of the day: Red
Incense of the day: Cinnamon

Nephthys

The Egyptian Nephthys was the sister of Isis, wife of Set, and mother of Anubis. When Set murdered and dismembered Osiris, she helped Isis search for him. Nephthys thus became a guardian of and mourner for the dead. A papyrus survives with the text of her lamentations for Osiris.

Like everyone else, we Pagans have to face death—relatives, friends, our fur (or feathered) babies. Most of us know about reincarnation and that cats have nine lives. But mourning is still hard. We need to process how we feel: alone, sad, angry, cheated.

Call on Nephthys for help and comfort. Do this in a meditation or, if you can, in a lucid dream.

*Blessed Nephthys, you who
know all the stages of life*

*And the afterlife, where we
rest between lives and dream
of past and future lives—*

*Gentle Nephthys, bring us
knowledge and comfort.*

*Wipe our tears, caress us, help
us dream of those we've lost.*

*Comfort them, comfort us,
comfort all in need of blessing.*
Barbara Ardinger

NOTES:

August 31
Wednesday

1st ♎

☽ v/c 6:43 am

☽ → ♏ 1:11 pm

Color of the day: White

Incense of the day: Bay laurel

Protection Spell for house and home

As summer winds down and we move into autumn, it is a good time to establish a yearly ritual to protect your home. The direction of the seasons is shifting from active to passive, but there is still plenty of energy around to tap into for a simple protection ritual.

You can use a sage smudge stick for this (being careful of stray sparks) or a bowl of salt and water. Move through each room of your house or apartment, starting at the front door. Either waft the sage stick or sprinkle the salt and water mixture with your fingertips. As you walk through your space, be mindful of any entrance or exit (windows, doors, etc.), and give them an extra bit of attention. As you do this, say:

My home is protected.

This space is protected.

All is well and all will be well.

So mote it be!

Deborah Blake

NOTES:

September

The equinox happens toward the end of this month, heralding the beginning of autumn in the Northern Hemisphere and the start of spring in the Southern Hemisphere. An equinox happens when the sun crosses the celestial equator, an imaginary line in the sky not unlike our Earth's own equator. It's on the equinox that the sun rises due east and sets due west. This is why people often go to famous landmarks to watch the rising or setting of the sun on the equinoxes and solstices. In our ever-changing world, it's nice to know there are at least some constants!

Astrologically, the autumnal equinox is when the sun sign of Libra begins. It's fitting, as this is the time when day and night are of equal length, and Libra is the sign of the scales. The full moon that corresponds with this event is called the Harvest Moon or the Corn Moon. The few days around the equinox and the full moon bring a period in which everything is ripening and full of energy. It all seems to be coming into fullness, preparing either for the coming of winter or the start of the growing season.

Charlie Rainbow Wolf

September 1
Thursday

1st ♏

Color of the day: Green
Incense of the day: Balsam

Athena Invocation

Athena is a very powerful goddess to invoke for anything. She's associated with conception, life, and death. To invoke her you'll need:

- An intention
- A brand-new solid red outfit or several new red accessories
- Curly hair (curly wand or natural)
- A reusable bag
- An owl or other feathered domino mask
- Some Greek olives
- A halved pomegranate
- 3 shot glasses
- Small containers of olive oil, honey, and river water
- Optional: Kyphi incense (with charcoal, matches, and a fireproof plate or censer)

Put on the red items. Place all the spell ingredients in the bag and take them to an oak tree trunk. Put on the mask. Step away, then spin around three times. (This is one of Athena's numbers.)

Stand still and shake your head from left and right several times to free the curls' energies. Spoon some olives and the pomegranate halves onto the earth.

Recite the following as you pour the three liquids in shot glasses:

Athena, please accept these gifts.

I give them in your honor.

This is for you.

Light the incense as you say:

I burn sweet incense for all that you do.

Extend your hands outward as you say:

Help me with my quest.

Bow your head.

Extinguish the incense and place everything back in the bag, then say:

Blessed be!

Sit and reflect quietly on your intent.

Stephanie Rose Bird

 **September 2**
Friday

1st ♏

☽ v/c 1:22 pm

☽ → ♐ 6:39 pm

Color of the day: Rose
Incense of the day: Violet

Fall Cleaning

Everyone thinks about spring cleaning, but few people think about fall cleaning. September is a good time to start switching from summer to fall things. The hottest days of summer are usually over, but the weather hasn't turned cold yet, so there's room for transition.

First, put away the summer toys and make sure swimming suits are washed before storage, etc. The lightest clothes such as shorts and tank tops can go, but leave versatile ones like T-shirts and ankle pants available for warm days. If you use seasonal altar cloths, take those down. Clean summer dust from the floors.

Next, bring out fall things. Make sure your clothes fit and are clean. Fall colors include red, yellow, orange, and brown. Clean your altar and reset it for fall. Watch stores for seasonal decorations such as gourds and decorative corn. You can find great altar plates with autumn themes like deer or acorns now.

Elizabeth Barrette

September 3
Saturday

1st ♐

2nd Quarter 2:08 pm

Color of the day: Blue
Incense of the day: Magnolia

Spell for Demeter

For many magickal folks, Demeter reigns supreme as the goddess of early autumn. Every year in early September, we give her a place of honor on our house's main altar and invoke her blessings for the harvest season.

For this spell you will need either a statue of Demeter or something that represents her. Demeter can be represented by a cornucopia, a sheaf of grain, a flower, or fresh produce. Place your Demeter statue (or object) in a prominent place in your home and then invoke her blessings:

> Great Demeter, goddess of the grain,
> Mother of the Earth, we honor you
> in this place and time and thank
> you for the many blessings you have
> given us. May what we have sown
> this past year be reaped in love and
> abundance. Hail great Demeter!

For best results, follow this by leaving an offering for Demeter outside.

Ari & Jason Mankey

September 4
Sunday

2nd ♐

☽ v/c 9:51 pm

☽ → ♑ 10:03 pm

Color of the day: Yellow
Incense of the day: Eucalyptus

Back to School Success Spell

For many people, both children and adults, the beginning of September means time to return to school. But whether you are attending formal classes or not, success in life often depends on the ability to keep learning and growing. That might mean success in a career, achieving spiritual goals, having healthier relationships, or simply becoming a better person.

Today, pick (at least) one area of your life where it feels as though you might have more to learn, and make a commitment to do so. Light a yellow candle to symbolize the conscious mind and say:

I wish to become wiser

And deeper in knowledge.

I commit to more learning

With life as my college.

Meditate on the flame for a while, then blow it out. Light it again when you need inspiration (always being mindful of fire safety).

Deborah Blake

September 5
Monday

2nd ♑

Color of the day: White
Incense of the day: Clary sage

Labor Day (US) –
Labour Day (Canada)

All hail Salt!

Salt is a common crystal on Earth and one of the most sacred. We depend on sunshine and water to stay alive, but we need salt too. Our eyes weep salty tears, our hearts pump salty blood, and our unborn children float in salty wombs. Salt has been used medicinally, as currency, and in sacred offerings, and our salted oceans are cauldrons of life. It's no wonder we attach such value to it.

Keep a vial of salt at hand, ready for a number of uses:

- *Purification:* Bury magical tools in salt or bathe them in salt water.

- *Cleansing:* Wash hands and face with salt water before ritual or spellcraft. Clean magical tools and spaces with salt solutions; sprinkle the solution to cleanse large spaces.

- *Setting space:* Use salt to outline magical space, holding defined energies in or out.

- *Protection:* Cast salt to create barriers or to protect doorways and thresholds.
- *Spellcraft:* Include salt in spells and charms for abundance, protection, or wealth.

Susan Pesznecker

NOTES:

September 6
Tuesday

2nd ♑

☽ v/c 5:43 pm

☽ → ♒ 11:41 pm

Color of the day: Maroon
Incense of the day: Ginger

Sparking a Connection

Tuesdays are a good time to work on romantic connections and relationships. If you have been unlucky in love, you can work on drawing to you the best partner.

First, on a piece of parchment paper, write down a list of characteristics you want in a partner. Be brutally realistic and honest with yourself. Next, create a sachet of love herbs. These can include cinnamon, apple, basil, thyme, clove, jasmine, and many more. Use the herbs you have on hand and that work for you. You can also add in some stones if you'd like, such as rose quartz. Burn the piece of parchment with your list of qualities on it. Add the ashes to your sachet and seal it up while you recite the following:

Let my one and only find their way and hear my hope that they never stray.

Keep the sachet in your bedroom in a safe space.

Charlynn Walls

September 7
Wednesday

2nd ♒

Color of the day: Topaz
Incense of the day: Honeysuckle

Demeter Offering

Perhaps it's no mistake that National Beer Lover's Day (today) falls in the middle of Virgo season, the sign symbolized by a virginal woman holding a sheaf of wheat. (It's important to note that in the ancient world, virginal didn't mean chaste but rather autonomous.) As the grain and earth mother, who is both fiercely protective and fiercely independent (so much so that she even rebelled against Zeus and won), Demeter is the quintessential Virgo. She is a powerful incarnation of the Great Mother Goddess and can be invoked for protection, prosperity, transformation, health, magical power, and healing from disordered eating. Today, light a brown, tan, or golden candle to Demeter. Place a glass of beer or barley water on your altar and pour one for yourself. Say:

Great Goddess Demeter, I call on you.
Great Goddess Demeter, I drink to you. Please help me with _____
(your intention). Thank you.

Mindfully drink your libation. Then extinguish the candle, go outside, and offer Demeter's beverage to the earth.

Tess Whitehurst

September 8
Thursday

2nd ♒

☽ v/c 8:34 am

Color of the day: Purple
Incense of the day: Myrrh

Plant for Tomorrow Spell

Now is the time to plant spring-blooming bulbs such as crocus, daffodils, and tulips. When you plant now for spring, it shows that you believe in tomorrow. The bulbs you plant now will appear dead, brown, and lifeless. But they contain the miracle of hidden life, which, like nature, will return in the spring. Within each bulb is the eternal life cycle: birth, death, and rebirth.

For this spell you'll need some spring-blooming bulbs of your choice. As you plant, think about nature's cycle. While planting, think or say:

The sun's reign is about to end,

The dark season will soon begin.

There's no need to grieve
or time for sorrow,

It's time to plant and
believe in tomorrow.

I return these bulbs to Mother Earth,

To continue the cycle of birth,
death, and rebirth.

In the spring, you'll enjoy seeing your belief come to life.

James Kambos

September 9
Friday

2nd ♒

☽ → ♓ 12:42 am

Color of the day: Pink
Incense of the day: Orchid

Blessed Feet, Blessed Path

Today the moon is in Pisces, the astrological sign that rules the feet. We often don't give love to our feet like we do to other parts of our body, even though they transport us every day. This spell uses massage oil to bless our feet and ask that they lead us onto the right paths.

Sit in a chair and rest one foot on the opposite knee. Pour about a teaspoon of oil into one of your palms. Raise your palm close to your mouth and speak this spell aloud so that your breath causes the oil to move:

Healing hands and healing oil,

Allow all tension to uncoil.

A blessing on me, toes to heel,

Direct me to the paths ideal.

Join your hands and then wrap them around one foot. Massage it with slow strokes. After a few minutes, pour more oil, speak the spell again, and switch feet.

Astrea Taylor

September 10
Saturday

2nd ♓

🌕 Full Moon 5:59 am

☽ v/c 8:29 pm

Color of the day: Black
Incense of the day: Rue

Balancing Your Intuition

The full moon is a potent time for accessing intuitive wisdom, and basking in the moonlight can help you balance this spiritual faculty, blocking out unhelpful energies and amplifying beneficial insights.

Sitting in a comfortable meditative position in the moonlight, feel this energy bathing your aura with healing and cleansing. Focus on your crown chakra, and allow the moonlight to enter the crown, cascading gently through your chakras from crown to root. As the energy travels, intend that each chakra is in perfect balance, connecting you with intuitive messages in a manner aligned with your highest good.

You might sense some chakras expanding and opening, while others find equilibrium by screening out an excess of input. Trust that your energy knows how to self-balance. When the process feels complete, send gratitude to the moon. If needed, place your palms on the earth to ground any excess energy.

Melissa Tipton

September 11
Sunday

3rd ♓

☽ → ♈ 2:47 am

Color of the day: Gold
Incense of the day: Frankincense

Twin Towers Talisman Altar

Just about everyone remembers where they were and what they were doing on September 11, 2001. Honor the memory of the events of that fateful day with this talisman altar.

You will need three safety pins and twenty silver seed beads (with holes big enough so they can be threaded onto the pins). The Twin Towers of the World Trade Center were tall and silvery; this talisman will mimic them in looks. Open the first safety pin and thread ten silver beads on the open needle as you recite these words:

Always remember, never forget,

The memory in my mind is set.

Repeat the process with the second safety pin. If you have some, light a stick of myrrh incense (to honor those who passed and their families) and dragon's blood incense (to banish negativity), and pass the safety pins through the smoke. Thread the two pins onto the needle of the last safety pin. Wear this portable altar in honor of this solemn day.

Natalie Zaman

September 12
Monday

3rd ♈

Color of the day: Silver
Incense of the day: Hyssop

Purify with Sound

As we move back into our houses after the free-flowing ease of summer, it's good to smudge and cleanse our home space. Reset the energy. Release what no longer works and bring in the new.

While sage, sweetgrass, and cedar all make great smudge material, many people have difficulty breathing smoke, and many homes have sensitive smoke detectors that make smoke smudging difficult, so use sound to purify your environment. A bell, a crystal bowl, clackers, or even clapping hands can be used to move energy. Sound has vibration, so it literally can reach into the corners of any room and help to stir up, disrupt, and remove any stagnant energy.

Consciously go from room to room in your home, ringing a bell, clapping your hands, or letting the crystal bowl hum and fill the space. Feel the shivers up your spine, and know that energy is shifting.

Dallas Jennifer Cobb

▽ September 13
Tuesday

3rd ♈

☽ v/c 12:53 am

☽ → ♉ 7:39 am

Color of the day: White
Incense of the day: Ylang-ylang

Our Living Earth

It's good to know what we're standing on where we live. It's useful to know what ground we're grounding ourselves in during rituals. Make a simple hands-on survey of your small part of the living earth. Dig up a handful of dirt from your yard. Hold this dirt, this bit of Mother Earth, in your hands. Feel its texture. It's not the same as potting soil. Is it hard and sticky? Sandy? Poke around in it. Are there little bits of compost in it? Tiny rocks? Insects or worms? (If there are, let them go.)

Place your earth in a green bowl on your altar. Set a green candle in it and light the candle. State your intention:

From today forward, I will honor our blessed, living Mother Earth and do whatever I can to protect her.

As the candle burns down safely, consider climate change, recycling, and overwhelming trash. What else comes to mind? Promise to pick up your trash and contribute to organizations that work to protect the planet.

Barbara Ardinger

NOTES:

September 14
Wednesday

3rd ♉

Color of the day: Brown
Incense of the day: Lavender

Invite Creativity Spell

September 14 is National Live Creative Day. If you think you must be an artist, designer, or musician or have some distinct "talent" to be creative, think again. Creativity comes in many forms—we just need to be open to it coming into our lives.

We find creativity when we work to find solutions to problems, when we share what we're passionate about, and when we let go of fear and take a chance. All you need is you.

To begin this spell, take three slow breaths to connect your body and spirit and say:

Spirits of creativity, I call upon you!

Touch your chest and head and say:

May my heart and mind be inspired.

Touch near your eyes and say:

May my eyes see new possibilities.

Touch your earlobes and say:

May my ears listen to new ideas.

Touch your lips and say:

May my mouth say yes to opportunity.

As you bring your hands together and open them out, say:

May my hands be ready to do the work.

So may it be!

Laura Tempest Zakroff

NOTES:

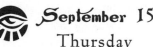

September 15
Thursday

3rd ♉

☽ v/c 8:59 am

☽ → ♊ 4:16 pm

Color of the day: Crimson
Incense of the day: Clove

Practical Bibliomancy

The ancient practice of bibliomancy is divination by means of any book. In this day of PDFs and e-readers, handheld books are something of a treasure.

First, have a question in mind. This should not be a yes-no question, but rather something into which you wish to gain insight. For example, "I wish to gain insight into my class presentation tomorrow."

Using your intuition, grab three books from your shelf, as well as a pen and paper. Sit at a desk and meditate on the issue.

When ready, speak to the first book:

I wish to gain insight into _____.

Close your eyes and open the book at random. Allow your finger to rest anywhere on the page. Open your eyes and write down the sentence that you've landed upon. Repeat this with the other two books, and see how the abstract messages lend insight into your question.

Raven Digitalis

▽ September 16
Friday

3rd ♊

Color of the day: Purple
Incense of the day: Vanilla

Collecting Rocks

Today is Collect Rocks Day. Stones represent the element of earth. They bring strength, stability, and other benefits. Searching for them adds an element of chance.

There are several ways to celebrate this holiday. First, you can take a walk and collect natural stones that you find. Second, you can paint some rocks, then go on a hike to distribute the ones you made while searching for those left by other people. Third, you can take a shopping trip to look for jewelry or other items with gemstones.

As you set out on your quest, tap your foot on the ground and say:

Mother Earth, send me the stones

Suited to my path today.

Pick them out and put them down

So I find them on my way.

Pay attention as you walk around, and choose the stones that call to you.

When you get home, take out a book about stone magic. Look up the stones you found. Try to identify them and learn about their qualities.

Elizabeth Barrette

September 17
Saturday

3rd ♊

☽ v/c 5:52 pm

4th Quarter 5:52 pm

Color of the day: Gray
Incense of the day: Pine

Magickal hops

L et's embrace Celtic Vine Moon
with an incredible vine: hops.
Celtic Moon brings awareness of
emotions. It helps us get more balanced. It's a time to refine our ambi-
tions and goals. We're engaging the
energy of hops not only because
we're in Vine Moon but also because
it's the first day of Oktoberfest in
Munich.

Today most everyone is familiar
with hops thanks to small beer companies. Hops are a time-honored,
multipurpose witch's medicine
beloved for their strong influence on
the nerves. They have a relaxing effect
on the mood, which we need during
Vine Moon. Moreover, as you do
your spells, being level-headed helps.

For this spell you will need:

• 2 cups purified or spring water

• 2 tablespoons hops

• A teacup with a cover

• Honey and lemon (optional)

Boil the water. Rub the hops flowers
in your hands, gently blowing in your
intent as they fall into the cup. (This
releases the herb's medicinal qualities
too.) Cool the water for one to two
minutes, then pour over the hops.
Place the cover on the teacup. Steep
for seven to nine minutes, then strain.
Add optional items if desired.

Stephanie Rose Bird

NOTES:

September 18
Sunday

4th ♊

☽ → ♋ 3:59 am

Color of the day: Orange
Incense of the day: Hyacinth

Praise for the Grapes (and Dionysus)

September is the time of the grape harvest where we live in California, and we like to commemorate this event by invoking the blessings of the Greek god Dionysus. For this spell you will need a glass of wine (or grape juice), preferably from near where you live.

This spell requires that you leave a libation to Dionysus, poured directly onto the earth. We recommend saying the blessing spell where you will pour the wine.

Great Dionysus, god of the vine, god of the grape, we thank you for these blessings of the harvest! As you give to us, so we give to you. Accept this offering of the sacred wine, and may the blessings of joy and abundance you bring wash over us and this space. So mote it be!

Take a sip of the wine and pour the rest of it on the ground for the god.

Ari & Jason Mankey

September 19
Monday

4th ♋

Color of the day: Lavender
Incense of the day: Lily

Harvesting Joy

It is the season of the harvest. We are between the harvest festivals of Lammas and Mabon, surrounded by the bounty of the fruitful earth. But as Witches, we know there are many kinds of abundance and many ways to reap the seeds we planted earlier in the year. Don't forget to take the time to celebrate all the things in your life that have brought you joy—the people, the animals, the successes, and even the failures that taught you something important. Celebrate the enduring presence of the gods and all the gifts of spirit. If you can, light a bonfire and dance around it. If that's not possible, just put on some drum music or any other music that inspires joy in you, and dance in celebration of the joy you have harvested so far this year. Embrace your harvest of joy, and plant the seeds for more to come.

Deborah Blake

 ## September 20
Tuesday

4th ♋

☽ v/c 11:57 am

☽ → ♌ 4:38 pm

Color of the day: Red
Incense of the day: Basil

Abundance!

It's harvest time, and our thoughts turn toward bounty. Celebrate your own abundance with this simple ritual. You'll need:

- Milk, fruit juice, wine, or beer
- A pitcher or measuring cup
- A 9-by-12-inch piece of construction paper (or a piece from a brown paper bag)
- Cellophane tape
- Salt (any type)
- A cinnamon stick
- Seeds or nuts
- Dried fruit
- Bread or grains

Pour the liquid of your choice into the pitcher or cup. Roll the paper into a cone, tape securely, and fill with the other items, cornucopia-style.

Carry the pitcher and cornucopia to the heart of your garden space. Lift the cornucopia to the sky, saying:

I honor this bounty: gifts of earth, air, fire, and water; gifts of soil and sun; gifts of energizing light and restorative night.

Set the cornucopia on the ground. Take a sip of the liquid, then pour the rest on the ground, saying:

In communion with you, deities of the harvest, I give thanks for this season's bounty, which will nourish and restore me.

Susan Pesznecker

NOTES:

September 21
Wednesday

4th ♌

Color of the day: Yellow
Incense of the day: Lilac

UN International Day of Peace

Everyday Peace Shrine

Today is the International Day of Peace. A shrine for peace can externalize our intentions for inner peace and remind us that we can choose it over reactionary emotions.

To make a shrine for peace, collect items throughout your home that help you feel peaceful, such as angelite, amethyst, chamomile, and lavender. Place a peaceful-smelling essential oil there, such as lavender or frankincense. Include small scraps of paper, a pen, and a jar.

When your shrine is complete, open the oil and take a deep breath. On a scrap of paper, write:

Today, I choose peace.

Place the paper in the jar and take another deep breath. Envision how you will choose peace.

Throughout the day, recall the peace you felt at the shrine. If you feel overwhelmed, imagine standing before it, and take a few deep breaths. Over time, the combined intention and action can reprogram our brains to be more peaceful.

Astrea Taylor

NOTES:

September 22
Thursday

4th ♌

☽ v/c 7:07 am

☉ → ♎ 9:04 pm

Color of the day: Turquoise
Incense of the day: Mulberry

Mabon – Fall Equinox

Finding Your Balance

The fall equinox is an ideal time to find balance, and this spell uses tarot or oracle cards to focus these equilibrating energies. If using the tarot, place the Temperance card in the center of your altar. For oracle decks, choose a card representing balance.

Shuffle the deck and ask to be shown the forces seeking equilibrium within you, then draw two cards. Place them on either side of the Temperance/balance card. Spend some time contemplating your initial impressions of the cards, then use the following incantation to go deeper:

Left and right, above and below,

Forces of balance, I seek to know,

What it is I'm meant to change

And how my soul yearns to grow.

Show me this, I ask of thee,

That I may find sweet harmony.

Spend time in meditation, opening to additional messages, and return to the cards throughout the day to see how your impressions evolve.

Melissa Tipton

NOTES:

❤ September 23
Friday

4th ♌

☽ → ♍ 3:53 am

Color of the day: White
Incense of the day: Yarrow

Let Go of a Relationship

If a relationship is over but it doesn't quite feel over, conditions are ideal today for clearing residual relationship energy so you can call your power back to you and begin anew. This can be done with any relationship (not just a romantic one).

First, go through your home and round up any pictures of this person, any notes or gifts from them, and anything this person once owned or co-owned with you. Then let these items go in a responsible way. Throw out, donate, sell, or recycle them accordingly. If you can't get them out of your possession right away, that's okay, but definitely pack them up and get them ready to move out.

Now safely light a stick of rose incense and a stick of palo santo wood. While holding a dish or plate beneath them to catch burning embers, move counterclockwise around each room and area in your home as you cleanse the space with smoke. Finish by cleansing yourself with the smoke as well. Then extinguish the incense.

Tess Whitehurst

September 24
Saturday

4th ♍

Color of the day: Indigo
Incense of the day: Ivy

Stop the Gossip Spell

For this spell to help stop gossip or rumors, you'll need one over-ripe apple and one sage leaf. Follow the instructions in the following verse. If possible, perform this spell on a windy autumn day.

*On an autumn day when
the woods are dying*

And the wild geese are flying,

Take an apple soft with age,

Rub it well with a silvery leaf of sage.

*Carry it to a place where the
grasses once stood tall,*

*But now are covered with
the russet leaves of fall.*

*Announce the lie on the autumn
wind with all your fury,*

*Then press the apple into the
earth, there let it be buried.*

*Turn your back and walk
away with a clear mind,*

*The lie shall fade and pass
away with time.*

The spell is done. One final tip: since sage has purification qualities, bury it with the apple. As they decay together, the gossip will fade.

James Kambos

NOTES:

September 25
Sunday

4th ♏

☽ v/c 8:49 am

☽ → ♎ 12:43 pm

New Moon 5:55 pm

Color of the day: Amber

Incense of the day: Juniper

Rosh hashanah begins at sundown

Clean Slate

Rosh Hashanah represents fresh starts, as it is the Jewish New Year. We can tap into the energies of fresh starts and the lunar phase of the new moon to give our magickal workings an extra boost. For this spell we will focus on letting go of our previous misdeeds in order to make a clean start.

You will need a small dish with sand in it. Use a chopstick or pencil to write in the sand the transgression that you want to eliminate. Once you have done so, see in your mind how you can correct it. Then smooth over the sand, erasing what was written there, while saying:

What once was is no more.

Now you can start fresh, with a clean slate.

Charlynn Walls

September 26
Monday

1st ♎

Color of the day: Ivory

Incense of the day: Rosemary

Circle of Spice Altar

Create this altar using warming spices and sugar to sweeten your autumn. Go outdoors and clear a one-foot space; you can mark it out with chalk. In the center of the space, pour a small amount of sugar and shape it into a two-to-three-inch circle. Sprinkle the following four spices around the sugar in concentric circles, invoking the power of each spice as you work:

Cloves to cleanse body and soul,

Ginger for prosperity, silver, and gold.

Cinnamon for lucky starts,

Cardamom to lift my heart.

Now walk around the circles clockwise three times as you recite this chant to sweeten your autumn:

Cooler days,

Darker nights.

Sweet sugar,

Warming spice.

I love the fall!

Natalie Zaman

 September 27
Tuesday

1st ♎

☽ v/c 12:21 pm

☽ → ♏ 7:15 pm

Color of the day: Gray
Incense of the day: Geranium

The Dark Madonna

As light wanes and darkness grows, invoke the Dark Madonna to guide your journey. Every culture has a personification of the dark mother, representing the seasonal descent into darkness and the symbolic journey into our psyche and shadow material. Call on Nyx, the Greek goddess of the night, or Hecate, goddess of the crossroads, witchcraft, and the moon. Invoke either Persephone or her mother, Demeter, to join you as you journey down, examining loss, abandonment, separation, and pain.

O Dark Madonna, journey with me.

O Dark Madonna, journey with me.

Mary, mother of Jesus, be with me in my grief.

Isis, mother of Horus, provide healing relief.

Demeter, help me release summer's light.

Persephone, be with me as I journey into night.

Nyx, stay by my side through the dark night of the soul,

And Hecate, guide my journey, that I may emerge whole.

O Dark Madonna, journey with me.
Dallas Jennifer Cobb

NOTES:

September 28
Wednesday

1st ♏

Color of the day: White
Incense of the day: Bay laurel

Fairy and Folk Tales

Are there days when you just want to get away from consensual reality? One way to do this is to turn yourself (temporarily!) into a fairy in a tale of princesses, princes, enchanted beasts, or wizards. Reread your favorites, such as the Grimm brothers' *Household Tales*, *The Lord of the Rings*, or *Wicked*, for starters. Watch *The Wizard of Oz* and *Into the Woods*. How soon do you notice that there aren't any fairies in these true and faux folk tales, novels, and plays?

Read your favorite story again. Cast yourself as a character. Become a real fairy. Who can you make friends with? Examine the world of the story. Of course it's not perfect. If it were, there'd be no plot. As a fairy, what can you do to change the story? Improve the life of the princess or the cinder girl? Create a happier ending? Here's your invocation:

I am the Good Fairy.

As I enter this story,

My intentions are good.

I bring good magic to balance the bad.

Barbara Ardinger

September 29
Thursday

1st ♏

☽ v/c 5:20 pm

Color of the day: Purple
Incense of the day: Carnation

Speed It Up

September 29 is National Coffee Day. Besides being many people's favorite magical brew to start the day, coffee has other metaphysical properties that are worth noting. As caffeine tends to speed things up, why not tap into that potential energy to hurry along something that could use a boost? Coffee is generally easy to come by, and it's also good for clearing and cleansing. You can add coffee to your spell in one of three easy ways:

- *Liquid:* Add black and freshly brewed coffee to other liquids, or pour it where it can be easily absorbed.

- *Coffee grounds:* Allow the grounds to dry, then sprinkle them in places where things are stuck, or mix them with incense.

- *Beans:* Add the beans to satchels, along with stones, herbs, coins, and other small items that wouldn't mix well with liquid or the fine particles of the grounds.

Laura Tempest Zakroff

♆ ☉$ September 30
Friday

1st ♏

☽ → ♐ 12:03 am

Color of the day: Coral
Incense of the day: Cypress

Something for the Pocketbook

It's a wise idea to carry some sort of financial charm with you, especially in your wallet or purse. This sort of magick is practiced across the globe in some form or another. Indeed, we are all dependent on this made-up thing called "money" for certain things in life. But, as with any other energy, we are allowed to open ourselves to it so that we can use it for the greater good.

Find a fancy piece of paper (papyrus and parchment are my favorites) and cut a square of ten centimeters (approximately four inches). On one side, write your country's symbol for currency. On the flip side, draw an infinity loop, with two arrows pointing to it.

Anoint the paper with patchouli and/or vetiver oil, and always store it with your cash or cards. Replenish the spell anytime by anointing it with the oil.

Raven Digitalis

October

Days that turn on a breath into rapidly waning light. Wispy, high dark clouds in an orange and turquoise sky. Bright orange pumpkins carved into beautiful art and lit from inside. The eerie music of screeching cats. These fond images of October burn at a Witch's heart, calling to her even across the seasons where she's busy setting up her tent for festival. By the time October finally arrives, Witches and other magic users have already had discussions about costumes and parties, rituals and celebrations, and we look forward with happiness to the whole month of both poignantly somber and brightly playful activities.

In Celtic Europe, our ancestors acknowledged October as the last month of the summer season, with winter officially beginning on Samhain. They carved slits in squashes to keep light in the fields so they could finish their day's work, and when the custom came to America, it eventually evolved into the tradition of carving jack-o'-lanterns. American Witches often use magical symbols to carve their pumpkins, creating beacons for their Beloved Dead. In the spirit of the turn of energies at this time, we give candy to children to ensure that they, our future, will remember the sweetness inside and be good leaders when their turn comes. May we all be so blessed.

Thuri Calafia

October 1
Saturday

1st ♐

☽ v/c 5:46 pm

Color of the day: Brown
Incense of the day: Magnolia

Bonfire and Flames

As we move deeper into the fall, the cooler air and darkening nights bring to mind the charm of being around a crackling bonfire. The smell of the wood smoke, the company of friends, the warmth of the fire…what could be better?

Whether or not you can have an actual bonfire, this is a perfect time to make a connection to the element of fire. Fire can be found in many different forms, from a single candle to a grouping of tealights, a barbeque, or a fireplace. Choose the one that works best for you and approach it mindfully and with appreciation for the gifts and power of fire. Kindle your flame and spend a few minutes basking in the light and warmth it gives off. Then say:

Fire so bright,

Fire so warm,

Share your light,

I feel your charm.

Deborah Blake

October 2
Sunday

1st ♐

☽ → ♑ 3:38 am

2nd Quarter 8:14 pm

Color of the day: Gold
Incense of the day: Marigold

Car Naming

If you own a car, does it have a name? October 2 is Name Your Car Day. While it might seem silly to give your car a name, many folks who own cars tend to spend an awful lot of time in them. Most magical folks I know name their cars and talk to them as well. (I certainly do!) If you can recognize that your vehicle has an energy of its own, you'll find you can head off major problems early and get more "life" out of it. You don't have to do a formal naming ceremony, but taking a day in both the spring and the fall to wash the outside, clean the inside, remove any debris, and reset/refresh any altars or talismanic items helps show that you respect and honor your car. (Every car I've ever owned has had at least one stuffed animal, several rocks/shells, a feather, and some plant matter.)

Laura Tempest Zakroff

October 3
Monday

NOTES:

2nd ♑

☽ v/c 11:49 pm

Color of the day: Gray
Incense of the day: Neroli

A Good, Short Banishing

Shakespeare invented a word that needs to be in wider use today: *rudesby*. It means exactly what it sounds like: an ill-mannered, uncivil person. Two of his strong female characters use the word. Katherine and Olivia dismiss hangers-on in their houses with "mad-brain rudesby" and "Rudesby, be gone!"

So who's been hanging around you lately? What pest is driving you berserk? Take or find a photo of the rudesby, set it on your altar, and speak the banishing words:

Rudesby, be gone!

Make the words a meme and post it. Be aware, however, that rudesby people are like ants, fleas, and flies: they don't pay attention. Human pests can be as bad as insects, but please don't use poison spray on them. Speak the words as often as necessary at your altar and in person. Visualize the rudesby gone to wherever you want them to go. Speak the words again. Do this as often as necessary. You may, alas, need to be more persistent than the rudesby is.

Barbara Ardinger

October 4
Tuesday

2nd ♑

☽ → ♒ 6:20 am

Color of the day: Black
Incense of the day: Ginger

Yom Kippur begins at sundown

Clearing Away

According to Jewish tradition, today is Yom Kippur, the Day of Atonement. It's a good time for clearing away past mistakes and negative energy. Asking forgiveness for wrongs helps to heal relationships too.

For this spell you will need a bowl of water, a pinch of salt, and a hand towel. Sprinkle the salt over the water and say:

By the tears of the sea,

Be pure and blessed be.

Rinse your hands with the water and say:

Where salt and water go,

May sacred clearing flow.

Sprinkle the water over your head and say:

May all beneath the rain

Be new and free of pain.

Recite the things you have done that you regret. Describe what you have done or will do to make amends, whether to the gods or to other people. When you finish, pour the water down the drain. Wash your hands in clean water and dry with the towel.

Elizabeth Barrette

NOTES:

October 5
Wednesday

2nd ≈≈

☽ v/c 6:46 pm

Color of the day: White
Incense of the day: Marjoram

Cord Magic Spell

Magic can be used to focus energy to effect change in the world, for the good of all. Cord magic is a great way to be clear in your intention and draw a desired effect into reality. Find a piece of string or cord about a yard long. As you tie nine knots in the string, say the following and let the power of your intention be focused and real:

By knot of one, this spell has begun.

By knot of two, it shall come true.

By knot of three, so mote it be.

By knot of four, I invoke more.

By knot of five, this spell is alive.

By knot of six, the magic is fixed.

By knot of seven, the magic leavens.

By knot of eight, I need not wait.

By knot of nine, this spell is mine.

Keep the knotted string on your altar, and renew the spell as needed.

Dallas Jennifer Cobb

October 6
Thursday

2nd ≈≈

☽ → ♓ 8:47 am

Color of the day: Crimson
Incense of the day: Nutmeg

Flowers for the Dead

October, how we love you! Blessed be the season of the Witch. As you likely know, Samhain is a time of honoring the ancestors, of banishing, releasing, divining, and communicating with the Otherworld.

As we begin to decorate our homes for Halloween, we also begin to set the altar. Common autumnal altar decor includes gourds, fallen leaves, pomegranates, veils, bones, and photos of our dearly departed.

Whether ancestral by blood or spirit, the deceased are with us always. This is the best time of the month to make an offering of flowers. Offer roses or whatever feels right, and place them in a vase without water so that they will be dead by Samhain. By the light of a single black candle, declare:

Mighty Ancestors, hear me now; the veil grows thin, we lift the shroud.

Accept this offering of flowers bright; you are loved, in darkness and light.

Extinguish the candle.

Raven Digitalis

October 7
Friday

2nd ♓

Color of the day: Rose
Incense of the day: Mint

Pillars of Protection

This spell creates four energetic pillars, one in each cardinal direction, anchoring your home in protective, balanced energy. Find a comfortable meditative position, roughly in the center of your home. Close your eyes and allow earth energy to rise upward, through your body and out the crown of your head. Simultaneously, allow sky energy to cascade through your crown and down through your root chakra.

When you feel centered and balanced, envision your home or property, and starting in the north, call up a pillar of earth energy, grounding and anchoring, as you say:

I call on the power of earth to
protect and balance this home.

Moving clockwise, repeat with a pillar of fire in the east, air in the south, and water in the west. Finish by visualizing all four pillars, strong and luminous, and thank the elements for guarding your home. Allow the earth and sky flows to taper off, returning your energy to a neutral state.

Melissa Tipton

 October 8
Saturday

2nd ♓

☽ v/c 7:10 am

☽ → ♈ 11:57 am

Color of the day: Indigo
Incense of the day: Patchouli

Altar Blessing

Now is a good time for an altar blessing. It is helpful to clear off your altar and clean it at least once a year. Gather some soft cloths and cleaners appropriate to the type of altar and tools you have.

First take everything off the altar. Wipe down the altar. If you have an altar cloth, you'll need to wash it. Ideally keep at least two, so you can put a fresh one on the altar right away. Clean the individual tools and put them back where they belong. Set fresh candles in the candleholders. Put some type of blessing incense in the censer and light it. Then say:

Altar of service, vessel of care,

Fire and water and earth and air.

Shrine of my spirit, seat of my Art,

Serve me with faith and I'll do my part.

Let the incense burn down to ash. When the censer cools, clean it again and restore it to the altar.

Elizabeth Barrette

October 9
Sunday

2nd ♈

Full Moon 4:55 pm

Color of the day: Orange
Incense of the day: Eucalyptus

Sukkot begins at sundown

A Full Moon Scrying Spell

An October full moon is a power-ful time to scry. For this spell you'll need a dark-colored bowl or a cauldron. You'll also need a silver coin and a white candle. The coin not only serves as a focal point but also symbolizes the full moon.

Begin by filling your container with water. Safely light the candle and set it beside the bowl or cauldron. Now drop the coin into the water. Gaze at the ripples in the water as you think of a question. When the water becomes still, focus intently on the coin. Soon the water will cloud over, then become clear. As it clears, an image should appear. Gaze for no more than ten to fifteen minutes. Slowly let the vision go. End by snuff-ing out the candle. Save the coin for scrying. You may record the image you saw, or any messages received, in a journal.

James Kambos

October 10
Monday

3rd ♈

☽ v/c 10:02 am

☽ → ♉ 5:04 pm

Color of the day: White
Incense of the day: Narcissus

Indigenous Peoples' Day –
Thanksgiving Day (Canada)

Payment to Pachamama

It's Indigenous Peoples' Day, Columbus Day, and Thanksgiving Day in Canada—so it's a complex day. Let's conjure the venerable mother goddess Pachamama, creatrix of all life and embodiment of the earth. She can be seen as a gorgeous Peruvian woman wearing a red dress and alpaca shawl and carrying a child.

We get everything we enjoy from the natural world from Pachamama. Let's do a ritual where you pay what you can in thanks for all she does in your life.

Do this ritual in a field. The altar you build at the beginning of the ritual pays homage to all that is indigenous, and it salutes Thanksgiving.

Gather these materials:

+ Stones

+ A basket (a cornucopia is ideal)

+ A variety of whole foods or herbs

+ Some pretty doll clothing

+ Spirits

+ Cacao leaves if possible; if not, then cacao nibs

Build an altar with stones and set the basket on it. Fill the basket with whole foods or herbs. Scatter the doll clothing, and hold the items down with rocks. Mindfully pour your libation. Crumble and let the cacao leaves or nibs hit the air before scattering. Say:

Pachamama, this is my payment to you for all that you do!

Stephanie Rose Bird

Notes:

October 11
Tuesday

3rd ♉

Color of the day: Maroon
Incense of the day: Cedar

Let Go of a Problem

Today, collect nine autumn leaves that have already fallen. (If there aren't any fallen leaves in your area, you can use rose petals instead.) Light a stick of cedar incense on your altar. Take some deep breaths, center yourself, and call on the Great Goddess. Bring to mind a problem, issue, or block from which you would like to liberate yourself. From your heart, ask the Goddess to help you heal, unravel, and dissipate this issue in all directions of time. Hold the leaves between your hands as you direct the energy of the challenge into the leaves. Breathe fully as you imagine draining your body and aura of all related stress or anxiety and sending all your tension and worry into the leaves. Once this feels complete, set the leaves down and safely bathe one leaf at a time in the incense smoke. Extinguish the incense, then go outside and release the leaves to the wind, into a body of water, or near the base of a tree.

Tess Whitehurst

October 12
Wednesday

3rd ♉

☽ v/c 5:42 pm

Color of the day: Brown
Incense of the day: Honeysuckle

Stay Out, Unwanted Spirits!

As the veil between the worlds begins to thin in early October, we like to do a little extra protection work to keep our house free of unwanted spirit visitors. For this spell you will need a couple of pinches of salt and a bowl of water. Say a cleansing blessing over the salt and water and then mix together.

Now walk the perimeter of your dwelling, sprinkling the salted water as you go. As you walk, state your intentions. We use these words:

Only those souls that are wanted and invited are welcome in this space! I cast out what is not wanted and shield this space from those that would cause mischief or harm.

Pay special attention to windows and doors, and don't be afraid to throw a little water to get to things above your reach. When done outside, repeat indoors.

Ari & Jason Mankey

October 13
Thursday

3rd ♉

☽ → ♊ 1:08 am

Color of the day: Green
Incense of the day: Carnation

A Spell for Mental Clarity and Growth

Our brains are constantly changing and developing, and every challenge we face offers us a chance to learn.

For this spell to encourage mental clarity and growth, you'll need:

- A purple candle and holder
- A small open bowl or jar
- A sharpened pencil
- Matches
- One or more of fluorite, amethyst, lapis, or tiger eye
- One or more of fresh or dried peppermint, turmeric, basil, or green tea
- A small bell

Place the candle, bowl, and pencil on your altar. Light the candle safely. Place the gems and herbs in the bowl or jar, then hold it in your hands, with eyes closed, and focus on clearing your mind. Think about an obstacle you face and what you need to do to surmount it. Set the bowl down, open your eyes, and hold the pencil. Repeat:

The sharp point of this pencil creates, while its softer end erases.

May I remember that in every action

There is no failure—

Only a chance to experience growth.

Ring the bell and pause, focusing on growth. Extinguish the candle. Leave the materials on your altar for contemplation.

Susan Pesznecker

NOTES:

October 14
Friday

3rd ♊

Color of the day: Coral
Incense of the day: Alder

Guardian Angel Buttons

It's been said (in buttonless circles) that a button is something for the devil to hang onto. Well, if the devil can hang onto a button, why can't a guardian angel do the same?

Take a quiet moment to talk to your guardian angel. (I like to do this on my morning walk and just have chat where I ask for guidance and protection throughout the day.) As you converse, what colors or patterns come to mind? Find or buy buttons in the colors or patterns that were shown to you—you may find that they just come into your hands! Sew the button into the inside of the left side of your coat or jacket (or any piece of clothing), right over your heart. As you sew, say or sing:

Near to my heart, angel of mine,

Bound by thread and love divine!

Carry your angel with you wherever you go!

Natalie Zaman

October 15
Saturday

3rd ♊

☽ v/c 12:11 am

☽ → ♋ 12:11 pm

Color of the day: Blue
Incense of the day: Sandalwood

Embrace Change

At this time of year, many people enjoy the enchanting sight of autumn leaves. Their fiery colors represent the beauty that arises from embracing change.

On your next walk, collect several autumn leaves. (You can also use green leaves, flowers, or a clipping of grass. They change with time too, so they will work.) When you return home, place them in a dish on your altar. With deep breaths, tap into their energy. Imagine their lives, from when they were first hidden in a branch, then grew into tiny green buds and into maturity. See how the sun and weather changed every day, and as the sunlight decreased, the leaves responded by changing color. Finally, envision the leaves letting go of what they knew and floating to the ground, peacefully surrendering.

Keep the dish of leaves as a reminder of how beautiful change is and how you can embrace it with grace. When you no longer need the reminder, place the leaves in a jar and use them in future magical works for change.

Astrea Taylor

October 16
Sunday

3rd ♋

Color of the day: Yellow
Incense of the day: Heliotrope

Sukkot ends

World Food Day

O n this day in 1945, the United
Nations founded the Food and
Agriculture Organization, dedicated
to dealing with the issues of poverty
and hunger. In 1979, World Food
Day was officially established as an
international celebration. Each year,
the day has a different theme and
focus, usually revolving around agriculture, and events are held in over
150 countries.

But you don't need to be part of a
worldwide organization to do your bit
toward ending hunger. Today, donate
to your local food pantry or, if you
garden, give a part of your harvest to
a food kitchen. If you know someone
who is struggling, drop off a bag of
groceries. No matter what else you
do, try to have a renewed appreciation for the food on your own table.
Remember to thank the gods and
those who worked hard to produce
the food, and be grateful.

Deborah Blake

 October 17
Monday

3rd ♋
4th Quarter 1:15 pm
☽ v/c 4:56 pm

Color of the day: Ivory
Incense of the day: Hyssop

Spread the Wealth

T he International Day for the
Eradication of Poverty is
observed by the United Nations every
year on October 17. Working to bring
a little more prosperity into the world
is the goal of today's spell.

We all can use a little help from
time to time. Today, carry some extra
cash in your pocket or purse. When
you are presented with the opportunity to do something for someone, do
so. You could pay for someone's meal
or donate money to a cause you care
about. Each time you give something
away today, say either out loud or in
your mind:

*Though this monetary gift may
be small, it is sure to snowball.*

When you share what you have with
the world, others will too and your
own kindness is likely to be returned
to you as well.

Charlynn Walls

·October 18
Tuesday

4♄ ♋
☽ → ♌ 12:45 am
Color of the day: White
Incense of the day: Bayberry

Let's All honor Each Other

Holding a big ball of rainbow-colored yarn, sit on the floor in a circle with friends. Sit so close that you're all touching. With the end of the yarn in one hand, toss the ball so it flies like a comet with a rainbow tail to someone across the circle. As you toss the yarn, speak an affirmation that Concordia, goddess of community harmony, whispers in your ear. The person who catches the yarn touches it to their heart, then tosses it to someone else, speaking another affirmation of harmony.

Keep tossing the ball back and forth around the circle and speaking words of harmony until all the yarn is loose. What you'll have now is a big, untidy web. It's really a cone of energy of community harmony hovering above and around your circle. Ground the energy into yourselves and figure out a way to preserve that web as a symbol of harmony of your magical and mundane communities.

Barbara Ardinger

 ·October 19
Wednesday

4♄ ♌
Color of the day: Topaz
Incense of the day: Bay laurel

New friends Spell

They say it's harder to make friends as we get older, but that likely has to do more with our work environment, family life, and busy schedule than our ability to actually find new friends. Sometimes we just need to make a little more of a window of opportunity and put that intent out into the universe.

This fun little satchel will help draw friendship to you. Collect the following:

- A cinnamon stick
- A rose quartz pebble
- A dried yellow rose bud or petals
- 2 wrapped candies of your choice
- 6 shiny pennies

Place all the items in an opaque cotton satchel, ideally one you make yourself out of a fun print that reminds you to be playful. Allow it to sit on your altar for at least three days, then carry it with you as you go about your day (in your car or in a coat pocket, purse, backpack, or briefcase).

Laura Tempest Zakroff

·October 20
Thursday

4th ♌

☽ v/c 6:35 am

☽ → ♍ 12:25 pm

Color of the day: Purple
Incense of the day: Apricot

Prosperity Tech

People often use technology as a means to prosperity. These days most folks carry a smartphone or tablet with which they can access financial resources. They do a lot of shopping online too. This has pros and cons. It's convenient, but it can be a weakness. It can also offer a line of attraction for your magic.

For this spell you will need your smartphone or other favorite device. You will also need a length of black yarn and a length of green yarn, in any synthetic fiber. (Match the materials to the type of magic you're doing, so use synthetic materials for a techno-magic spell.) Wrap the black yarn around your phone or device and tie a knot. Then say:

As this black yarn I wind,

All evil things I bind.

Slip off the black yarn, whole. Bury it far away.

Wrap the green yarn around your phone or device and tie a knot. Then say:

As this green yarn I tie,

Money comes by and by.

Slip off the green yarn, whole. Keep it in your purse or wallet.

Elizabeth Barrette

NOTES:

October 21
Friday

4th ♏

Color of the day: Pink
Incense of the day: Rose

Leaf It All Behind

Now that we are in the midst of the season of releasing, take a walk in a quiet place with trees whose leaves are in the process of changing color. Walk slowly, deeply inhaling the alluring, mystical scent of seasonal decay. This autumnal energy stands strong in the heart of the Witch.

As you notice leaves that have fully changed color and are on the verge of falling to the earth, pluck them one by one. As you pick each leaf, hold it in your right hand, crumple it up, and declare:

This season I hereby release _____.

Toss the crumpled leaf on the ground. Continue this for as long as it feels right. Feel free to release various things in your own life that no longer serve you, such as inner pain or confusion. It's also a good idea to release things that are baneful in the world, such as apathy, racism, and greed.

Raven Digitalis

October 22
Saturday

4th ♏

☽ v/c 2:17 pm
☽ → ♎ 9:24 pm

Color of the day: Black
Incense of the day: Sage

Cleansing Altar Spray

Your altar is a representation of the microcosm and your relationship to these forces. Regularly cleansing and tending to this space is an important magical hygiene practice that will keep your life and your magical workings running more smoothly.

Choose a purifying or cleansing herb, such as sage, angelica, or rosemary, and place a few pinches in a bowl of spring water. Ask the spirit of the plant(s) to impart their powers of cleansing to the water, then leave the bowl in a sunny spot for a few hours. Strain out the plant material and pour the infused water into a spray bottle.

Mist your altar with the cleansing spray, visualizing all harmful or unwanted energy dissolving and returning to the cosmic cycle, leaving your sacred space fresh and revitalized.

Melissa Tipton

October 23
Sunday

4th ♎

☉ → ♏ 6:36 am

Color of the day: Amber
Incense of the day: Hyacinth

Leave a Treasure

If you've ever found something— a penny on the ground with a special date, money when you needed it, a long-lost object—it got to your hand or entered your orbit somehow. Magic comes in all forms, and sometimes we are the means by which it is delivered.

What small object in your possession calls to be released and put into the hands of someone who needs it or would be uplifted by it? Find your object (keep it small) and carry it with you when you're out and about. Wait for it to tell you when it's time to let go. When that happens, drop or place it wherever it's going to go with these words:

Go with good energy and
for positive effect!

You may never witness the resultant magic, but trust that it is there.

Natalie Zaman

October 24
Monday

4th ♎

☽ v/c 8:36 pm

Color of the day: Silver
Incense of the day: Rosemary

Wintering In

We're well into autumn, and winter is just around the corner. It's the season for wintering in, when country folk would prepare for winter, gathering what they needed to get through the cold months until the storms stopped and the light returned.

Carry out your own wintering in ritual to help you get through the dark months.

You'll need a favorite mug, your choice of hot beverage, a favorite book, warm mittens, and a white, gray, or dark blue candle in a holder.

Bring everything to a table or to your altar. Light the candle safely and put on the mittens. Repeat:

Warmth and comfort,

Candle bright,

Keep me through

The long dark night

As I await the

Return of light.

Sip your hot beverage. Focus for a minute on the brightness of the candle, the comfort of the mittens, and

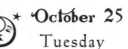

the soothing warmth of your drink. Envision yourself as a warm cocoon in the midst of winter. Settle in and read your book while enjoying the beverage. Extinguish the candle when you're done.

Susan Pesznecker

NOTES:

October 25
Tuesday

4th ♎

☽ → ♏ 3:18 am

New Moon 6:49 am

Color of the day: Scarlet
Incense of the day: Basil

Solar Eclipse

Finding Your Shadow Self

S hadows fill the sky today as a solar eclipse covers much of Europe, the Mediterranean, and the Middle East. It's also the night of the new moon. All of this energy makes it a perfect time to confront our shadow self, the part of our psyche that makes us uncomfortable and is often repressed or ignored. Simply acknowledging our shadow can often be a challenge.

Find a dark place where you won't be disturbed, and place a lit candle in a spot between you and a wall. Ideally you want to be in a spot where you cast a giant shadow. In the darkness, stare into your shadow and write down everything you see, positive or negative. Hold nothing back and be honest with yourself. Using your list as a guide, work on integrating both sides of yourself from now until Imbolc.

Ari & Jason Mankey

October 26
Wednesday

1st ♏

Color of the day: Yellow
Incense of the day: Lilac

Dream Breakthrough Spell

This dream spell is for breaking through a stubborn challenge or moving forward in any area of life where you've been feeling blocked. Do this just before bed.

If you have runes, pull the Dagaz rune (ᛞ) out of your set. Otherwise, draw it on a stamp-size scrap of cardboard. Hold the rune (letter side) against your forehead. Relax and bring to mind whatever you'd like to shift in a positive way. Don't try to be positive about it: feel everything you feel about the issue. Also bring to mind the options as you see them (or the lack thereof). Then set the intention to direct all the energy of your thoughts and feelings about the situation or challenge into the rune, letting them drain from your body and mind. Place the rune under your pillow. As soon as you wake up in the morning (and if you wake up in the night), immediately write down any dreams you remember. The key to your breakthrough will be contained within them.

Tess Whitehurst

October 27
Thursday

1st ♏

☽ v/c 12:27 am

☽ → ♐ 6:55 am

Color of the day: White
Incense of the day: Balsam

Bless This Desk

During the winter months I spend more time at my writing desk, where many magical parts of me come together. Today, let us bless our desks. Clear the desktop and wipe it down with a damp cloth. Say:

> May water bless this desk with fluidity.

Gently stir the air over the desk as you say:

> May air bless this desk with new beginnings, the birth of ideas, and the joy of creation.

Set a lamp and your computer on the desk and say:

> May fire bless me with clarity, vision, and connectivity.

Place a rock or crystal on the desk and say:

> May earth bless this desk with stability.

As you sit down at your desk, bless yourself and your creativity:

> May I be happy and prolific in my creation, speaking and writing what

needs to be said. May I be kind and wise so that my writing inspires and encourages those in need. So be it.

> Dallas Jennifer Cobb

Notes:

October 28
Friday

1st ♐

Color of the day: Rose
Incense of the day: Yarrow

Xochiquetzal's Spicy Chocolate

It's National Chocolate Day. Chocolate, called the food of the gods, has a rich history in Mexico, beginning in the Aztec and Mayan cultures. So let's create the drink of Aztec goddess Xochiquetzal. She has dominion over sex, childbearing, creativity, flowers, hummingbirds, and butterflies. She manifests for feather-workers and metalworkers. Xochiquetzal loves weavers, painters, sculptors, florists, homemakers, sex workers, mothers, pregnant women, and midwives.

For plant energy, pin Aztec marigold (*Tagetes erecta*) to your clothing, hair, or hat. Then make the spicy chocolate.

Ingredients:

* ¾ cup quality dark chocolate chips

* 3 cups milk

* 1½ teaspoons ground cinnamon

* 1½ teaspoons vanilla

* Pinch of coarse sea salt

* 1 chili pepper, cut vertically and seeded

* 4 Mexican cinnamon sticks

* Sweetener (optional)

Whisk the chocolate chips in ¾ cup milk in a pot on a stove set at medium. Whisk in the rest of the milk briskly for several minutes until well blended. Then whisk in the ground cinnamon, vanilla, and sea salt. Blend well.

With the heat on medium high, steep the chili pepper and a halved cinnamon stick in the mixture for ten minutes in the pan with the cover on. Then remove the cover and discard the solid ingredients. Whisk in sweetener if desired. Pour the spicy chocolate into three small cups and serve with Mexican cinnamon sticks.

Stephanie Rose Bird

NOTES:

October 29
Saturday

1st ♐

☽ v/c 9:10 am

☽ → ♑ 9:21 am

Color of the day: Gray
Incense of the day: Pine

Feline Protection

Today is National Cat Day in the United States. Though you may not have a cat of your own, you can connect and work with feline energies during this time. One energy of the cat that you can tap into is that of protection. A familiar works with their witch and looks out for them. Bast is an excellent goddess to work with, and you can call on her for help when you need protection for yourself or others. Create a small representation of Bast to carry with you. You can use clay, as it is easily molded and dries quickly. Focus on Bast as you mold your clay and say:

> Goddess Bast, enchant this charm.
> Allow it to shield me from harm.

Charlynn Walls

 October 30
Sunday

1st ♑

Color of the day: Orange
Incense of the day: Almond

Jack-o'-Lantern Spell

One of my favorite childhood memories is carving a jack-o'-lantern and setting it outside for the whole neighborhood to see. A jack-o'-lantern's warm glow can imbue magical feelings and deter negativity—they hide magic in plain sight.

This spell requires a pumpkin, a sharp serrated blade, a spoon, a bowl, a tealight candle, and a lighter.

Cut a circle on the top of the pumpkin. Remove the seeds with a spoon, place them in a bowl, and dispose of them outside if possible to give a treat to wildlife. Carve a face in the pumpkin that feels magical and alert. When you're done, light the tealight and place it inside the pumpkin. Tap the knife against the pumpkin three times to awaken its spirit. Say:

> Jack-o'-lantern, I call you forth to create a magical community! May all who see you feel pure magic! Protect us against those who mean harm.

Place the jack-o'-lantern outside somewhere safe facing the street. Replace nightly with a fresh tealight to recharge the magic.

Astrea Taylor

October 31
Monday

1st ♑

☽ v/c 11:14 am

☽ → ♒ 11:43 am

Color of the day: Ivory
Incense of the day: Clary sage

Samhain – halloween

hecate Candle Spell

On Samhain night you can ask Hecate to help you communicate with your deceased loved ones. You'll need a black candle, some salt water, and a piece of purple fabric.

Begin this ritual at midnight. Drape the fabric over your altar. Lightly rub the candle with the salt water to keep negative spirits away. Then safely light the candle. Sit before the candle and gaze at the flame. Now call upon Hecate by saying:

Hecate, queen of the Witches,
queen of the night,

Bring to me the power of second sight.

Let me see in this candle's glare,

Spirits of the family tree I share.

Softly say the names of the departed souls you wish to communicate with. Gaze at the candle's flame and its halo. Soon you'll begin to see faces, some you may not recognize. When you wish to stop, thank the spirits, snuff out the candle, and thank

Hecate. When the candle is cool, throw it away. Record any communication in your Book of Shadows.

James Kambos

NOTES:

November

The sounds of nature begin to quiet down in November, but this month is far from silent. Yes, the cheery morning birdsong of spring is gone, and crickets are no longer fiddling on warm summer afternoons, but November has its own "voices." On a frosty November morning, you'll hear a faint, faraway gabble. Raise your eyes toward the sky, and coming over the horizon, in a V formation heading south, is a flock of wild geese. The sound makes you pause and wonder: how do they know it's time to migrate? As you rake leaves, the late autumn breeze stirs them, and they softly rustle as they click and swirl up the street. Few sounds say November like the wind. It may be as gentle as a baby's breath or it may roar, carrying the weight of the coming winter as it howls in the night. During the night you can also hear November's most haunting voice: the lone hooting of an owl. Yes, this month has many voices, but every evening I hear the most comforting voice of all. That voice belongs to the crackling of burning logs as my hearth fire wards off the chill of a dark November night.

During this mysterious month, let the voices of November speak to you, igniting your imagination and your magic.

James Kambos

November 1
Tuesday

1st ♒

2nd Quarter 2:37 am

Color of the day: Gray
Incense of the day: Ylang-ylang

All Saints' Day

Caring for Our Ancestors

Today is a day to remember those who have passed. The veil is still thin, and if you can go out and commune with your ancestors at their resting place, do so. Take the time to show your appreciation for them and what they did for you in this lifetime. Clean and cleanse their gravesite in order to remove all physical and spiritual residue that may have accumulated over the past year. Once you have physically cleaned the space, use dragon's blood incense or sage to remove the spiritual residue. Say the following verse several times while using the incense:

Dearest ancestor, take heart.
Negative energies now depart.

Leave your loved one flowers or another gift that would speak to them.

Charlynn Walls

▽ **November 2**
Wednesday

2nd ♒

☽ v/c 7:08 am
☽ → ♓ 2:46 pm

Color of the day: Brown
Incense of the day: Lavender

Flush Away Negativity

This spell blends (toilet) humor with intention to help you shed negative energy and move on with your life. You'll need toilet paper (thicker varieties are easier to work with) and a ballpoint pen. If there's something you need to let go of, such as a nasty comment someone left on social media or a hurtful offline interaction, write it out on toilet paper.

You might record the nasty comment verbatim or simply pour out any thoughts and feelings you've been ruminating on. Once you've captured the full essence of the crappy situation, use the following incantation before unceremoniously tossing the paper in the bowl and giving it a good cathartic flush!

Sticks and stones won't break my bones,
These words, they cannot hurt me.
I flush this crap right down the drain,
And only peace and love remain.
So mote it be!

Melissa Tipton

November 3
Thursday

2nd ♓

Color of the day: Turquoise
Incense of the day: Mulberry

Ocean Jar Spell

Today, put a few seashells and some blue glass marbles in a Mason jar. Add eight shiny dimes and eight shiny pennies. Add purified water until the jar is one-half to three-quarters full. Hold your hands over the jar. Say:

Great Mother of the Waters, goddess of the rivers, oceans, and seas, I call upon your generosity and your lavish abundance now. I ask that you fill this water with your gifts of nourishment and infinite flow. Thank you.

Seal the Mason jar securely with the lid and turn it upside down to serve as a homemade ocean globe. Place it near your workspace or in the wealth sector of your home (that's the rear-left corner of your home while standing at your front door, facing inward). Say:

I now align with the vibration of increase, and call it into my life. I am in the flow of divine blessings, and my life is flooded with wealth.

Tess Whitehurst

November 4
Friday

2nd ♓

☽ v/c 6:05 pm
☽ → ♈ 7:07 pm

Color of the day: Purple
Incense of the day: Vanilla

Samhain's Rest

For many in the magickal community, the celebration of Samhain (or Halloween) is a true highlight of the year. When it's over, instead of just packing up the Halloween decorations without a second thought, we like to turn this bittersweet time of year into a magickal event.

Before putting away the various Halloween items you decorate with, sprinkle them with salt (or salted water) to cleanse them of any residual energy. As you pack them away, hold them in your hands and appreciate the energy and joy they bring. Visualize the items coming out again next fall to decorate your home.

Place all the items you are going to store in one place, then draw an invoking pentagram over them while thinking happy thoughts of next Samhain and saying:

Samhain's celebration has now come to its rest.

But it shall return next year, for we are blessed!

Ari & Jason Mankey

November 5
Saturday

2nd ♈

Color of the day: Blue
Incense of the day: Patchouli

house for Sale Spell

If you're looking to sell a house, the spirit to invoke is St. Joseph. Bury a statue of St. Joseph upside down in your yard when you put your house up for sale, making sure to dig it up once the house has been sold. If you can't get your hands on a St. Joseph statue, invoke him with some fig cookies. (Fig Newtons work nicely!). Trace a builder's square (one of Joseph's symbols) into the cookie with a toothpick, then ask for his help and leave the cookie in the yard for him. When your house sells, make sure you leave another cookie for him as a thank-you.

But what if you're in the market for a new place to live? Some folks ask Joseph for his help in this area as well, but St. Anthony may be the one to invoke, as he is good at finding things, lost or otherwise:

St. Anthony, who finds it all,

Help me find a new and happy home!

How do you thank St. Anthony once your wish comes to pass? Pay it forward with a charitable donation. (He is also the patron saint of those in need.)

Natalie Zaman

 November 6
Sunday

2nd ♈

☽ v/c 5:30 pm

Color of the day: Yellow
Incense of the day: Juniper

Daylight Saving Time
ends at 2:00 a.m.

Wooden Spoon Enchantment

It may seem old school, but an essential element to kitchen witchery is the wooden spoon. It was a familiar sight in both my mother's and my grandmother's kitchens— for good reason. A wooden spoon can take on flavors as well as enhance what it stirs, and it reacts better with acids than metals or plastics do, which is why it is the stirring spoon for our family tomato sauce.

Experiment with different woods to see how they feel to you, as each tree has its own energy to lend. Wooden spoons require a little more care than more modern utensils, but it's worth it. Wash and dry your spoon immediately versus soaking it. You can also apply edible oil for protection (hemp, sesame, or flax are common suggestions) once a year to keep the spoon in good shape. Enchant your spoon:

Mortar and pestle, cauldron, wooden spoon,

Magic stirred under the light of the moon.

*Blessed gift of tree, keep
strong, smooth, and light,*

*May all the brews you touch
be true and right.*

                    Laura Tempest Zakroff

NOTES:

 November 7
Monday

2nd ♈

☽ → ♉ 12:15 am

Color of the day: Lavender
Incense of the day: Lily

Protect Your Sleep

To cope with stress, we need to protect our sleep. Getting regular, good-quality sleep improves our mood, sharpens the mind, boosts memory, lowers blood pressure, steadies blood sugar levels, and fights germs. Sleep is crucial in healing physical injury and rebuilding muscle tissue.

Turn your bedroom into a sanctuary devoted to sleep. Banish all screens and phones from your room. Make your bed with pretty linens and blankets, lightly scent your pillows and sheets, and create a haven of relaxation. Regularly cast this protection spell:

This bed is for my peaceful sleep, my ease promoted by scented sheets.

This pillow is to rest my head, I sleep and dream and heal in bed.

This blanket keeps me safe and warm, protected from worry, fear, and harm.

This room is my sacred space, I rest and renew in this place.

I call protection around my sleep. Blessed be.

                    Dallas Jennifer Cobb

November 8
Tuesday

2nd ♉

☊ Full Moon 6:02 am

Color of the day: Red
Incense of the day: Cinnamon

Election Day (general) –
Lunar Eclipse

Eclipse Portal Spell Jar

During today's lunar eclipse, the earth will float between the Sun, Mercury, and Venus and the Moon and Uranus. This may cause turbulent emotions, but it can also reveal a unique perspective.

This portal spell jar requires a translucent jar, water, parsley, flower petals, grain, loose change, a magnet, and a fingernail clipping. You will also need paper and a writing utensil.

Under the light of the full moon, combine all the ingredients in the jar except for the water. Write down all of your accomplishments from the past six months and drop the paper in. As you pour water into the jar, consider how your emotions have supported you on this journey.

Catch the moon's reflection on the surface of the water, then set the jar in the moonlight. Meditate on the future and the successes coming your way.

When you're done, cap the jar and put it on your altar as a memento of your perseverance and what's to come.

Astrea Taylor

▽ **November 9**
Wednesday

3rd ♉

☽ v/c 7:00 am

☽ → ♊ 8:37 am

Color of the day: White
Incense of the day: Honeysuckle

Float Away Your Troubles

This year, a very important Thai festival of lights takes place today. Loy Krathong is a beautiful way of engaging and making offerings to water spirits while doing personal magick. Rivers and waterways are the most appropriate place for your ritual, but some people also use lakes, canals, brooks, and streams. What you will do is write down your trouble(s) and then watch them float away on a candlelit floral vessel.

Make a small boat using a loaf of banana bread or cork as the bottom. Insert your little sheet of paper. Put a votive candle on the base, along with a pretty flower. Wrap the bottom loosely with a banana leaf.

As you watch the vessel float away, imagine the wake bringing you a fresh start. If you need a substitute for the banana leaf, such as a corn husk or palm leaf, that's okay, but make sure whatever you use is completely biodegradable.

Stephanie Rose Bird

November 10
Thursday

3rd ♊

Color of the day: Purple
Incense of the day: Jasmine

The Wild Hunt Spell

The Wild Hunt is the Wild Huntsman (the God) and his cavalcade of horsemen who ride across the sky on windy autumn nights. They come from the Otherside to gather the souls of the recently departed. The lesson they teach is about change and transition. Call for their help when you're afraid to make a change. You'll need your wish written on plain white paper and one red apple. On a windswept night, hide your wish outside and place the apple on the paper. The apple is your gift to the Huntsmen. As you hide your wish, say:

The riders of the Wild Hunt ride untamed

Upon night stallions with flowing manes.

I ask, bring me the change I seek,

Only to you I reveal the secret I keep.

Tell no one about your wish. The next day, if your wish and apple are still there, hide the paper until your change occurs and compost the apple. If they're gone, your wish is already working in the Unseen Realm.

James Kambos

November 11
Friday

3rd ♊

☽ v/c 5:28 pm

☽ → ♋ 7:22 pm

Color of the day: Pink
Incense of the day: Thyme

Veterans Day –
Remembrance Day (Canada)

The Power of Giving Service

Is there any magic stronger than helping others? I think not. Veterans Day in the United States is a day when we honor those who have served and protected our country. Celebrate this with a ritual of honoring and awareness.

You will need one or two of your favorite tools (shovel, scissors, rolling pin, etc.).

Start in the morning at sunrise. Hold your tools, facing east, and repeat the following:

To those who have served this country, I honor you.

To those who serve others every day, even in the simplest of roles, I honor you.

May I show this through my actions.

May I be inspired by the giving hearts of those around me.

May I use my time and skills to help others.

May these tools guide my hands.

May my work be a gift to the world.

Now take your tools and get to work, making someone's life a little better.

Susan Pesznecker

NOTES:

November 12
Saturday

3rd ♋

Color of the day: Indigo
Incense of the day: Rue

All Things Shall Be Well

As we wander through the waning light of November, it's easy to feel the dark season approaching. While some people are afflicted by seasonal affective disorder (SAD), which leads to depression and similar feelings, it doesn't have to be that way. We can cheer up. We can be optimistic even as the year's light fades.

If you're feeling sad, set comical things on your altar, such as a favorite toy or a picture of a child or a kitten or puppy. As you light a bright-colored candle, repeat the words of Dame Julian of Norwich, a medieval English anchorite. (I've added to her words to make this spell.)

All is well.

All things shall be well.

All manner of things shall be well.

All can only be well.

Hold this spell in your heart and repeat it to yourself every morning, every evening, and any other time you're feeling a bit darkish. (Be sure to extinguish the candle.) We know the light will return. Hold this thought that all can only be well.

Barbara Ardinger

 ### November 13
Sunday

3rd ♋

Color of the day: Orange
Incense of the day: Marigold

Celebrate the Festival of Feronia

On this day, the Romans celebrated the Festival of Feronia. They worshipped her as the goddess of the harvest and abundance. They held a fair in her honor, with a market and entertainment. They offered the fruits of the harvest to her in a sacred grove.

This is a good time for a spell of gratitude. If possible, visit a farmers' market to choose the best offerings from the current harvest. If you have a garden, you can also make offerings of things you have grown. Make an altar covered with an autumn-colored cloth. Place the fruits of the harvest in a cornucopia or basket. Then say:

Feronia, goddess of plenty,

Accept the gifts of my hand.

Thank you for a bountiful harvest

And abundance from the land.

Afterward, you may use the fruits of the harvest to make a sacred feast.

Elizabeth Barrette

November 14
Monday

3rd ♋

☽ v/c 5:41 am

☽ → ♌ 7:48 am

Color of the day: Silver
Incense of the day: Hyssop

healing hands

Y ou don't have to be a professional massage therapist or a
Reiki Master to be able to use your
hands for healing. There is a natural
human instinct to place our hands on
a place that hurts, whether it is on
ourselves or others. We all have the
innate ability to do basic energy work
with a little practice, and sometimes a
simple back rub or foot massage can
both heal and soothe.

To do energy healing, try rubbing
your hands together until you can
feel them heat up a bit, then hold
them about a foot apart, bringing
them together slowly until you can
feel a ball of energy forming between
them. Then hold your hands above
the place that needs healing and concentrate on sending that energy out.
If you want, before doing any form
of healing, you can say:

Goddess, guide my hands
so they might heal.

Deborah Blake

November 15
Tuesday

3rd ♌

Color of the day: Scarlet
Incense of the day: Cedar

Symbols of healing Love

F or this self-love healing spell,
you'll need a washable marker in
the color of your choice. Spend some
time in meditation, asking your higher
self what within you needs healing
right now. If it's a mental-emotional
situation, get a sense of where in your
body you feel the strongest connection to this issue.

Then ask your higher self what
healing words or symbols would be
most beneficial right now. It could be
something like "love," "forgiveness,"
or "be gentle with yourself," or you
might see an image of a Reiki symbol,
rune, astrological glyph, etc.

Focusing on your healing intention, use the marker to write or draw
your healing symbol on the body area
you identified in meditation. Intend
that these words or symbols will
release the perfect amount and form
of healing energy until you wash the
marking off.

Melissa Tipton

🟊 November 16
Wednesday

3rd ♌︎
4th Quarter 8:27 am
☽ v/c 6:55 pm
☽ → ♍︎ 8:04 pm

Color of the day: Yellow
Incense of the day: Marjoram

Our Lady of the Gate of Dawn

Our Lady of the Gate of Dawn, whose feast day is celebrated today, is the protector of a small Lithuanian village that was nearly destroyed, save for her help. Personal identity is precious, our very foundation. When you feel that yours is in danger, call on this gentle but awesomely powerful mother figure with a simple request adopted from an ancient prayer in her honor:

Tota pulchra es, tu
honorificentia populi nostri.

Mater prudentissima,
Mater clementissima.

Ora pro nobis.

(You are all beautiful, you
give honor to our people.

Mother most intelligent,
Mother most merciful.

Pray for us.)

Natalie Zaman

🟊 November 17
Thursday

4th ♍︎

Color of the day: Crimson
Incense of the day: Myrrh

Daily Spiritual Alignment

Many Witches and other spiritual folks around the world practice daily rituals, prayers, meditations, and other activities that help them align with Spirit (in whatever form) and get through the day.

In addition to any morning routines you may have established, consider using a natural ink, pen, or marker to bless your physical body. Mark areas that will be later hidden by clothing.

Each magickal practitioner feels aligned with particular things. Everyone is unique. Think about the symbols that resonate with you personally, based on your own pantheon, interests, and spiritual callings.

As you mark each place on your body with a chosen sacred symbol, say an affirmation that confirms your reason for doing so, such as:

I mark the bottoms of my feet with the
symbol of earth, keeping me grounded
and connected to the sacred path.

Raven Digitalis

November 18
Friday

4th ♏

Color of the day: White
Incense of the day: Mint

heal a Broken heart

Grief and heartbreak cannot be rushed. Still, you can magically bolster the heart-healing process by cutting cords of attachment to your former partner and removing unhelpful patterns from your energy field and subconscious.

Today, add ¼ cup rose water to a warm bath along with ¼ cup sea salt and a rose quartz. Swirl the water in a counterclockwise direction to dissolve the salt. Light an unscented or rose-scented soy candle and get into the bath. As you soak, call on the goddess Aphrodite. Speak words from your heart about why you are asking for her help. Tell her how you've been feeling and ask that she clear and dissolve any remaining energetic connections to your former partner. Also ask that she remove any unhealthy relationship patterns or patterns of negative self-talk from your mind, spirit, and aura. Relax and imagine soft pink light healing and restructuring your heart and emotions on every level of your being. Thank the goddess before getting out of the tub.

Tess Whitehurst

November 19
Saturday

4th ♏

☽ v/c 3:47 am
☽ → ♎ 5:58 am

Color of the day: Gray
Incense of the day: Magnolia

Peppermint Oil Invitation

Late November and December are a popular time of year for parties and family get-togethers. If your friends and family are anything like ours, they often forget to RSVP and may not arrive at events on time. However, you can help your friends and family be a bit more prompt with just a couple drops of peppermint oil!

When sending out paper invitations, put a little bit of (diluted) peppermint oil on the tips of your fingers while you work, and refresh the oil every fifteen minutes or so. This will ensure that your invitations all go into the mail with a bit of peppermint oil on them.

Your family and friends will think your invitations smell nice, but peppermint oil is great for jogging the memory. The smell of the oil will put the date and time of your event firmly in the minds of everyone you invite!

Ari & Jason Mankey

November 20
Sunday

4ᵗʰ ♎

Color of the day: Amber
Incense of the day: Frankincense

honoring TDoR Vigil

November 20 is Transgender Day of Remembrance (TDoR), an observance that honors the memory of the transgender people whose lives have been lost in acts of anti-transgender violence. Healing isn't just for the living; we can do work that aids those who have passed on as well, whether we knew them or not, through vigils and similar rituals.

For TDoR, the vigil typically includes lighting a candle and reciting a list of names of all those lost in the past year. Look up those names (visit https://www.glaad.org/tdor) and prepare a white candle to burn on your altar. A contained tealight or glass votive will both work well. Light the candle, say the names, and pass along this message:

To those who have been lost,
you are not forgotten.

May this light be a beacon of hope
that shines in all dark places,

Guiding all to deeper
understanding and compassion.

Blessed be your spirit!

Laura Tempest Zakroff

November 21
Monday

4ᵗʰ ♎
☽ v/c 6:14 am
☽ → ♏ 12:16 pm

Color of the day: Ivory
Incense of the day: Clary sage

Onion Magic for Cleansing

Onions are associated with the underworld because they grow beneath the ground's surface and have a sharp aroma. They're used in magic to absorb negative energy and protect people from harm.

Cut an onion in quarters, leaving the skin on, and place the quarters in a shallow dish of salt. The dish could be placed under the bed of someone who is physically or emotionally sick, or anywhere you feel negative energy. This practice is best performed under a waning moon, but any lunar phase will work. Say:

With onion bulb and waning moon,

I ask for protection of this room.

The negative energy will be drawn into the onion. When it has done its work, usually a day later, throw the onion away outside or take the trash out of your home. Clap your hands seven times to represent that the work is done. Finally, wash your hands with aromatic soap and take a deep breath, knowing the negativity is gone.

Astrea Taylor

November 22
Tuesday

4th ♏

☉ → ♐ 3:20 am

Color of the day: Maroon
Incense of the day: Geranium

St. Cecilia's Day:
Let's have More Music!

We've always needed music. The music of Orpheus charmed all living things and even stones. When guilds were formed in the Middle Ages, St. Cecilia (who had magically caused an organ to burst into song) was adopted by musicians as their patron saint.

Bring harmony and joy—music—into your life more often. What music do you love? Find your favorite song on YouTube. Sing along! Can you attend a concert tonight? Sing and dance all day long today. Cast your circle with song and dance and celebrate the healing beauty of music with some lines from Shakespeare:

Give me some music;
music, moody food

Of us that trade in love.
(Antony and Cleopatra)

If music be the food of love, play on;
Give me excess of it. (Twelfth Night)

Barbara Ardinger

November 23
Wednesday

4th ♏

☽ v/c 1:16 pm

☽ → ♐ 3:16 pm

New Moon 5:57 pm

Color of the day: Topaz
Incense of the day: Bay laurel

New Moon Sweetgrass Cleansing

Welcome the new moon and its potential for great beginnings today. Let's align with the sweetness of *Hierochloe odorata*, which means "holy grass" and "fragrant." The common name for this herb, believed to be the braid of Mother Earth, is sweetgrass.

As one of the Four Sacred Medicines, sweetgrass is a special herb. Unlock its healing potential with a respectful offering to the ancestors by burning tobacco. Next, tap sweetgrass's ability to create good vibrations. Light an end and tamp out the flame to create a smoldering incense. Begin at the north door of your home and travel south, waving the smoke in open, closed, and corner spaces. Leave some sweetgrass at your southernmost door.

Use sweetgrass to cleanse the aura and sacred objects, bless a space, yield protective energies by carrying it in a pouch on your body, or hang it up indoors as a protective amulet.

Stephanie Rose Bird

November 24
Thursday

1st ♐

Color of the day: White
Incense of the day: Clove

Thanksgiving Day

Just Desserts for Abundance

Thanksgiving is often associated with overindulgence. However, it is also a time of abundance and appreciation. You can weave a little magick throughout your day. Create a little kitchen magick when baking your desserts for the day. While creating your dessert, you can chant this verse as you stir with a clockwise motion:

*Abundance is my wish for my
guests. May they ever be blessed.*

This is the perfect way to serve up to your guests your desire for them to cultivate abundance in their lives and give them a sweet treat. You can also create a decorative centerpiece with colorful flowers that incorporates cinnamon, clove, and nutmeg into it for a scent that permeates the house. Not only will it blend in with the pumpkin pie being served later, but the energies will work well with the desire for abundance!

Charlynn Walls

November 25
Friday

1st ♐

☽ v/c 2:22 pm
☽ → ♑ 4:18 pm

Color of the day: Rose
Incense of the day: Orchid

healing Meditation

Sit comfortably in a chair, with your back supported, and breathe. Place your palms on your thighs. Close your eyes. Feel your feet firmly on the earth and know you are grounded. Breathe deeply, pulling energy up from the earth.

Feel your backside and thighs on the chair and know you are supported. Feel your ribs and shoulders against the chair and know you are embraced. Feel your head sitting atop the structure of your body and know you are balanced. With each deep breath, draw from the earth, pulling strength and resilience up through your body. Move your hands up the middle of your body like you are doing up a zipper. Then with arms overhead, exhale and release energy from the top of your head, your arms sweeping out and around your body, creating your own personal space. Repeat, reinforcing your natural force field. Know you are grounded, supported, embraced, and balanced. You are love.

Dallas Jennifer Cobb

November 26
Saturday

1st ♑

Color of the day: Black
Incense of the day: Pine

A Fireside Divination

As the wind howls through the trees and rattles the storm door, a November night is a good time to settle in and divine by the fire. If you don't have a fireplace, a candle flame or a small fire in your cauldron are fine substitutes. Safely light your fire. Sit before it, think of a question, then speak these words into the fire:

I sit before the fire watching the flames,

*I watch the sparks and
the smoke as it rises.*

I'll gaze for letters, symbols, or names,

*So shall my fate be revealed
in many disguises.*

You might see only symbols, faces, or words, or you might see an entire image. When done, if you used a candle, safely snuff it out. You may use the candle again for scrying. If you built a fire, watch it as it goes out on its own. Some people continue to gaze into the dying embers.

James Kambos

November 27
Sunday

1st ♑

☽ v/c 3:11 pm

☽ → ♒ 5:07 pm

Color of the day: Gold
Incense of the day: Heliotrope

Bedknobs and Broomsticks

We spend a third of our lives asleep. While we dream, our body heals and our mind tries to make sense of our waking life. Sometimes we are able to resolve issues from the past while dreaming, and other times we are able to gain prophetic glimpses into the future.

It's wise to maintain a bubble of protection around our beds, especially as magickal folk. Anoint each corner of your bed with lavender essential oil (not synthetic "fragrant" oil). Do the same under your pillows and anywhere on your blankets that feels right. Place four pieces of amethyst under your bed or mattress at all corners. By the light of one candle (ideally violet), raise your arms above your bed and visualize a protective dome that is the color of lavender and amethyst. Declare:

*This rampart here is peaceful and
protecting of all my dreaming
and astral projecting!*

Extinguish the candle.

Raven Digitalis

November 28
Monday

1st ♒

Color of the day: White
Incense of the day: Neroli

Blessing the Traveler

The Rural Dionysia was a festival of fertility, travel, and entertainment. People baked phallic bread loaves and poured offerings of wine and water. They traveled from town to town visiting friends. They held games, contests, plays, concerts, and other revelries.

During the modern holiday season, people also travel, so now is a good time for a blessing. For this spell you will need wine or grape juice, plus a bit of ivy, such as a sprig of silk leaves, a metal brooch, etc.

Raise the ivy to the four directions in turn, saying:

For protection against dangers from the east, from the south, from the west, and from the north.

Sprinkle a few drops of wine or grape juice over the ivy. Then say:

Dionysus, god of revelry, guard the traveler along the journey. Let none be waylaid by mischance and all reach their destination safely.

Carry the ivy for protection while traveling.

Elizabeth Barrette

November 29
Tuesday

1st ♒

☽ v/c 1:53 am
☽ → ♓ 7:15 pm

Color of the day: Red
Incense of the day: Ginger

The Family You Create

The holidays can be difficult for people who don't have good relationships with their family, or even for those who do but who live far away from those they wish they could be with. Thankfully there is more than one kind of family. There is the family you were born to and the family you create. For many Witches, some of those folks may be part of the local Pagan community, if they have one. They might also be friends or people you work with or even your pets. This can be a good time to strengthen those ties or to open your home to other people who might need a "family" to share the holidays with. If this is something you want to work on this year, try lighting a candle and say:

Family made of friendship bright,

Help me make this season light.

Make sure to snuff out the candle when done.

Deborah Blake

November 30
Wednesday

1st ♓

2nd Quarter 9:37 am

Color of the day: Yellow
Incense of the day: Lilac

A Bathtime Rebalancing

There's nothing like a soak in the tub for relaxation, and if you can also cleanse and balance your personal energies, even better!

Gather these items:

- 1 cup kosher or sea salt
- ½ teaspoon or more of frankincense, juniper, lavender, or rosemary essential oil
- A bowl
- 3 bay leaves
- A white candle and holder
- An unbreakable cup
- A clean towel
- Clean pajamas

Place the salt and essential oil(s) in a bowl. Use your fingers to mix well.

Run a bath to your desired temperature, adding the salt mixture and the bay leaves directly under the water stream. Light the candle and place it safely near the tub.

When the tub is full, remove your clothes and toss them into the laundry. Step into the bath, feeling the cleansing waters close around you. If you can't immerse yourself, use the cup to pour water over your head. Feel your stress and tensions being washed away.

Step out, drying yourself with the towel and donning the pj's. Embrace a sense of freshness, renewal, and balance. Extinguish the candle.

Susan Pesznecker

NOTES:

December

Ｄecember features a palette of cool colors: white snow, silver icicles, evergreen, and, of course, blue—the bright cerulean sky on a clear, cold winter's day, or the deep navy velvet of the darkening nights, culminating on the longest night of the year, the winter solstice. This hue is reflected in December's birthstones: turquoise, zircon, tanzanite, and lapis. The notion of a stone representing each month has been linked to ayurvedic beliefs that suggest correspondences between the planets and crystals. It wasn't until the eighteenth century that associating stones with a birth month became a popular practice in the Western world.

Even if you weren't born in December, you can still tap into the power of this month's special stones. Zircon increases bone stability, which is good for moving over icy terrain. Use turquoise, a rain-making stone, to summon snow. Turquoise also heals and brings peace. Engage tanzanite's powers for psychic visions for the impending new year. Lapis—the mirror of the winter night sky, and a stone that can be found in the breastplate of the high priest—brings wisdom and awareness.

Natalie Zaman

December 1
Thursday

2nd ♓

☽ v/c 9:44 pm

☽ → ♈ 11:41 pm

Color of the day: Turquoise

Incense of the day: Balsam

Citrine Protection Spell

We love the holiday season, but it can be stressful and chaotic, turning otherwise good folks into giant balls of negative energy. We tend to encounter this negativity most often when we go Yule shopping. It would be one thing if people could keep their negativity to themselves, but that's seldom the case. Luckily, we always carry a secret weapon with us: a citrine crystal.

Citrine is a pale yellow quartz, and it's our favorite crystal to use for protection. Before going shopping, place a piece of citrine in your pocket or purse. When you feel the bad energy of others starting to creep up on you, grab the citrine with your dominant hand and say either aloud or in your head:

My citrine is a shield.

Bad energy must yield!

The citrine will act as a shield, blocking the negative energy.

Ari & Jason Mankey

December 2
Friday

2nd ♈

Color of the day: Pink

Incense of the day: Cypress

Holiday Spirit

Early winter is the holiday season. Many cultures feature major holidays at this time: some fixed, like Christmas, some based on astronomical events, like Yule, and others more variable, like Hanukkah. If you have friends from many traditions, you could wind up celebrating all month long. This creates a sense of holiday spirit. Sometimes all the excitement can get exhausting, though.

Here is an invocation for the Holiday Spirit to help you through this time. You will need a symbol of your favorite winter holiday, such as a sprig of mistletoe or a holly-shaped pin for Yule. Hold your hands over the symbol and say:

I invoke the Holiday Spirit. Watch over me in your season as I celebrate Yule. [Add any other holidays you plan to observe, too.]

Let my mind stay calm, my heart joyful, and my body full of energy. As I will, so mote it be.

Afterward, hang the symbol in your home if you will be hosting events, or wear it if you plan to visit more.

Elizabeth Barrette

December 3
Saturday

2nd ♈

Color of the day: Indigo
Incense of the day: Ivy

Sigil Bell Spell

Bells are often used in witchcraft to call forth blessings, to bring a change, or to call spirits. Bells are even more powerful when they're charged with a sigil. This historical practice has roots in witchcraft. This spell requires a bell, paper, and a marker (fine-tipped if possible).

Ring the bell and determine your intention for the bell. Speak your intention out loud with confidence, and write it down on the paper. Next, write down seven words associated with the intention. Draw symbols for each word. Combine the symbols to form a sigil.

When your sigil is done, hold the bell, close your eyes, and really feel your intention. Envision your sigil floating before you, then see it catch fire and sustain the flame.

With the marker, draw the sigil on the inside of the bell. Imagine the flame touching this sigil too.

Ring the bell, and as the sound travels, envision that the sigil's meaning is being carried forth. Ring the bell nine more times to complete the spell.

Astrea Taylor

December 4
Sunday

2nd ♈

☽ v/c 12:46 am

☽ → ♉ 6:38 am

Color of the day: Orange
Incense of the day: Juniper

Drawing the Sugarplum Faeries

When Witches think about "drawing," we often think of invocation, such as Wicca's poetic "Drawing Down the Moon" written by Doreen Valiente. For this spell, we will actually be drawing with pencils, pens, markers, paints, or whatever suits your fancy.

Winter is renowned to be a time when faeries and Upper World spirits interact with those on the mortal plane.

Go outside to a place where you can sit comfortably. Make an offering to the fae, such as cookies, milk, honey, or anything sweet. Ask the wintertime faeries to surround you with their abundance and joy, and tell them you'd like to sketch their image. Smile and ask politely!

Take time drawing one or more images of whatever comes to mind. You will likely find yourself entering a trancelike state while doing so. Place these images on your wintertime altar or keep them in a sacred space so their magick can be preserved.

Raven Digitalis

December 5
Monday

2nd ♉

Color of the day: Lavender
Incense of the day: Narcissus

holly Blessing Spell

Holly is a popular Yuletide seasonal plant because of its bright red berries and evergreen leaves. It is ruled by Saturn and is often used in magic for protection, drawing good fortune, warding off storms, and repelling the evil eye. If you're looking for a beneficial bush or small tree to plant near the front door of your house, holly is definitely a friend to Witches. Remember to give it small offerings throughout the year (even just some kind words praising its strength and beauty) and tend to its needs.

If you cannot plant anything where you live, take advantage of the season to procure a small bunch of holly branches to hang on your door. Bind them together with a festive ribbon, and upon hanging, say:

Holly, holly, berry bright,

Please guard our home, day and night.

Laura Tempest Zakroff

December 6
Tuesday

2nd ♉

☽ v/c 2:02 pm

☽ → ♊ 3:49 pm

Color of the day: White
Incense of the day: Bayberry

A Blue Christmas Spell

For many people, the holiday season isn't cheery or bright. For some, it's a blue and sad time. Loneliness, grief, and joblessness are more deeply felt now. This spell will help you find those in need and make the season more bearable for them.

First sit at your altar and safely light a red candle. Red is the color of the life force. Visualize the candle flame spreading out and touching those in need with its warmth. Ask the Divine to guide you to the right person or place that will connect you with those in need. Then safely snuff out your candle and begin your search for ways to help. You could start at your county department of job and family services. They have lists of items needed by their clients, or maybe they need volunteers to wrap gifts, etc. Local schools will know of children in need, too. Keep visualizing your kindness spreading to help others.

James Kambos

December 7
Wednesday

2nd ♊

Full Moon 11:08 pm

Color of the day: Brown
Incense of the day: Marjoram

Writing Down the Moon

The full moon is a time of power. It's a great time to do work that manifests energy or requires introspection. One powerful approach to looking within is freewriting, a process that opens the channels between the brain, hand, and paper, allowing access to ideas and memories that otherwise might remain hidden.

For this exercise you'll need:

- A fluorite or moonstone
- A cup of peppermint tea
- Paper
- Pen or pencil
- A location from which you can see the full moon

A few minutes before the moon is full tonight, sit down. Raise your stone to the moon and feel the rising energies. Sip the tea, heightening your mental clarity.

As the moon becomes full, start writing. Pick a subject, or just write about whatever comes to mind. Write without stopping to edit or make corrections. Don't worry about forming full sentences—just write. Let the lunar energies flow through you and onto the page, and write in whatever direction it takes you, perhaps veering into unknown corners to find once-lost memories and details.

You are inspired, writing down the moon.

Susan Pesznecker

NOTES:

December 8
Thursday

3rd ♊

Color of the day: Green
Incense of the day: Mulberry

Goddesses of Light

Lucina was an early Italian goddess of light who merged with Juno and Diana to bring us the light that overcomes the dark. In the fourth century, Lucina was renamed as St. Lucy, a Sicilian girl who vowed to distribute her family's wealth to the poor. Somehow Lucy and her sacred light were carried to Scandinavia, where the winter nights seem endless. For her feast, little girls wear garlands and everyone carries Lucy candles. Let us celebrate Lucina and Lucy.

Cast your full moon circle and light silver candles. (The moon was full late last night.) Breathe the light of the full moon and the candles into your heart and then be silent. See and feel the full moon's light coming closer and bringing the lunar magic into your heart and hands. When you're ready, invoke the full moon:

Under the full moon's light

And with clearest sight,

I see and love

With understanding,

Without illusions,

With an open heart.

I love and honor

The people in my life,

The work I do,

My blessed life.

Barbara Ardinger

NOTES:

December 9
Friday

3rd ♊

☽ v/c 1:13 am

☽ → ♋ 2:49 am

Color of the day: Coral
Incense of the day: Violet

Rosemary Aura Strengthening

Today's Cancer moon means you're likely to feel extra emotional and sensitive, which is not a bad thing. Still, as we quickly approach the coldest and darkest point on the Wheel of the Year, it may be desirable to give your mind, heart, and energy field a magical boost.

Today, bring home a living rosemary plant in a pot. Some stores sell rosemary in the shape of a holiday tree at this time of year, but any rosemary will do. Gently snip a tiny sprig of rosemary. Sit comfortably, breathe deeply, and rub the rosemary between your fingers to release the scent. Then inhale and feel that you are breathing bright green energy into your body. Continue to breathe in the fresh scent as you feel it awakening your mind, fortifying your heart, and fueling your body and aura with vibrant health. Send gratitude to the rosemary plant. Vow to take wonderful care of it, and know that you can come back to this simple ritual whenever you'd like.

Tess Whitehurst

December 10
Saturday

3rd ♋

Color of the day: Brown
Incense of the day: Pine

Pendulum Decision Spell

Harness your inner wisdom, and use a pendulum to amplify your energy, making it visible. A crystal on a chain, a ring on a string, or even a necklace with a charm can be used as a pendulum. Hold the chain, string, or cord in your dominant hand (the one you write with). Begin with a statement you know to be true, such as this:

My name is _____ (your name).

Observe the movement of the pendulum. This is your "yes." (Many people find that the pendulum moves like our head moves when we indicate yes and no. It moves forward and back for yes, and side to side, left to right, to indicate no.) Practice statements that are true and false, and observe the pendulum's response. There will be a distinct "yes" and a distinct "no." It takes a while to "train" a pendulum and learn to read its responses, but with regular use you will have a divination tool to amplify and help you read energy. A pendulum can be useful to test foods, determining which foods are "good" and which are "bad" for you.

Dallas Jennifer Cobb

December 11
Sunday

3rd ♋

☽ v/c 1:49 pm

☽ → ♌ 3:09 pm

Color of the day: Amber
Incense of the day: Almond

Mountain of Memories Altar

Today, on International Mountain Day, begin the construction of a ritual altar that will take you into the next year. You can also create this altar for just today, this week, this month, or whatever makes the most sense to you and your situation.

You'll need a pen, some sticky notes, and a blank wall (the front of a refrigerator works well too!). Cleanse and clear the space you will use. At the end of the day, write a note or draw a picture that represents what happened that day, whether it be cheerful or challenging, supportive or painful (keep it real), and place it on your chosen surface. You can also create multiple notes and images if the day was memorable for many reasons. Day after day, the mountain will grow. Build up the base and watch it take shape. You can arrange the notes in a triangular shape (although not all mountain formations are like that) or let it grow organically.

Next December 11 (or for however long you've decided to build your altar), "climb" the mountain by reviewing each memory. Meditate on how it has shaped your present and helped you grow, and give thanks. Safely burn the notes and scatter the cooled ashes to release them.

Natalie Zaman

NOTES:

December 12
Monday

3rd ♌

Color of the day: White
Incense of the day: Rosemary

Meditation for Peace

The holidays can be crazy and more than a little stressful. There are expectations and obligations, and even the fun parts take energy. It can be overwhelming, even if you enjoy this time of year (and not everyone does). Some folks fight with depression, anxiety, or loneliness. Whether you love the holidays or hate them, everyone can benefit from taking a break and doing this easy meditation for peace and calm. If you want, you can light a candle in a fire-safe container and gaze at the flames. Then read or say these words:

> I am calm and at peace,
>
> Although chaos may be all around me.
>
> I am the eye at the center of the storm.
>
> I am the quiet breath and
> the softly falling snow.
>
> I am calm and at peace.
>
> I am calm and at peace.
>
> Ahhhhhh.

Then just breathe for a few minutes before blowing out the candle.

Deborah Blake

December 13
Tuesday

3rd ♌

☽ v/c 10:52 am

Color of the day: Gray
Incense of the day: Cinnamon

Waning Gibbous Moon
Purging Ritual

The waning gibbous moon is a fascinating lunar phase. During this time, the moon is only partially illuminated, as it's decreasing in size. Here are some things to do as the moon gets smaller:

* Reduce some unwanted characteristics and habits.
* Learn to become more attentive.
* Dedicate more energy to positive intentions.
* Relinquish or delegate tasks.
* Reduce stress and aggravation.
* Shun bad vibes.

On a piece of paper, make a list of what you want to change in your life. On a separate sheet of paper, write down how you will go about making those changes.

Take the first paper outside at dusk. Dig a shallow space in the earth. Say:

Under the diminishing light of Luna, I submit to change.

Bury the first sheet of paper (containing the things you want to change) and say:

My habits, obligations, life, dear Luna, I leave it all to you to rearrange.

Your power is in your ability to evolve, and so is mine.

Please help me with my changes, line by line.

Fold the second sheet up tightly and place it beneath your pillow.

Stephanie Rose Bird

NOTES:

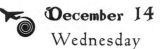

December 14
Wednesday

3rd ♌

☽ → ♍ 3:45 am

Color of the day: Topaz
Incense of the day: Lavender

Spirited Communication

Wednesdays are good for communication, as they tap into the energy of the planet and Roman god Mercury. Working with Mercury or his Greek counterpart, Hermes, is a perfect choice today, as he is the messenger between the worlds. He can help you communicate with others on the mortal plane or with those who have passed on.

Take a piece of paper and write what you wish to communicate to the other party on it. Fold the paper in half and draw the wing of Hermes's shoes to indicate your desire to work with him to deliver your message. As you draw the image, say:

Lord Mercury, take this written
passage and deliver my message.

You can then burn the paper in a fireproof container so that the message is spirited away.

Charlynn Walls

December 15
Thursday

3rd ♍

Color of the day: Purple
Incense of the day: Clove

Chamber of Healing

At night, while sitting in bed, come into a light meditative state and visualize your bedroom transforming into a magical healing chamber that is perfect for you in every way. Perhaps the mattress and linens are aglow with a matrix of healing light or your bed becomes a float tank filled with beautiful rose petals, where you are effortlessly supported by the water.

Allow yourself to surrender to the healing energy, intending that you will receive what is correct and good for you while you sleep. Sweet dreams!

The next morning, give thanks for the healing energy, and after you climb out of bed, wipe the image of the healing chamber from the screen of your mind, like erasing a chalkboard, returning your room to a neutral state. Know that you can call up the healing chamber whenever you need to.

Melissa Tipton

December 16

Friday

3rd ♏

4th Quarter 3:56 am

☽ v/c 2:13 pm

☽ → ♎ 2:49 pm

Color of the day: Rose

Incense of the day: Vanilla

A Blessing for the home

In winter, everything is cold and dark. When no one is home, the houses, too, stand dark, covered in unmelting snow—but those with people inside shine bright and warm, spilling golden light through their windows. Now is a good time to bless your home.

For this blessing you will need a slice of bread (preferably homemade) and a pinch of salt (preferably sea salt). First hold the bread and say:

I bless this bread, the staff of life,

May it be free of loss and strife.

Then hold the salt and say:

I bless this salt, so bright and clean,

No evil in its sight be seen.

Sprinkle the salt over the bread and say:

I bless this home with salt and bread,

Its hearth and hall, its bath and bed.

Let those who dwell within be blessed

With peace and love in every breast.

Eat the bread. Then walk through the rooms of your home and repeat the last verse once in each room.

Elizabeth Barrette

NOTES:

 December 17
Saturday

🜍 ♎

Color of the day: Blue
Incense of the day: Sandalwood

Saturnalia Feast Blessing

The Roman holiday Saturnalia begins today. It honors Saturn, the god of wealth and agriculture. Historically, it was a time of feasting, drinking, dancing, games, and role reversal of kings and servants. Evergreen boughs were brought inside and candles were lit.

This meal blessing recalls some of the merriment associated with that time. All you need is a meal, beverages, an evergreen bough, taper candles, and a lighter.

Set the table with the greenery and the candles in the middle. Light the candles and raise your drink. Say:

Today we feast as royalty

On the land's great bounty.

*May all who dine here
find some pleasure*

*In dancing, drinking,
gaming, and leisure.*

For Saturn calls us to rejoice,

Have fun and frivolity in raised voice.

Cheers to Saturn and the Golden Age!

May we relish these fruitful days!

Enjoy every bite and sip. Set aside some for Saturn, then play games or dance to celebrate life and your successes. When the day is done, extinguish the candles.

Astrea Taylor

NOTES:

December 18
Sunday

4th ♎
☽ v/c 5:35 pm
☽ → ♏ 10:31 pm

Color of the day: Gold
Incense of the day: Eucalyptus

hanukkah begins at sundown

Safe Travels Amulet

At this time of year, many of us travel to see family and friends, often navigating winter weather conditions, busy airports and depots, and crowded highways. Craft this handy amulet to take with you to smooth your path, keep things on time, and reduce stress levels.

You'll need:

- A 3 x 3-inch square of blue fabric
- A shiny dime or similar silvery coin
- 1 teaspoon dried feverfew flowers
- A pinch of lavender flowers
- 18 inches of green ribbon or thread

Lay out the fabric, then place the coin and herbs in the center. Draw up the four corners and gently twist them clockwise, creating a "neck." Tie the green ribbon around the neck, knotting it once to close. Then wrap the loose ends from both directions until you have just enough for one more knot, saying as you wind the thread:

Clear ways be mine,
stress-free, on time.

Laura Tempest Zakroff

NOTES:

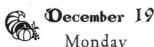

 December 19
Monday

4th ♏

Color of the day: Silver
Incense of the day: Clary sage

Thirteen Bucks for Luck

In honor of the season of giving, this is a fun spell to perform that not only creates good luck for yourself but also blesses others with a small auspicious surprise.

Get thirteen dollar bills (or the smallest currency note in your country), and anoint each one with essential oil of patchouli or vetiver. Make sure they are nice and scented! Place these in an envelope on which you have drawn sacred symbols of abundance, luck, and joy.

Face the direction north while declaring:

Prosperous spirits of abundance, hear my call! Bless these thirteen bucks with infinite luck. As I will, so mote it be!

Walk around town and secretly place these bills where people will find them with a smile. If you have a bit of extra cash to spare, consider doing this with two-dollar bills or five-dollar bills, or a different monetary amount, depending on your country's currency.

Raven Digitalis

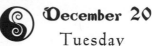

 December 20
Tuesday

4th ♏
☽ v/c 9:45 pm

Color of the day: Red
Incense of the day: Ginger

The Power of Two

Twosomes are dynamic duos and even-Steven. They represent the balance of give-and-take and perfect partnerships. As we stand on the threshold of winter, invoke the power of two to help you balance as the season shifts. Write today's date on a piece of paper, adding up the numbers until they funnel down to two:

1+2 (Dec.) 2+0 (day) 2+0 2+2 (year)

3+2 2+4

5+6

1+1

2

Fold up the paper and carry it with you. At the hour of the solstice, burn the paper safely in a fireproof dish. When all the embers are out and the ashes have cooled, scatter them to release the energy.

Natalie Zaman

December 21
Wednesday

4th ♏

☽ → ♐ 2:12 am

☉ → ♑ 4:48 pm

Color of the day: White

Incense of the day: Bay laurel

Yule – Winter Solstice

Yule Candle Spell

This spell invokes the power of Yule into your home. It can be done before starting a Yule ritual, a celebratory gathering, or a dinner. You'll need one taper candle in whatever color reminds you of Yuletide. Place your candle in a prominent place wherever you are doing your work. Take a deep breath and think of the beauty of the holiday season. Envision the sun growing in the sky and the joy present on so many faces this time of year. With those images in your mind, light your candle and say:

I invoke the blessings of this time of year,

Merriment, mirth, and all people of good cheer!

Gifts, peace, growth, and wonder I do invoke,

Timeless Yuletide magick for all of the folk!

Your space will be filled with the magick of Yule while the candle burns. Extinguish it when done.

Ari & Jason Mankey

December 22
Thursday

4th ♐

☽ v/c 3:16 pm

Color of the day: Crimson

Incense of the day: Apricot

A Pine Purification Spell

Pine is physically and emotionally clearing and healing. In this spell it's used to clear away emotional stress, which is common at this time of year. You'll need one pine cone, a small pine branch with soft needles, a white piece of fabric, and a fireproof container.

First cover your altar with the fabric. Place your fireproof container in the center of the altar, then place the pine cone and the pine branch on either side of the container. Now hold the pine cone and project your stressful feelings/problem into it. Place the pine cone in the container and carefully ignite it. It'll flare quickly, then burn out. Next, brush yourself lightly from head to toe with the pine branch. This will get rid of any lingering negativity. When the pine cone ashes are safely cool, throw them away. End by placing the pine branch at the base of any tree as an offering to nature and the Divine.

James Kambos

December 23
Friday

4th ♐

☽ → ♑ 2:49 am

New Moon 5:17 am

Color of the day: Pink
Incense of the day: Mint

Metaphorical Seeds (Wishes)

As we know, the new moon signals the beginning not only of the lunar cycle but of something in our lives. To help that something be born, we can plant seeds, either real or metaphorical. If metaphorical, what do you want to plant and grow? Write your wishes ("seeds") on small pieces of paper and hide them along with a tiny crystal in a small biodegradable box or container. Hold your container in your receptive (non-dominant) hand as you cast your circle outside under the new moon, if you can do so in private and without the interference of neighbors.

Speak these words to the new moon:

Here I plant my seeds,

Here I plant my dreams,

Here I set my wishes.

Here I sprout new plans—

As I will it,

Let it grow.

I will see my seeds

Growing, growing, growing,

As the moonlight grows,

Budding, blooming, fruiting.

As I will it,

So let it be.

Bury your container of seeds in your yard.

Barbara Ardinger

NOTES:

December 24
Saturday

1st ♑

☽ v/c 10:11 pm

Color of the day: Indigo
Incense of the day: Rue

Christmas Eve

Gifting hope

Christmas Eve is a time for gatherings and merriment with those who are closest to us. It can also be a good time to focus on the hope that you have for your friends and family who are gathered or will be gathering during the Yuletide season. Some traditions have a single gift opened on Christmas Eve. You can turn this into a way to gift hope to others during this season.

Take a small jar and fill it with items that make you feel hopeful or have a tie to the individual you are gifting it to. Seal the jar with a lid and wax if you'd like. Each one of these gifts will be unique and special. On a piece of parchment, write what you hope the recipient will see within the next year. Finish by tying to the lid a small red ribbon with the piece of parchment attached.

Charlynn Walls

December 25
Sunday

1st ♑

☽ → ♒ 2:14 am

Color of the day: Yellow
Incense of the day: Marigold

Christmas Day

Gift Giving

Today is Christmas, which marks the birth of Jesus Christ, from whom the holiday gets its name. Whether or not you were raised a Christian, you probably celebrate this time with gift giving. It is said that three wise men traveled a long distance to bring the new child gifts, but you don't have to spend a lot of money on frankincense and myrrh in order to celebrate the holiday. While it is always nice to have a fancy wrapped box under your Christmas (or Yule) tree, remember that there are other gifts we have to give. The gift of love is priceless, as is the gift of time and energy to spend with those who need us. Acceptance, friendship, and shared knowledge are also gifts. Remember that this holiday isn't about who can buy the biggest present, but rather how present you are with those you love.

Deborah Blake

December 26
Monday

1st ♈ ♒

☽ v/c 1:19 pm

Color of the day: Gray
Incense of the day: Neroli

hanukkah ends –
Kwanzaa begins –
Boxing Day (Canada & UK)

Sharing the Unity of Kwanzaa

It's the first day of Kwanzaa, and today celebrants honor the concept of unity. You can honor this day magically with a ceremony of unity for your family and ancestors.

Prepare by creating a list or a family tree of your family members, as many as you know or can recall.

You'll also need a special cup or goblet, a beverage to be shared, family photographs, and a candle. Ask each family member attending to bring a favorite item that reminds them of the family.

Gather your family members at the dining table, inviting them to place their items on the table with the photos. Light the candle safely. Ask everyone to share a favorite family memory, then read aloud the list of family members sharing memories. Pour the libation into the cup, and pass it around the table. Ask everyone to drink in honor of family, past and present.

Join hands and say:

Together, our family is strong.
Present and past, we endure.
May it always be so.

Extinguish the candle.

Susan Pesznecker

NOTES:

December 27
Tuesday

1st ♒

☽ → ♓ 2:34 am

Color of the day: Scarlet
Incense of the day: Basil

Traveling with Tea

This period of time over the holidays, with kids out of school and workplaces holding those dreaded parties, might leave you in need of peace and quiet and some time alone. But maybe your home is still filled with people, or perhaps you are visiting relatives in their space.

Put on the kettle, choose your favorite mug from the cupboard, and get ready for the power of tea. Black tea has antioxidants and other compounds that improve cardiovascular and neurological health. Plus it provides comfort. Pour boiling water on a tea bag and let steep for five minutes. Mix in milk, sugar, or lemon, then pause.

Wrap your hands around the mug and feel the warmth. Close your eyes and inhale the fragrant steam. Now sip and taste and appreciate the tea, knowing that even in this busy season, there are moments of comfort, safety, and ease. And you've made one.

Dallas Jennifer Cobb

December 28
Wednesday

1st ♓

Color of the day: Yellow
Incense of the day: Honeysuckle

Tea with the Mighty Dead

The Mighty Dead are the spirits of accomplished magical practitioners, teachers, and honored guides who have crossed over. They may or may not be related to us by blood or lineage, but they are powerful beings we can look to for inspiration and guidance. If you didn't know them in life, then it's good to start with an introduction before formally setting them up on your altar and working with them. To do this, review the work they did (books, songs, art, speeches, etc.) that has inspired you. Frame a photo or other image of them and place it on a table you can sit at, facing you. Prepare two cups of tea (appropriate for the hour), one for yourself and one for them. Between you, set and light a white candle, and say:

> I welcome you, (name of Mighty Dead). Please join me for tea.

Sit quietly, enjoying your tea and focusing on their image. Make note of whatever words or feelings come to you to determine if you can work with them further. Extinguish the candle.

Laura Tempest Zakroff

December 29
Thursday

1st ♉ ♓

☽ v/c 1:21 am

☽ → ♈ 5:36 am

2nd Quarter 8:21 pm

Color of the day: Green
Incense of the day: Jasmine

Smoke Gazing

As we head into the new year, let's do some smoke divination with copal. Copal's aroma can quickly put you in a trancelike state, and for that reason it's revered by visionaries, shamans, and energy healers. This food of the gods in several venerable cultures should be used in a very well-ventilated area or outdoors. Once lit, copal produces copious amounts of smoke, and it will relax your senses. Let's look into copal smoke's shape formations to see what's revealed.

To begin the ritual, light an incense charcoal and put it in a sturdy shell or on a fireproof plate. Put a small copal nugget on the white-hot charcoal. Invoke the Corn Mothers as you wave a whole maize in the copal smoke. Say:

Maize, I ask you respectfully to open the way. Reveal to me all that I need to see to ensure success and abundance in the coming year.

Place the maize next to the smoldering copal and gaze deeply into the smoke. Let the aroma permeate your thoughts. Reflect on the smoke signals and notice shapes that appear. Seek out messages in the signs, symbols, and shapes created by the smoke, inspired by the aroma. When done, extinguish the incense.

Stephanie Rose Bird

NOTES:

December 30
Friday

2nd ♈

Color of the day: Purple
Incense of the day: Alder

The Power of Quitting Cleanly

The end of the year is an ideal time for practicing something I call "quitting cleanly." Often we have a long list of things we feel we should be doing, yet we find ourselves endlessly procrastinating. When we allow ourselves to consciously release these lingering "shoulds," this frees our energy and focus for more soul-aligned pursuits.

Quitting cleanly doesn't necessarily mean that you'll never decide to do this thing again; it simply means that right now you're liberating yourself from the energy-draining pressure of "should" so you can start fresh.

On a piece of paper, write down any nagging projects you're ready to quit cleanly. Roll the paper into a scroll, rolling away from your body, then safely light the paper on fire in a heat-proof dish. Feel the energy separating from these commitments, reentering the cosmic cycle, where it can be used for other purposes. Let the ashes cool, then bury them or throw them away with gratitude.

Melissa Tipton

December 31
Saturday

2nd ♈
☽ v/c 7:44 am
☽ → ♉ 12:08 pm

Color of the day: Black
Incense of the day: Magnolia

New Year's Eve

Self-Love Manifesto

You don't have to love yourself in order for other people to love you. But loving yourself sure does make a positive difference in every aspect of your life! And no matter how much you love yourself now, you can always love yourself more.

Today, pave the way for greater self-love than ever before. Light some cinnamon incense. Then, in a journal, list every self-loving thing you can think of that you did for yourself this year. How did you set boundaries? In what ways did you speak kindly to yourself? How did you take care of yourself? Now, with kindness and nonjudgment, list the areas where you didn't love yourself as much as you'd like and the ways you could have loved yourself even more. Finally, write a self-love manifesto in which you commit to loving yourself unconditionally in the year ahead. In what ways will this manifest? How will it look? How will it feel? Sign your manifesto and date it. Extinguish the incense.

Tess Whitehurst

Daily Magical Influences

Each day is ruled by a planet that possesses specific magical influences:

Monday (Moon): peace, healing, caring, psychic awareness, purification

Tuesday (Mars): passion, sex, courage, aggression, protection

Wednesday (Mercury): conscious mind, study, travel, divination, wisdom

Thursday (Jupiter): expansion, money, prosperity, generosity

Friday (Venus): love, friendship, reconciliation, beauty

Saturday (Saturn): longevity, exorcism, endings, homes, houses

Sunday (Sun): healing, spirituality, success, strength, protection

Lunar Phases

The lunar phase is important in determining best times for magic.

The new moon is when the moon and sun are conjunct each other. It corresponds to all new beginnings and is the best time to start a project.

The waxing moon (from the new moon to the full moon) is the ideal time for magic to draw things to you.

The full moon is when the sun and moon are opposite each other. It is the time of greatest power.

The waning moon (from the full moon to the new moon) is a time for study, meditation, and little magical work (except magic designed to banish harmful energies).

Astrological Symbols

The Sun	☉		Aries	♈
The Moon	☽		Taurus	♉
Mercury	☿		Gemini	♊
Venus	♀		Cancer	♋
Mars	♂		Leo	♌
Jupiter	♃		Virgo	♍
Saturn	♄		Libra	♎
Uranus	♅		Scorpio	♏
Neptune	♆		Sagittarius	♐
Pluto	♇		Capricorn	♑
			Aquarius	♒
			Pisces	♓

The Moon's Sign

The moon's sign is a traditional consideration for astrologers. The moon continuously moves through each sign in the zodiac, from Aries to Pisces. The moon influences the sign it inhabits, creating different energies that affect our daily lives.

Aries: Good for starting things but lacks staying power. Things occur rapidly but quickly pass. People tend to be argumentative and assertive.

Taurus: Things begun now do last, tend to increase in value, and become hard to alter. Brings out an appreciation for beauty and sensory experience.

Gemini: Things begun now are easily changed by outside influence. Time for shortcuts, communications, games, and fun.

Cancer: Stimulates emotional rapport between people. Pinpoints need, supports growth and nurturance. Tend to domestic concerns.

Leo: Draws emphasis to the self, to central ideas or institutions, away from connections with others and emotional needs. People tend to be melodramatic.

Virgo: Favors accomplishment of details and commands from higher up. Focus on health, hygiene, and daily schedules.

Libra: Favors cooperation, compromise, social activities, beautification of surroundings, balance, and partnership.

Scorpio: Increases awareness of psychic power. Favors activities requiring intensity and focus. People tend to brood and become secretive under this moon sign.

Sagittarius: Encourages flights of imagination and confidence. This moon sign is adventurous, philosophical, and athletic. Favors expansion and growth.

Capricorn: Develops strong structure. Focus on traditions, responsibilities, and obligations. A good time to set boundaries and rules.

Aquarius: Rebellious energy. Time to break habits and make abrupt change. Personal freedom and individuality are the focus.

Pisces: The focus is on dreaming, nostalgia, intuition, and psychic impressions. A good time for spiritual or philanthropic activities.

Glossary of Magical Terms

Altar: A table that holds magical tools as a focus for spell workings.

Athame: A ritual knife used to direct personal power during workings or to symbolically draw diagrams in a spell. It is rarely, if ever, used for actual physical cutting.

Aura: An invisible energy field surrounding a person. The aura can change color depending on the state of the individual.

Balefire: A fire lit for magical purposes, usually outdoors.

Casting a circle: The process of drawing a circle around oneself to seal out unfriendly influences and raise magical power. It is the first step in a spell.

Censer: An incense burner. Traditionally a censer is a metal container, filled with incense, that is swung on the end of a chain.

Censing: The process of burning incense to spiritually cleanse an object.

Centering yourself: To prepare for a magical rite by calming and centering all of your personal energy.

Chakra: One of the seven centers of spiritual energy in the human body, according to the philosophy of yoga.

Charging: To infuse an object with magical power.

Circle of protection: A circle cast to protect oneself from unfriendly influences.

Crystals: Quartz or other stones that store cleansing or protective energies.

Deosil: Clockwise movement, symbolic of life and positive energies.

Deva: A divine being according to Hindu beliefs; a devil or evil spirit according to Zoroastrianism.

Direct/retrograde: Refers to the motion of a planet when seen from the earth. A planet is "direct" when it appears to be moving forward from the point of view of a person on the earth. It is "retrograde" when it appears to be moving backward.

Dowsing: To use a divining rod to search for a thing, usually water or minerals.

Dowsing pendulum: A long cord with a coin or gem at one end. The pattern of its swing is used to answer questions.

Dryad: A tree spirit or forest guardian.

Fey: An archaic term for a magical spirit or a fairylike being.

Gris-gris: A small bag containing charms, herbs, stones, and other items to draw energy, luck, love, or prosperity to the wearer.

Mantra: A sacred chant used in Hindu tradition to embody the divinity invoked; it is said to possess deep magical power.

Needfire: A ceremonial fire kindled at dawn on major Wiccan holidays. It was traditionally used to light all other household fires.

Pentagram: A symbolically protective five-pointed star with one point upward.

Power hand: The dominant hand; the hand used most often.

Scry: To predict the future by gazing at or into an object such as a crystal ball or pool of water.

Second sight: The psychic power or ability to foresee the future.

Sigil: A personal seal or symbol.

Smudge/smudge stick: To spiritually cleanse an object by waving smoke over and around it. A smudge stick is a bundle of several incense sticks.

Wand: A stick or rod used for casting circles and as a focus for magical power.

Widdershins: Counterclockwise movement, symbolic of negative magical purposes, sometimes used to disperse negative energies.

About the Authors

Barbara Ardinger, PhD (www.barbaraardinger.com), has been writing for the Llewellyn annuals for nearly a decade and has been creating and leading rituals for nearly thirty years. She is the author of *Secret Lives*, a novel about a circle of crones, mothers, and maidens, plus goddesses, a talking cat, and the Green Man. Her earlier books include the daybook *Pagan Every Day*, *Goddess Meditations*, *Finding New Goddesses* (a parody of goddess encyclopedias), and *Quicksilver Moon* (a realistic novel…except for the vampire). Her day job is freelance editing for people who have good ideas but don't want to embarrass themselves in print. Barbara lives in Southern California with her two rescued cats, Heisenberg and Schroedinger.

Elizabeth Barrette has been involved with the Pagan community for more than thirty-one years. She served as managing editor of *PanGaia* for eight years and dean of studies at the Grey School of Wizardry for four years. She has written columns on beginning and intermediate Pagan practice, Pagan culture, and Pagan leadership. Her book *Composing Magic: How to Create Magical Spells, Rituals, Blessings, Chants, and Prayers* explains how to combine writing and spirituality. She lives in central Illinois, where she has done much networking with Pagans in her area, such as coffeehouse meetings and open sabbats. Her other public activities include Pagan picnics and science fiction conventions. She enjoys magical crafts, historical religions, and gardening for wildlife. Her other writing fields include speculative fiction, gender studies, and social and environmental issues. Visit her blog, *The Wordsmith's Forge* (https://ysabetwordsmith.dreamwidth.org/), or website, PenUltimate Productions (http://penultimateproductions.weebly.com). Her coven site, which includes extensive Pagan materials, is Greenhaven Tradition (http://greenhaventradition.weebly.com/).

Stephanie Rose Bird has written for several Llewellyn annuals and written four Llewellyn books, including the award-winning and bestselling *Sticks, Stones, Roots & Bones* and *365 Days of Hoodoo*. Her soon-to-be published ancestry magick book is called *Spirits in My Bones*. She has written several other books on magick and anthropology and is also the author of several magical realism fantasy YA novels. Bird is an eclectic pagan, practicing shamanism, green witchcraft, and hoodoo. She lives with her husband, family, and animals in Chicagoland. Her website is http://www.stephanierosebird.com. Follow her on Instagram @s.r.bird,

Twitter @stephanierosebi, and Facebook at https://www.facebook.com /stephanierosebirdauthor.

Deborah Blake is the award-winning author of eleven books on modern Witchcraft from Llewellyn, including *The Goddess Is in the Details*, *Everyday Witchcraft*, and *The Little Book of Cat Magic*, along with the popular Everyday Witch tarot and oracle decks. *Modern Witchcraft: Goddess Worship for the Kick-Ass Woman* was published by St. Martin's Press in 2020. She has published many articles in the Llewellyn annuals, and her ongoing column, "Everyday Witchcraft," is featured in *Witches & Pagans* magazine. She is also the author of the Baba Yaga and Broken Rider paranormal romance series and the Veiled Magic urban fantasies from Berkley. Deborah can be found online at Facebook, Twitter, Instagram, her popular blog (*Writing the Witchy Way*), and her website, www.deborahblakeauthor.com. She lives in a 130-year-old farmhouse in rural upstate New York with various cats who supervise all her activities, both magickal and mundane.

Dallas Jennifer Cobb lives in a magical village on Lake Ontario. A Pagan, mother, feminist, writer, and animal lover, she has conjured a sustainable lifestyle with a balance of time and money. Widely published, she writes about what she knows: brain injury, magick, herbs, astrology, abundance, recovery, and vibrant sustainability. When she isn't communing with nature, she likes to correspond with like-minded beings. Reach her at jennifer.cobb@live.com.

Raven Digitalis (Hawaii/Montana) is the author of *The Everyday Empath*, *Esoteric Empathy*, *Shadow Magick Compendium*, *Planetary Spells & Rituals*, and *Goth Craft* (Llewellyn). Originally trained in Georgian Witchcraft, Raven has been an earth-based practitioner since 1999, a Priest since 2003, a Freemason since 2012, and an empath all his life. He holds a degree in cultural anthropology from the University of Montana and co-operated a nonprofit Pagan temple for sixteen years. He is also a professional Tarot reader, DJ, card-carrying magician, and animal rights advocate. Visit him at www.ravendigitalis.com, www.facebook.com/ravendigitalis, and www.instagram.com/ravendigitalis.

James Kambos is an herbalist, artist, and writer. He became interested in the power of spells and the changes they can create in the physical world as a child. He'd watch his mother and grandmother perform folk magic rituals from their native Greece. He writes and paints from his home in the beautiful hill country of Southern Ohio.

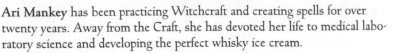

Ari Mankey has been practicing Witchcraft and creating spells for over twenty years. Away from the Craft, she has devoted her life to medical laboratory science and developing the perfect whisky ice cream.

Jason Mankey has written eight books for Llewellyn and is a frequent speaker and teacher at Pagan festivals across North America. He lives in Northern California with his wife, Ari, where they run two local covens. You can follow him on Instagram and Twitter at @panmankey.

Susan Pesznecker is a mother, writer, nurse, and college English professor living in the beautiful Pacific Northwest with her poodles. An initiated Druid, green magick devoteé, and amateur herbalist, Sue loves reading, writing, cooking, travel, and anything having to do with the outdoors. Previous works include *Crafting Magick with Pen and Ink*, *The Magickal Retreat*, and *Yule: Recipes & Lore for the Winter Solstice*. She's a regular contributor to the Llewellyn annuals. Follow her on Instagram as Susan Pesznecker.

Astrea Taylor is an eclectic/intuitive pagan witch whose life goals include empowering other witches and encouraging them to use intuition in their witchcraft. She's the author of *Intuitive Witchcraft* and *Air Magic*. Her work has been published in *The Witch's Altar*, *Llewellyn's Witches' Companion*, *Witchology*, *Soul & Spirit*, and *Lune Bleue*, and she blogs as *Starlight Witch* on Patheos. When she's not co-leading the Aurora Fire dance group, she presents workshops and rituals at festivals across the country. Learn more at www.AstreaTaylor.com.

Melissa Tipton is a Structural Integrator, Reiki Master, and founder of Jungian Magic, which utilizes potent psychological insights to radically increase the success of your magic. She is the author of *Llewellyn's Complete Book of Reiki* and *Living Reiki*. Learn more and find Jungian Magic courses designed to improve your magic and your life at http://realmagic.school.

Charlynn Walls is an active member of her local community and a member of a local area coven. A practitioner of the Craft for over twenty years, she currently resides in central Missouri with her family. She continues to expand upon her Craft knowledge and practices daily. She shares her knowledge by teaching online and at local festivals and by writing articles for the Llewellyn annuals.

Tess Whitehurst is the award-winning author of *The Magic of Flowers*, *You Are Magical*, *Holistic Energy Magic*, and many other books. She's also the cohost of *Magic Monday Podcast* and the founder and facilitator of the Good Vibe Tribe Online School of Magical Arts. Find lots more of her spells, as well as free guided meditations, sabbat ideas, inspiring videos, and more, at TessWhitehurst.com.

Laura Tempest Zakroff is a professional artist, author, dancer, designer, and Modern Traditional Witch based in New England. She holds a BFA from RISD (the Rhode Island School of Design), and her artwork has received awards and honors worldwide. Her work embodies myth and the esoteric through her drawings and paintings, jewelry, talismans, and other designs. Laura is the author of the bestselling Llewellyn books *Weave the Liminal* and *Sigil Witchery*, as well as *Anatomy of a Witch*, the *Liminal Spirits Oracle* (artist/author), and *The Witch's Cauldron*, and co-author of *The Witch's Altar* with Jason Mankey. Laura edited *The New Aradia: A Witch's Handbook to Magical Resistance* (Revelore Press). She blogs for Patheos as *A Modern Traditional Witch* and for *Witches & Pagans* as *Fine Art Witchery* and contributes to *The Witches' Almanac, Ltd.* She is the creative force behind several community events and teaches workshops worldwide. Visit her at www.LauraTempestZakroff.com.

Natalie Zaman is the author of *Color and Conjure* and *Magical Destinations of the Northeast* (Llewellyn), coauthor of *Sirenz* and *Sirenz Back in Fashion* (Flux) and *Blonde Ops* (Thomas Dunne Books), and a contributor to various Llewellyn annuals.